1-2-3®
To Go!

1-2-3® To Go!

21 Business Templates for Instant Productivity

Steven J. Bennett
Peter G. Randall
Alan P. Wichlei

A Brady Utility

A Brady Utility
Published by Prentice Hall Press
A Division of Simon & Schuster, Inc.
Gulf + Western Building
One Gulf + Western Plaza
New York, New York 10023

PRENTICE HALL PRESS is a trademark of Simon & Schuster, Inc.

Manufactured in the United States of America

10 9 8 7 6 5 4 3 2 1

Library of Congress Cataloging-in-Publication Data

Bennett, Steven J., 1951–
     1-2-3 to Go! «computer file».

     1 computer disk; $5\frac{1}{4}$ in. + reference manual.
     System requirements: IBM PC, XT, AT or Lotus
compatible computer; 384k (512 preferred); PC DOS 2.0
or higher or MS DOS 2.1 or higher; Lotus 1-2-3,
version 1A, 2, or 2.01; 2 disk drives (1 hard disk
preferred); monochrome monitor printer capable of
condensed print (15 characters per in. or smaller)
recommended; graphics monitor; or graphics cards
recommended; graphics printer or plotter recommended.
     Title from reference manual.
     "A Brady utility."
     Not copy protected.
     Summary: Provides twenty-one ready-to-run applications
for small business and beginning computer users
interested in using the potential of Lotus 1-2-3.
     1. Business—Data processing—Software. 2.Small
business—Data processing—Software. I. Randall,
Peter G., 1951–. II. Wichlei, Alan P.
III. Lotus 1-2-3 (Computer program) IV. Title.
V. Title: One-Two-Three to Go! VI. Title: 1-2-3
to Go!
HF5548.4.L67B46 1987   658'.0028'5   87-7116

ISBN 0-13-636697-X

CONTENTS

Trademarks

Limits of Liability and Disclaimer of Warranty

ACKNOWLEDGMENTS

This book represents a true team effort—not just among ourselves, but among the people who helped mold and test the ideas into a finished book/diskette package. We'd like to first express our appreciation to our editor, Terry Anderson, who believed in the project from the start and helped shape what we hope is a very practical and exciting tool for the business user. Our gratitude also goes to Joe Esposito, for his guidance in developing the underlying concept of Ready-to-Run, and to Mike Snell, our agent, who offered his wisdom in making the book more readable to the general business user.

Hats off to Peter Kinder, Bob Moran, Bruce Sunstein, and Greg Plimpton for helping to test the templates as they were created, and to Nancy MacDonald for reviewing the documentation.

Last but not least, we'd like to thank our families and friends for bearing with us so patiently while we clicked away into the autumn nights.

QUICK START

If you are an experienced Lotus 1-2-3 user, you can probably skip the introduction. The following information is all you need to begin using the Ready-to-Run templates:

- The templates are not copy protected. Copy them to a working diskette or into a directory of your hard disk.
- Each template has a printer setup string of \027\015, the IBM/Epson standard for condensed print.
- The Main Menu of each template is accessed by pressing **ALT-M**.
- Each chapter is designed to function as a stand-alone chapter, and covers:

  Template layout
  Menu Options
  Data Entry (auto and/or manual)
  Printing Reports
  Title Lock
  Screen Lock (windowson/off, panelon/off, for Release 2)
  Saving the File
  Common Questions and Problems

- The data base templates do not have data or formats set beyond the first row. The formulas and formats are copied and set each time data is input through the auto-entry feature (a Main Menu option). If you do not plan to use the auto-entry feature, you must copy the formulas throughout the worksheet and format the cells appropriately. (Note: If you do not use auto-entry, make sure that at a minimum all cells in the data entry sections have a label prefix in them; empty cells will cause the sort, extract, and print routines to act erroneously, since they function by using {end} to anchor the range.)
- A description of key macros is included in Appendix A, and a listing of range names used in each template is included in Appendix B.

INTRODUCTION

About Templates

Lotus 1-2-3 has become an indispensible tool for today's business world; it enables you to convert virtually every calculation task you now do by hand to electronic form. That not only means greater speed, efficiency, and accuracy, but the ability to carry out "what-if" scenarios without tedious rounds of manual calculation. In an instant you can see how different patterns of numbers affect the bottom line, giving you the ability to respond to change and better plan for the future.

But power often has its price, and in the case of 1-2-3 and other sophisticated spreadsheet tools, the price is complexity. The average business person has better things to do than figure out how to write formulas like:

```
((G9*@SUM(L8..L1000))-
(@SUM(A3..A1000)*@SUM(B8..B1000)))/
((G9*@SUM(M8..M1000))-
(@SUM(A8..A1000)*@SUM(A8..A1000)))
```

which recalculates the slope of the graph for a sales forecast or write macros (automated keyboard sequences) like:

```
RECALC      /wgpd{goto}PROC~/xcSCREENOFF~/wgpd
            /reA26.H1000~/xiTERM>2~/xgENDCALC~
            /dfLOOPSUM~(TERM)+13~1~{goto} LOOPSUM~
            {edit}{home}'~{goto}A
LOOPSUM
            ~
            FLAG~{goto}A25~/c.{end}{right}~
            .{end}{down}~
ENDCALC     {calc}{home}/wgpe/xcTLOCK~
            /xcSCREENON~/xmMENU~
```

which recalculates the amortization tables for a simple interest loan.

This book eliminates the need for learning such arcane babble. Rather than teaching you how to write 1-2-3 formulas and macros (there are plenty of fine books, tutorial disks, and video tapes on the market), Ready-to-Run offers 21 templates on the diskette attached to the back cover. A template is a 1-2-3 program that has structures and formulas built into it, but no data. You enter your own data, so you can instantly put 1-2-3 to productive use.

Ready-to-Run templates are extremely easy for the new computer user to learn and operate, yet they contain sophisticated formulas for performing advanced spreadsheet functions. All of the templates are "menu-driven," that is, you choose options such as Enter, Print, Graph, Sort, and Extract. In templates where data entry can be tricky or tedious, you will find an "auto-entry" option that prompts you to place data in the correct places, and prepares the cells with the correct formulas and formats. Most users should be able to put the templates to work in 10 to 30 minutes, depending on their computing experience.

Applications

Each Ready-to-Run template is dedicated to a specific business function, as described below:

- **Loan Amortization** (Chapter 2). Enables you to quickly calculate the principle and interest due on a loan. The template allows you to vary the loan amount, interest rate, and term.
- **Depreciation Schedule** (Chapter 3). Permits you to calculate the depreciation of capital assets using nine popular accounting methods.
- **Capital Asset Inventory** (Chapter 4). Allows you to create an "electronic log" of equipment, furniture, or other capital assets. Calculates the depreciated value of each item as well as total inventory.
- **Net Present Value—Continuous Flow** (Chapter 5). Enables you to quickly calculate net present value of an investment that involves regular cash flows and intervals.
- **Net Present Value—Variable Flow** (Chapter 6). Determines net present value when cash flows and/or cash flow intervals are irregular.
- **Time Billing** (Chapter 7). Provides an electronic log sheet for recording start and stop time of billable tasks. Computes total time and amount due. Sorts and totals by client, employee, project, or task.

- **Auto Mileage Reimbursement Calculator** (Chapter 8). Offers an easy means for recording auto mileage, parking, and tolls. Template automatically calculates reimbursement amount and generates comprehensive mileage log.
- **Travel Expense Recorder** (Chapter 9). Allows employees to enter travel expenses in basic categories, divided into company and personal cash outlays. Travel reports calculate amount due company or employee based on amount of travel advance.
- **1099-Miscellaneous Income Tracker** (Chapter 10). Allows you to record nonwage income for consultants and casual help, making it easy to fill out 1099 forms at the end of a year.
- **Commission Calculator** (Chapter 11). Determines commission amounts based on product mix. Also factors in user-specified group performance bonuses.
- **Direct Mail Revenue Calculator** (Chapter 12). Compares effects of response rates on the gross and net profits from a direct mail marketing campaign. Includes line graphs.
- **Sales Forecast Generator** (Chapter 13). Projects sales revenues based on past sales performance, using least squares line fit method. Includes line graphs of historical data and forecast.
- **Budget Planner** (Chapter 14). Compares projected and actual revenues and expenses for each month of the year, and computes variance and net profit. Includes bar graph.
- **Accounts Receivable Template** (Chapter 15). Features basic AR tracking systems with invoice search capabilities and total and selected invoice aging. Generates bar graphs.
- **Accounts Payable** (Chapter 16). Includes basic AP system with extensive search and sort features and bar graphs. Automatically ages payables.
- **Gantt Chart** (Chapter 17). Provides simple month-to-month project management program that computes end date or project length and displays result in Gantt Chart format.
- **Portfolio Valuation** (Chapter 18). Tracks current value of an investment portfolio, showing current position and unrealized short-term and long-term capital gains and losses.
- **The Business Planning and Analysis Series** (Chapter 19). Consists of four templates: The Master Financial Analyzer (a calendarized income statement and balance sheet that integrate to produce financial ratio calculations and a breakeven analysis); The Cash Flow Planner; The Financial Ratios Calculator;

and The Breakeven Analyzer. The templates cover many important business functions.

Whether you're a solo professional who needs to keep track of a small consulting practice or a sales manager of a medium-sized company who needs to project sales performance, this book has something for you.

What You Need to Use The Templates

Required Software and Hardware

1. Lotus 1-2-3, Release 1A, 2, or 2.01
2. An IBM PC, XT, AT, or Lotus-certified compatible computer with at least 256K of RAM.
3. A printer capable of condensed (15 characters per inch or smaller) print. (Note: all of the templates can in fact be used without a printer; however, to take full advantage of their power, you should have the capability of printing reports.)

Optional Equipment

1. Graphics monitor or graphics card. Several templates (Direct Mail Revenue Calculator, Sales Forecast Generator, Budget, Accounts Receivable, Accounts Payable, and the Business Planning and Analysis Series) generate graphs. To view the graphs on screen, both a graphics monitor or a graphics card is needed.
2. Graphics printer or plotter. To print Ready-to-Run graphs, your printer must be capable of generating graphs.

How to Use This Book

The book is organized as a set of stand-alone manuals. Each chapter covers the basic information you need to use the templates.

Chapter 1 describes Ready-to-Run functions that are common to each template—it is important to read the chapter before using any of the templates. Appendix A lists the major macros used in the templates, and Appendix B lists each template's range names and macros.

While Ready-to-Run does not require prior experience with Lotus 1-2-3, it does assume that the 1-2-3 system has been properly installed and that you have a formatted diskette to use to make a working copy of the distribution diskette included with this book.

If you are unfamiliar with 1-2-3, we suggest that before using a Ready-to-Run template you work through the tutorial supplied by Lotus to get acquainted with the program's keystrokes and screen displays. Then look at the following section, which summarizes the major concepts and keystrokes you will use when running the Ready-to-Run templates.

For users who are familiar with 1-2-3, skip the next section, but read the section on version compatibility as it contains some important information about Release 2 features included on the Ready-to-Run templates. Then proceed to Chapter 1 for an overview of Ready-to-Run macro functions.

LOTUS 1-2-3: Key Concepts For Using Ready-to-Run Templates

The Worksheet

Start Lotus 1-2-3 by typing **123 ‹RETURN›**, as explained in the manual supplied by Lotus Development Corp. Once the program has displayed the title screen with the 1-2-3 logo, a blank "worksheet" will appear. A worksheet (also called a "spreadsheet" by other software manufacturers), is a matrix with letters running across the top border, and numbers running down the left border. Each intersection of a number and a letter is called a cell, and its "address" is described by the intersecting letters and numbers. Hence, cell A1 (the *Home* cell) is located at the intersection of column A and row 1. G17 is located at the intersection of column G and row 17, and so on, as shown in Figure 0.1).

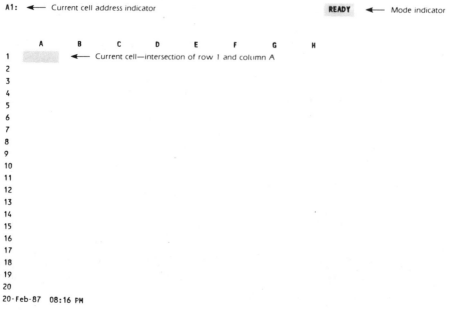

Figure 0.1 *Anatomy of a Lotus 1-2-3 Worksheet.*

When the column letters reach Z, they repeat, so that AA follows Z, BA follows AZ, and so on. Release 1A has 256 columns and 2,048 rows, while Release 2 has 256 Columns and 8,192 rows. The maximum size spreadsheet that can be created, however, will depend on the amount of RAM available in your computer.

Navigation

One of the cells in the worksheet will always be highlighted. This is called the "cell pointer" or "pointer," and it indicates which cell is the "current cell"; that is, the cell into which you are entering data. The address of the current cell is always displayed in the upper-left-hand corner of the worksheet screen (see Figure 0.1). The cell pointer can be moved throughout the worksheet by using the cursor keys (up arrow, down arrow, left arrow, and right arrow). Each time one of the cursor keys is pressed, the pointer will move one cell in the direction corresponding to the arrow designation.

Lotus 1-2-3 also makes use of certain special keys and key combinations so the pointer can be moved more quickly across the worksheet space. The most important keys are:

Single Keys

Home. Located in upper-left corner of the numeric key pad. The ⟨**Home**⟩ key moves cell pointer to cell A1. It is a useful key for reorienting yourself if you are lost in a worksheet.

PgUp. Moves cell pointer up one page (20 lines).

PgDn. Moves cell pointer down one page (20 lines).

F5 (GoTo Key). Special function key located on left side of keyboard. When **F5** is pressed, 1-2-3 prompts you to enter cell address to "go to." Enter the cell address and press ⟨**RETURN**⟩, and the pointer will move to the desired cell. (Note: you can also enter a "range name" after pressing **F5** or press **F3** to get a menu of range names. A range name is a rectangular block of cells that is given a name. When you tell 1-2-3 to go to a range name, it takes the pointer to the cell in the upper-left corner of the range. Many range names are used in the Ready-to-Run templates. A table of range names used by each template appears in Appendix B.)

Key Combinations

End + Cursor. **End** is located in lower-left corner of the numeric key pad. **End** takes the cell pointer to the end of a consecutive row or column of cells that have data in them (for example, if there are data in cells A1 through A60, and the cell pointer is in A1, pressing **End + Down [Cursor]** will move the pointer directly to cell A60. If the cell pointer was in A60 and **End + Up [Cursor]** was pressed, the pointer would go directly to cell A1.) The **End + Cursor** combination can also be used to find the first nonempty cell in a row or column.

Ctrl + Left [Cursor]. Moves cell pointer one screen to the left. **Shift + Tab** achieves the same results.

Ctrl + Right [Cursor]. Moves cell pointer one screen to the right. The **Tab** key is used for the same purpose.

Commands

Lotus has many commands for manipulating the contents of worksheet cells, such as erasing, copying, and moving. The only command needed to use Ready-to-Run templates is **File Retrieve**—everything else is built into the menu options described in Chapter 1. (Note: one exception involves setting up the printer. If the printer does not use the IBM/Epson standard, the setup commands are used to enter the appropriate codes to make it print in condensed mode. The procedure for doing this is simple, and is explained shortly.)

To invoke a 1-2-3 command, first press the "slash" (/) key. Note that the slash goes from bottom left to top right, which is the opposite of the "backslash" (\). When the slash key is pressed, a series of choices in a horizontal menu will show up across the top border of the worksheet, in an area called the "control panel." (See Figure 0.2.)

When the menu is first displayed, the cell closest to the left in the menu will be highlighted with the pointer. To select that option, simply press **<RETURN>**. To select other options, use the cursor keys to "slide" the cell pointer along the menu. When it highlights the option you want, press **<RETURN>**. (Refer to Chapter 1 for a discussion of common menu choices offered in Ready-to-Run templates.)

An alternative method to selecting menu items is to type the item's first letter; it is not neccessary to press return. Some people develop a "slide and **RETURN**" reflex, others prefer the first letter approach.

If you do not want to make any menu choices and want to return the cell pointer to the worksheet area, press **ESC**.

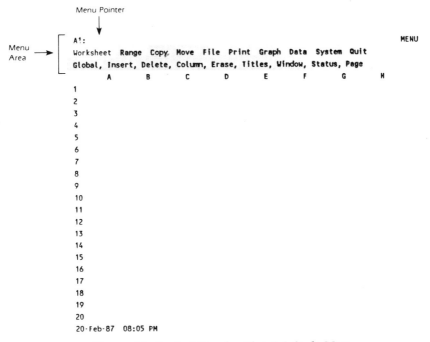

Figure 0.2 *Control Panel with 1-2-3 Style Menu.*

File Retrieve

You can retrieve a file by either typing / and using the pointer to select **File** and then **Retrieve** or by typing /**FR**. Either way, you will be presented with a list along the top border of the worksheet showing the available files (see Figure 0.3). Slide the cell pointer along the list, using the cursor keys, until you highlight the file you want to load. Then press **〈RETURN〉**. Alternately, after selecting **File Retrieve**, type in the file name, using its *exact* spelling.

Once you've retrieved a template, the built-in menu structures take over, and you will not have to use the slash key again until you have finished working on the template. At that point you can retrieve another template using the / **File Retrieve**. If you use the **File Retrieve** command to load another template, it will overwrite the template you are currently running. For that reason, make sure you have saved the data in the template you are currently using!

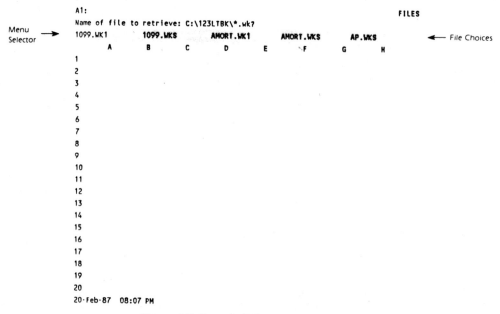

Figure 0.3 *Sample /File Retrieve Listing.*

Printer Set Up

Most Ready-to-Run templates, except where otherwise indicated, are designed to print out in condensed mode (15 characters per inch or smaller). The templates are preset with the IBM/Epson standard for condensed print, which is code 015. If you have an IBM printer, an Epson printer, or a printer that emulates the IBM/Epson standard, you can use any Ready-to-Run templates as is. Check your manual if you are not sure whether your printer uses the command code 015 for condensed print.

If your printer does not use 015, look up the condensed code in your manual and insert it in each template. This is a simple procedure, and only has to be done the first time the template is used. Here's how to do it:

1. Select the template you wish to use, with the **/ File Retrieve** command.
2. A title screen will be displayed. Press **‹RETURN›** to begin using the template. (The only exception is the Budget Tem-

plate. You must indicate whether you are using Release 1 or Release 2, after which the template will go through a one-time set up procedure that requires 60 seconds.)

3. Press **ESC**.
4. Type / and then type **PPOS** (or use the cell pointer to select) **Print Printer Options Setup**.
5. Use the backspace key to erase the 015 code and then type the appropriate code for your printer. (See your Lotus 1-2-3 manual if you need further help.) Press **‹RETURN›**.
6. Press **Q**uit twice to escape the print menu.
7. Press and hold the **Alt** key and then press **M**. This will bring up the Main Menu of the template, and you can begin computing. (Note: in order for the condensed code change to be permanently embedded in your template, you must save the file. This is done by selecting the **F**ile **S**ave option from the template's Main Menu).

At this point you know everything you need about Lotus 1-2-3 to use any of the Ready-to-Run templates. Before you boot up your system, though, read on to learn some additional important information about the macro concept, version compatibility, and making a working copy of the diskette included with this book.

About Macros

It is not necessary to know how to write macros to use the Ready-to-Run templates—they are all written. Nevertheless, it is worth taking a few moments to learn what macros are and what they do, since you'll frequently encounter the term in each chapter. A "macro" is a sequence of keystrokes executed by pressing **Alt** plus one other key, or by selecting a menu option. For example, pressing **Alt** + **M** in any template invokes a string of individual commands that create and display the Main Menu. Each menu option selected, such as **P**rint, **E**nter, or **G**raph, also invokes a string of individual key strokes. Some macros are extremely complex, and involve many keystrokes, such as the following, which sets up a print range and then prints it.

```
PRINT{goto}H1000~{end}{up}/ppcrr.{end}{up}{end}{left}
~,agpq{home}/xmMENU~
```

This chain of keystrokes is set off by selecting the **P**rint option from the Main Menu of the Loan Amortization Template. Translated into English, the sequence means: Find the bottom-right-hand corner of the data you want to print. Follow the right edge up to the top and then top edge over to the left corner. (This has defined the range to print.) Now align the printer and print it. When finished, eject the page, return to cell **A1** and restart the Main Menu macro. As you can see, the macro sequence is much easier than typing all of the keystrokes.

Version Compatibility

At the time of this writing, there are three versions of Lotus 1-2-3: Release 1A, which is no longer on the market but is still widely in use; Release 2; and Release 2.01 (which fixes bugs in Release 2, simplifies installation, and speeds up the file retrieve process). Release 1A places the extension .WKS after each file name. Release 2 and 2.01 place the extension .WK1 after a file name.

Release 1A files can be run on Release 2 and 2.01, but you cannot directly run Release 2 or Release 2.01 files with Release 1A. (Release 2 and 2.01 are interchangeable both ways). To run a Release 2 or 2.01 file with Release 1A, you must first use the Conversion function provided with Release 2 and 2.01.

While Ready-to-Run templates are compatible with all three versions, they are supplied on the distribution diskette as Release 1A files with the extension .WKS. If you are using Release 2 or Release 2.01, the first time you save the file, 1-2-3 will beep and indicate the file will be saved with a .WK1 extension. By pressing **〈RETURN〉** at that point you will convert the template to Release 2 or 2.01 format.

The only Release 2 functions used in Ready-to-Run that cannot be accessed by Release 1A users are "windowson/windowsoff" and "panelon/paneloff." These functions are used in the "Lock Screen" option, which freezes the screen while macros are running (see discussion in Chapter 1).

Installing and Running Ready-to-Run Templates

Making a Working Copy of the Distribution Diskette

As with any software package, never use the distribution diskette as the main copy; floppy disks are easily damaged, and should anything happen to the distribution copy you may find yourself in a frustrating situation.

The Ready-to-Run diskette is not copy protected. To make a working copy, take a formatted double-sided, double density diskette and copy all the files from the distribution disk, using the **DISKCOPY** or **COPY *.*** command. Be sure to store the distribution diskette in a safe place.

Two Drive Floppy Systems

If you are using a floppy system, make a second set of working diskettes that only include the templates you wish to use. (The templates and their corresponding file names are listed in Table 0.1.) Allow enough room for the templates to expand as you add data or save multiple copies. Your working diskettes will be run from the "B" drive, while the 1-2-3 program diskette will be booted from the "A" drive.

Table 0.1 *Templates with Corresponding File Names*

Chapter	Template	1-2-3 File
2	Loan Amortization	AMORT.WKS
3	Depreciation Schedule	DEPRE.WKS
4	Capital Asset Inventory	INVENT.WKS
5	Net Present Value Continuous Flow	NPV_C.WKS
6	Net Present Value Variable Flow	NPV_V.WKS
7	Time Billing	TIMEBILL.WKS
8	Auto Mileage Reimbursement Calculator	MILEAGE.WKS
9	Travel Expense Recorder	TRAVEL.WKS
10	1099-Miscellaneous Income Tracker	1099.WKS
11	Commission Calculator	COMMIS.WKS
12	Direct Mail Revenue Calculator	DIRECT.WKS
13	Sales Forecast Generator	SALEFORE.WKS
14	Budget Planner	BUDGET.WKS
15	Accounts Receivable	AR.WKS
16	Accounts Payable	AP.WKS
17	Gantt Chart	GANTT.WKS
18	Portfolio Valuation	PORTFOLI.WKS
19	The Business Planning and Analysis Series	
	Master Financial Analyzer	MASTER.WKS
	Cash Flow Planner	CASHFLOW.WKS
	Ratios Calculator	RATIOS.WKS
	Breakeven Analyzer	BRKEVN.WKS

Hard Disk Systems

To load Ready-to-Run templates onto a hard disk, copy the files into your Lotus 1-2-3 data directory. Alternately, you can create a new subdirectory using the **Make Directory** (**MD**) command. (See your DOS manual.) Copy all the templates you wish to use to the new directory, and update the default directory in 1-2-3 using the **/WGDD** command (refer to your 1-2-3 manual for details).

Loading Ready-to-Run Templates

Ready-to-Run templates are loaded the same way as any other 1-2-3 file, using the **/File Retrieve** command. Refer to Table 0.1 for a listing of file names. Once a template is loaded, a title screen confirming your template choice will be automatically displayed (see Figure 0.4).

```
*                                                                    *
*                        1-2-3 READY-TO-RUN:                         *
*                           21 TEMPLATES                             *
*                        FOR THE BUSINESS USER                       *
*                                                                    *
*                                                                    *
*                 * * *  LOAN AMORTIZATION  * *                      *
*                                                                    *
*                                                                    *
*                   Press <Return> to Continue                       *
*                                                                    *
*                   Written by Peter G. Randall                      *
*          With: Steven J. Bennett & Alan Wichlei                    *
*                                                                    *
*Copyright (c) 1987 Steven J. Bennett, Peter G. Randall,  *
*                   and Alan P. Wichlei                              *
```

Figure 0.4 *Title Screen, Loan Amortization Template.*

As the title screen indicates, press **‹RETURN›** to proceed. The template's Main Menu will then be automatically displayed (see Chapter 1 for details).

You are now ready to run.

Steven J. Bennett

Peter G. Randall

Alan Wichlei

1 | USING READY-TO-RUN TEMPLATES

Ready-to-Run templates have a number of unique macros that will save time and allow you to use the most powerful 1-2-3 functions without having to learn a new language. Some of the macros, such as those used to simplify data entry and deletion, are used in more than one template, and are described here. For a more detailed explanation of how the macros work, refer to Appendix A.

Menus

All Ready-to-Run macros are executed by selecting appropriate options from the template's Main Menu, either by typing the first letter of the option or moving the cell pointer to the desired option and pressing **⟨RETURN⟩**. The Main Menu will automatically ap-

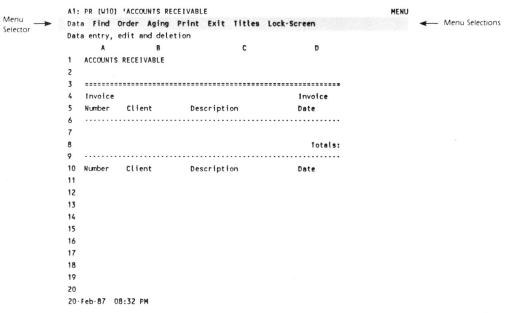

Figure 1.1 *Sample Menu, Accounts Receivable Template.*

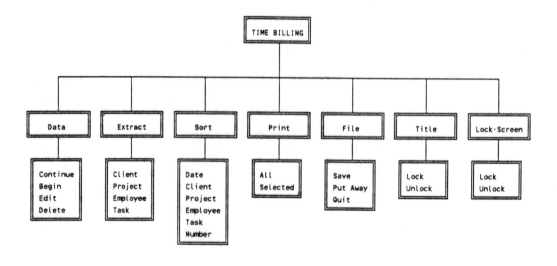

Figure 1.2 *Menu Tree, Time Billing Template.*

pear after the title screen is displayed and you press ⟨RETURN⟩. (See sample Main Menu, Figure 1.1). Some Main Menu options branch into submenus, and occasionally into sub-submenus (see Sample Menu Tree, Figure 1.2). Submenu and sub-submenu options are selected the same way as Main Menu options. If you have selected a menu option that branches to a lower menu, return to the higher level by pressing the **ESC** key. By pressing **ESC** at the Main Menu, the Main Menu will disappear from the control panel, and the template will be under manual cursor control. The Main Menu can be restarted at any time from any cell in the worksheet by pressing and holding the **ALT** key and then pressing the **M** key.

To go directly under manual control when the title screen is displayed, press and hold the **CTRL** key and then simultaneously press the **BREAK** key. The Main Menu will not appear; the cursors or various multiple-key combinations can be used to maneuver around the spreadsheet. With Release 2.0 and 2.01, pressing **CTRL-BREAK** will cause an error message to be displayed in the mode indicator box in the upper-right-hand corner. This can be cleared by pressing **ESC**.

Any Ready-to-Run macro can be stopped at any time by pressing the **CTRL-BREAK** key. If the macro is requesting text data, or is in menu mode, pressing the **ESC** key will also terminate the macro sequence. All data cells are identified as either (T)ext or (N)umeric in each chapter.

The following pages describe many of the Main Menu options used in Ready-to-Run templates.

Data Entry Macros

Data entry is facilitated in the database-oriented templates by use of an "auto-entry" macro that moves the cursor through a row of cells each time **‹RETURN›** is pressed, prompting you to enter appropriate data. The prompt is displayed above the worksheet (see Figure 1.3). The sequence of prompts corresponds to the column headings in each template, and is listed in the Data Entry section of each chapter. After entering a row of data with an auto-

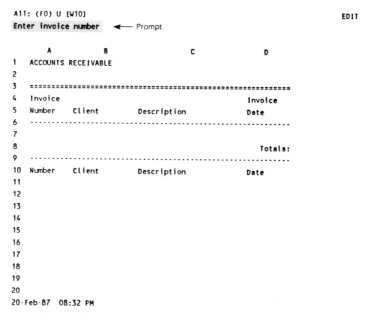

Figure 1.3 *Sample Auto-entry Prompt, Accounts Receivable Template.*

entry macro, you will have created a database "record" comprised of one "field" in each column. (Refer to your 1-2-3 manual and tutorial for more information about 1-2-3's database capabilities.)

Auto-entry macros are used in the following Ready-to-Run templates to create database records:

> Capital Asset Inventory (Chapter 4)
> Net Present Value: Variable Flow (Chapter 6)
> Time Billing (Chapter 7)
> Auto Mileage Reimbursement Calculator (Chapter 8)
> Travel Expense Recorder (Chapter 9)
> 1099 Miscellaneous Income Recorder (Chapter 10)
> Accounts Receivable (Chapter 15)
> Accounts Payable (Chapter 16)
> Portfolio Valuation (Chapter 17)

(Note: Most of the remaining Ready-to-Run templates have data entry macros. Unlike the macros described in this section, however, they are unique to one template, and are described at length in their respective chapters.)

As an example of how the auto-entry macro works, consider the Capital Asset Inventory Template, which allows you to catalog your equipment, furniture, and other assets, and to calculate their depreciated value. The template has column headings for the following kinds of information (see Figure 1.4):

> Item #
> Description/Serial Number
> Purchase Date
> Source
> Purchase Price
> Depreciation Life
> Depreciation Method
> Item Code

The auto-entry macro prompts you to enter information in each field, and will automatically move the cell pointer to the next field in the record when you press **‹RETURN›**.

Starting Auto Entry Macros

To use the auto-feature, select **Data** from the Main Menu. A sub-menu shows the following choices:

```
Continue Begin Edit Delete
```

Continue and Begin

Continue and **Begin** move the cell pointer to the first column on the left, prompting you to enter the item number of the asset. (**Begin** is used the first time data are entered into the template, and should not be used after that. **Continue** is used to enter input data during subsequent data entry sessions. See below for more details.) The auto-entry prompt is located in the control panel section of the worksheet (refer to Figure 1.3). When you press **<RETURN>**, the cell pointer moves to the cell to the right and prompts you (in the control panel) to enter the description and serial number of the item. When you press **<RETURN>**, the system continues to prompt you for the appropriate information, moving the cell pointer one cell to the right each time you enter data and press **<RETURN>**.

When the *Item Code* is entered the row is complete, and the cell pointer returns to the first column of the next row and displays a menu with two options:

```
Continue Stop
```

Press **<RETURN>** to accept the **Continue** option and the macro will cycle through another row, prompting you for information at each

```
CAPITAL ASSET INVENTORY  Valuation Date:
===================================================================================================
 Item                              Purchase                Purchase Deprec. Deprec. Deprec.  Depreciated  Item
 Number  Description and Serial Number  Date   Source      Price  Life   Method  Year       Value   Code
.......................................................................................................

                                        Totals:
.......................................................................................................
```

Figure 1.4 *Capital Assets Column Headings.*

cell. If you are done entering data, or wish to go back and edit the previously entered row, select the Stop option. Stop not only disengages the auto-entry macro, but restarts the Main Menu.

In addition to prompting you for appropriate data, the auto-entry macro locks a horizontal title in place (refer to Titles section following) so that you can see the column headings regardless of how many rows of data you have input.

General Auto-Entry Considerations

When using the auto-entry macros bear in mind the following important considerations and caveats:

1. When alphanumeric data are required, you may enter a blank response by pressing **‹RETURN›** without making an entry. When numeric data are required, however, you cannot enter a blank. If you do not want to enter a value, type "0" and **‹RETURN›**. The Data Entry section of each chapter indicates which cells require alphanumeric input and which are numeric only.

2. During auto-entry, press **ESC** to exit the macro only if you are in a cell that accepts alphanumeric data. If you are in a cell that requires numeric input, you must use the **CTRL-BREAK** key combination to end the macro. (Again, refer to the Data Entry section of each chapter for a listing of which cells are alphanumeric and which are numeric.)

3. When you input a date, the program will prompt you to enter the month, and will then prompt for the day and the last two digits of the year. For a logically impossible date, such as 13 01 87, the template will display an "Invalid Date" error message in the control panel. Press **‹RETURN›** and you will be prompted to input a correct date.

   Note: With the exception of the Accounts Receivable and Accounts Payable templates, you cannot input a blank date. With the Accounts Receivable and Payable templates, you will need to insert blank dates for invoices and bills that have not yet been paid. With those templates entering month = 1, day = 1, and year = 1 (i.e., "1/1/1") will produce a blank cell.

lllBradyLine

Insights into tomorrow's technology from the authors and editors of Brady Books.

You rely on Brady's bestselling computer books for up-to-date information about high technology. Now turn to BradyLine for the details behind the titles.

Find out what new trends in technology spark Brady's authors and editors. Read about what they're working on, and predicting, for the future. Get to know the authors through interviews and profiles, and get to know each other through your questions and comments.

BradyLine keeps you ahead of the trends with the stories behind the latest computer developments. Informative previews of forthcoming books and excerpts from new titles keep you apprised of what's going on in the fields that interest you most.

- Peter Norton on operating systems
- Jim Seymour on business productivity
- Jerry Daniels, Mary Jane Mara, Robert Eckhardt, and Cynthia Harriman on Macintosh development, productivity, and connectivity

Get the Spark. Get BradyLine.

Published quarterly, beginning with the Summer 1988 issue. Free exclusively to our customers. Just fill out and mail this card to begin your subscription.

Name _____

Address _____

City _____ State _____ Zip _____

Name of Book Purchased _____

Date of Purchase _____

Where was this book purchased?   *(circle one)*

Retail Store   Computer Store   Mail Order

F
R
E
E

Mail this card for your free subscription to BradyLine

If you want to enter a blank date in any other template, you must edit the worksheet.

> **Caution!** To create a blank date cell in a spreadsheet other than the Accounts Receivable and Payable templates, enter a single quote label prefix ('); otherwise the sorting macros, which depend on unbroken ranges, may not work properly.

4. Whenever a percentage is required, enter it in a conventional format. "Nine-and-a-half" percent would be entered as "9.5" not "0.095." The template will do the math for you.

5. During auto-entry, *you must NOT try to run another macro or execute any 1-2-3 commands!* Otherwise, you may "crash" or permanently damage the Ready-to-Run template, or cause unexpected results. As a reminder that the template is under macro control, the "CMD" indicator will be displayed in the lower-right-hand corner of the screen when the **Continue** or **Begin** options are selected.

6. If you have already entered data and use **Begin** instead of **Continue**, the cell pointer will move to the first data row of the template, and you will overwrite any existing data if you proceed. Stop the macro using **ESC** or **CTRL-BREAK** as described in step 2, and restart the macro with **Alt-M** and select **Continue**.

Manual Data Entry

You can enter data manually by stopping the Main Menu with the **ESC** key, and then moving the cell pointer to the desired cell with the cursor keys. If you choose to enter data manually, you must ensure that the formulas and formats are properly copied to the new data rows. In order to keep the templates as small as possible for distribution, only the first rows of data are preformatted. The auto-entry macro formats new data rows as it proceeds. Therefore, if you manually enter new rows of data, you must copy the necessary formats and formulas from a previously created rows of data to the new rows. This is done by using 1-2-3's /Copy command (See the 1-2-3 manual).

Edit

The **Edit** option breaks the auto-entry macro and positions the cell pointer at the home cell. Use the cursor keys to move the pointer to any desired cell in the worksheet, change or add data, then use the **ALT-M** key combination to recall the Main Menu.

When editing a date entry in a data base template, press **Alt-D** and you will be prompted to enter the month, day, and year in mm **⟨RETURN⟩** dd **⟨RETURN⟩** yy **⟨RETURN⟩** format. Otherwise you must enter in the standard Lotus 1-2-3 date format (@date(yy,mm,dd)).

Finally, note that several of the templates, Loan Amortization, Net Present Value, and Depreciation, use special editing routines to permit rapid "what-if" analysis. The procedures are explained in detail in the chapters associated with those templates.

Delete (row of data)

The easiest method for deleting entries is to simply overwrite the data you wish to be deleted in each cell with new information. To delete an entire row, use the **Delete (row)** function by first choosing **Data** from the Main Menu, and then selecting **Delete** from the sub-menu. The macro then instructs you to press **⟨RETURN⟩** and then move the cell pointer to the first column (A) of the row you want to delete. Press **⟨RETURN⟩** again, and the row will be deleted. Please observe the following important cautions:

1. When using the **Data/Delete** function, the cell pointer *must* be in column "A;" otherwise you may damage the worksheet.
2. Do not use the **Data/Delete** function with the last two rows of the worksheet if you are using Release 1A; otherwise you may encounter a "Memory Full Error." Users of Release 2 do not have this minor limitation.
3. Do not use 1-2-3's **Range Erase** function as an alternative to the **Delete** function, as it may leave blank cells that will disrupt various macro routines. The same holds for 1-2-3's **Delete Row** function, which can misalign the worksheet or delete portions of the macros, so that the macros fail to work properly.

Printing

Make sure that your printer is online before attempting to print a Ready-to-Run template, otherwise you will generate an error message. Note that some templates may pause for a few moments before printing, because each template recalculates all formulas when a print command is executed.

Screen Control

Most Ready-to-Run templates use the title and lock-screen functions to manage the scrolling and redrawing of the screen. The title feature makes it easier to enter data, and the lock-screen function reduces the amount of cursor movement displayed during macro execution (only in Release 2.0 and 2.01).

Title

The Title option "freezes" the worksheet column title at the top of the worksheet, or in some cases, the row titles on the left edge of the worksheet. This is helpful when you are working below row 20, and cannot see the column headings. With the Title option, the headings will remain in view at the top of the screen as you scroll down. When you select the Title option from the Main Menu, you will be presented with a submenu that has two choices:

`Lock Unlock`

Lock freezes the title. Unlock releases the title. Note that when title lock is in place, you cannot move the cell pointer into the titles area. (The title feature is also automatically invoked when you select the **Begin** or **Continue** data entry option. When you press **CTRL-BREAK** to exit, you are still in title lock mode. If you do not want the column headings locked, you will have to select the **Un**-lock option.) In some templates, you may wish to edit the column or row labels. You must first turn off the title lock to move the cursor in the titles area to manually edit these cells.

(Note: If you save and then retrieve a file with the titles unlocked, 1-2-3 will beep when the file is loaded. This is because one of the first automacro steps is to unlock the titles prior to displaying the introductory screen. If the titles were not locked, the redundant unlock causes a beep. This does not indicate a problem with the template.)

Lock-Screen

The Lock-Screen function is useful for users of Release 2.0 and 2.01. It locks the screen during recalculation and other lengthy macros, preventing the screen flashing as the macro performs its tasks. It cannot be used with Release 1A. When you select the Lock-Screen option from the Main Menu, you will be given the following two choices:

```
Lock Unlock
```

Lock

Lock holds the screen still during calculations, so that you do not have to view the cell pointer rapidly moving from cell to cell, a feature of the Lotus macro that many people find annoying. The Lock option also slightly speeds up various macros, by eliminating the need to redraw the screen. When you select the Lock option, the cell pointer will move during calculations to a portion of the screen that displays:

```
"PROCESSING DATA"
```

Once the calculation is complete, the cell pointer will return to the *data* section of the template. Note that during lengthy calculations, the "PROCESSING DATA" screen may be displayed for several minutes. Don't be concerned at the apparent lack of activity; much is going on in other parts of the spreadsheet. One tip off that the template is processing your data is that the "CMD" (Command Mode) indicator will be displayed and the mode indicator in the upper-right corner will say "WAIT."

CAUTION!!: The screen Lock feature *can only be used with Release 2*. If you select it while using Release 1A, 1-2-3 will give you an error message during recalculations. In that case, select the Unlock option to reset the template for Release 1A use.

Unlock

Unlock frees the screen during recalculation, so that cell pointer movement can again be viewed. You would select Unlock if you converted a worksheet from Release 2 to Release 1A with the Lotus conversion utility (refer to your 1-2-3 manual for conversion details). The Unlock option can be used either before or after conversion.

Saving Your Work and Leaving the Program

You can save your work or quit any Ready-to-Run template by selecting the File option from the Main Menu. When you select File, your template will display a submenu with the following options:

```
Save  Put Away  Quit
```

Save

The Save option saves the file to a name of your choice, and then returns to the Main Menu. When you select Save, 1-2-3 will display the file name to be saved with a .WKS extension if you are using Release 1A, and a .WK1 extension if you are using Release 2 (the first time you save a Release 1A file with Release 2 or 2.01, 1-2-3 will warn you that the .WKS file will be saved as a .WK1 file.) If you are saving the worksheet under the same name, the system will ask if you wish to replace the old file. Press **R** to replace, and the template will return to the Main Menu.

In general, you should save your worksheet under a different file name than that supplied on the Ready-to-Run disk, so that you preserve the original template. Enter the new name and press <RE-TURN>. Press <RETURN> again and the Main Menu will return to the screen. (Note: In the future when you save the file under the new name, you will be asked whether you want to Cancel the save operation or Replace the file. Select Replace to complete the save operation and return to the Main Menu.)

Put Away

Put Away operates the same as the Save option, but instead of returning to the Main Menu, it ends the 1-2-3 session after saving your data and returns to DOS.

Important Note! Don't wait until you are finished entering your data to save your work. Power surges, outages, computer failures, and keyboard mistakes can cause you to lose your data at any time. Until you save your template to disk, the information is vulnerable to loss. Therefore, Save your work frequently! (Frequently means as soon as you do not want to have to reenter your data.)

Quit

The Quit option exits to DOS without saving. Make sure you really want to abandon your worksheet changes before invoking Quit—once you invoke the command, there is no way to retrieve your worksheet!

A Note About Data Consistency

It is important to enter information consistently in the database-oriented programs, otherwise the Extract and Sort functions will not operate properly. The Extract function allows you to specify a criterion, such as all records with the same client name or product code, and copy those records to a separate area of the worksheet (called the "output range.") You can then view or print the selected records. The Sort function organizes entries alphabetically according to criteria of your choosing. (Each database-style template offers unique Extract and Sort choices.)

Consider what would happen with the Time Billing Template if sometimes you entered a client as "A.O. Smith & Co." (with periods), sometimes as "A.O. Smith & Co" (no period after "Co"), other times as "AO Smith & Co" (no periods at all), and yet other times as "A O Smith & Co" (no periods, and space between the "A" and the "O"). While each of these might be a valid way of entering the Smith company, 1-2-3 would treat each one as a different entry. Therefore, if you tried to extract all the A.O. Smith & Co. records, you would not find those that lacked periods or added spaces. If you tried to sort on the client's name, 1-2-3 would not group any of those records together, even though they are associated with the same client.

In addition to consistency, you must be careful about "case-sensitivity" if you are using Release 1A. This is because Release 1A is case-sensitive, meaning that the A.O. Smith Co. (upper and lower case) will be treated differently from the A.O. SMITH CO.

One measure that will help with consistency and case problems is to keep a list of "legal" entry formats and spellings near the computer. This will be especially useful if several people will be entering data into the template, as it will reduce the likelihood of each operator creating new data entry styles on the fly. Make sure the list reminds everyone that punctuation marks and spaces count as valid characters, and that spelling must be exact.

Conventions Used in This Book

The following typographic styles and formats are used to convey information and instruct you in the mechanics of using the templates:

1. When the text asks you to enter data, it is presented in quote marks (e.g., enter "1"). Do not include the quote marks in your entry.
2. Column headings are typeset in italics, such as *Description*.

3. The Return key is set off in brackets as **‹RETURN›**. On some keyboards **‹RETURN›** refers to the key labeled "Enter."

Worksheet Protection

The templates use the 1-2-3 range protection feature to prevent accidental erasure or overwriting of formulas and macros. Cells that have been protected appear in normal intensity, while cells that have been explicitly unprotected, permitting user input, appear in highlighted form (see Figure 1.5). While it is possible to turn off worksheet protection using the /Worksheet Global Protection Disable command in order to edit labels, this is generally not recommended and should only be done with great caution. If you must turn off protection, be sure to reset it with the /Worksheet Global Protection Enable command when you are finished with your editing.

LOAN AMORTIZATION

```
=======================================================================================================
Loan Amount:          $20,000.00    Loan Date:    12-May-87
Loan Term (Months):           12    Loan Type:    Computer
Annual Interest Rate:     10.50 %      Source:    1st National
Monthly Payment:       $1,762.97
=======================================================================================================
```

Month	Monthly Payment	Cumulative Payments	Interest Portion	Cumulative Interest	Principal Portion	Cumulative Principal	Balance Outstanding
......	....	....	....	....	....	....	....

LOAN AMORTIZATION

```
=======================================================================================================
Loan Amount:          $20,000.00    Loan Date:    12-May-87
Loan Term (Months):           12    Loan Type:    Computer
Annual Interest Rate:     10.50 %      Source:    1st National
Monthly Payment:       $1,762.97
=======================================================================================================
```

Month	Monthly Payment	Cumulative Payments	Interest Portion	Cumulative Interest	Principal Portion	Cumulative Principal	Balance Outstanding
......	....	....	....	....	....	....	....
1	1,762.97	1,762.97	175.00	175.00	1,587.97	1,587.97	18,412.03
2	1,762.97	3,525.94	161.11	336.11	1,601.86	3,189.83	16,810.17
3	1,762.97	5,288.91	147.09	483.19	1,615.88	4,805.72	15,194.28
4	1,762.97	7,051.88	132.95	616.14	1,630.02	6,435.74	13,564.26
5	1,762.97	8,814.85	118.69	734.83	1,644.28	8,080.02	11,919.98
6	1,762.97	10,577.82	104.30	839.13	1,658.67	9,738.69	10,261.31
7	1,762.97	12,340.79	89.79	928.92	1,673.18	11,411.87	8,588.13
8	1,762.97	14,103.76	75.15	1,004.06	1,687.82	13,099.70	6,900.30
9	1,762.97	15,866.73	60.38	1,064.44	1,702.59	14,802.29	5,197.71
10	1,762.97	17,629.70	45.48	1,109.92	1,717.49	16,519.78	3,480.22
11	1,762.97	19,392.67	30.45	1,140.37	1,732.52	18,252.30	1,747.70
12	1,762.97	21,155.64	15.29	1,155.67	1,747.68	19,999.97	0.03
13	1,762.97	22,918.61	0.00	1,155.67	1,762.97	21,762.94	(1,762.94)
14	1,762.97	24,681.58	(15.43)	1,140.24	1,778.40	23,541.34	(3,541.34)
15	1,762.97	26,444.55	(30.99)	1,109.25	1,793.96	25,335.30	(5,335.30)
16	1,762.97	28,207.52	(46.68)	1,062.57	1,809.65	27,144.95	(7,144.95)
17	1,762.97	29,970.49	(62.52)	1,000.05	1,825.49	28,970.44	(8,970.44)
18	1,762.97	31,733.46	(78.49)	921.56	1,841.46	30,811.90	(10,811.90)
19	1,762.97	33,496.43	(94.60)	826.96	1,857.57	32,669.47	(12,669.47)
20	1,762.97	35,259.40	(110.86)	716.10	1,873.83	34,543.30	(14,543.30)
21	1,762.97	37,022.37	(127.25)	588.84	1,890.22	36,433.53	(16,433.53)
22	1,762.97	38,785.34	(143.79)	445.05	1,906.76	38,340.29	(18,340.29)
23	1,762.97	40,548.31	(160.48)	284.57	1,923.45	40,263.74	(20,263.74)
24	1,762.97	42,311.28	(177.31)	107.27	1,940.28	42,204.01	(22,204.01)

Figure 1.5 *Protected and Unprotected Cells (bold indicates the protected cells).*

2 | LOAN AMORTIZATION TEMPLATE

CONTENTS

SPECIFICATIONS

File Name **AMORT.WKS**

Functions

- Calculates monthly payments and generates the amortization table for a user-specified principal, interest rate, and loan period.

Usage

- Calculates loan amortization for any type of business or personal loan.
- Compares various loan packages to determine which is most advantageous.
- Determines interest expense for a given tax period.
- Determines principal outstanding at any point to evaluate refinancing options.

Features

- Quick calculation of monthly payments.
- Generates comprehensive loan amortization tables including interest portion and principal portion of each payment.
- Automatically sizes loan table to print out four years per page.

Introduction

The Loan Amortization Template makes it easy to calculate a loan payment schedule for business or home use. You can vary the principal, interest, and the period of the loan, and then use the template either to calculate the monthly payment or generate a complete amortization table showing your cumulative monthly payments and indicating what portion of your payments is for interest and what portion is for principal. The table also shows cumulative interest and the outstanding balance on your loan.

Since it is so easy to change the numbers you are testing, you can use the template to quickly compare the financial implications of varying interest rates and loan periods. The template also provides a place for you to indicate what type of loan you are analyzing, and the loan source. This information is included in the printed reports, so that you can create valuable loan files for your permanent records.

Figure 2.1 shows a sample loan amortization printout. The basic loan information and your criteria are listed at the top, while the monthly breakdowns are shown vertically for the time period you indicated.

Template Layout

The Loan Amortization Schedule Template is divided into three sections (see Figure 2.2):

1. *Loan Data*. This is where you enter the numbers you wish to vary (amount borrowed, interest rate, and term) and note the date of the loan, the description, and source. This section also shows the calculated monthly payments.
2. *Amortization Table*. This section is where the actual amortization table will be generated. (See Figure 2.1 for a completed table.)
3. *Macros*. This section contains the various macros that drive the menu and recalculation functions of the template.

LOAN AMORTIZATION

```
=============================================================================================
Loan Amount:            $20,000.00   Loan Date:      12-May-87
Loan Term (Months):             24   Loan Type:  Computer
Annual Interest Rate:       10.50 %     Source:  1st National
Monthly Payment:          $927.52
=============================================================================================
```

Month	Monthly Payment	Cumulative Payments	Interest Portion	Cumulative Interest	Principal Portion	Cumulative Principal	Balance Outstanding
......	....	....	....	....	....	....	....

LOAN AMORTIZATION

```
=============================================================================================
Loan Amount:            $20,000.00   Loan Date:      12-May-87
Loan Term (Months):             24   Loan Type:  Computer
Annual Interest Rate:       10.50 %     Source:  1st National
Monthly Payment:          $927.52
=============================================================================================
```

Month	Monthly Payment	Cumulative Payments	Interest Portion	Cumulative Interest	Principal Portion	Cumulative Principal	Balance Outstanding
......	....	....	....	....	....	....	....
1	927.52	927.52	175.00	175.00	752.52	752.52	19,247.48
2	927.52	1,855.04	168.42	343.42	759.10	1,511.62	18,488.38
3	927.52	2,782.56	161.77	505.19	765.75	2,277.37	17,722.63
4	927.52	3,710.08	155.07	660.26	772.45	3,049.82	16,950.18
5	927.52	4,637.60	148.31	808.58	779.21	3,829.02	16,170.98
6	927.52	5,565.12	141.50	950.07	786.02	4,615.05	15,384.95
7	927.52	6,492.64	134.62	1,084.69	792.90	5,407.95	14,592.05
8	927.52	7,420.16	127.68	1,212.37	799.84	6,207.79	13,792.21
9	927.52	8,347.68	120.68	1,333.05	806.84	7,014.63	12,985.37
10	927.52	9,275.20	113.62	1,446.67	813.90	7,828.53	12,171.47
11	927.52	10,202.72	106.50	1,553.17	821.02	8,649.55	11,350.45
12	927.52	11,130.24	99.32	1,652.49	828.20	9,477.75	10,522.25
13	927.52	12,057.76	92.07	1,744.56	835.45	10,313.20	9,686.80
14	927.52	12,985.28	84.76	1,829.32	842.76	11,155.96	8,844.04
15	927.52	13,912.80	77.39	1,906.71	850.13	12,006.09	7,993.91
16	927.52	14,840.32	69.95	1,976.65	857.57	12,863.67	7,136.33
17	927.52	15,767.84	62.44	2,039.10	865.08	13,728.74	6,271.26
18	927.52	16,695.36	54.87	2,093.97	872.65	14,601.39	5,398.61
19	927.52	17,622.88	47.24	2,141.21	880.28	15,481.67	4,518.33
20	927.52	18,550.40	39.54	2,180.74	887.98	16,369.66	3,630.34
21	927.52	19,477.92	31.77	2,212.51	895.75	17,265.41	2,734.59
22	927.52	20,405.44	23.93	2,236.44	903.59	18,169.00	1,831.00
23	927.52	21,332.96	16.02	2,252.46	911.50	19,080.50	919.50
24	927.52	22,260.48	8.05	2,260.50	919.47	19,999.98	0.02

Figure 2.1 *Completed Loan Amortization Table.*

Loan Data
A1..E7

Macros
J1..P103

Loan Table
A14..H1000

Figure 2.2 *Layout of the Loan Amortization Table Template.*

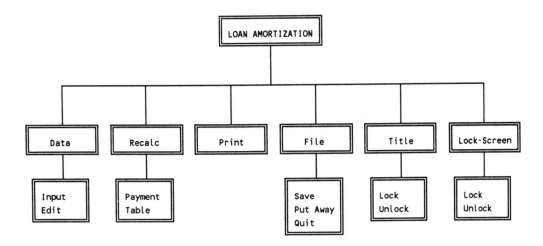

Figure 2.3 *Menu Tree, Loan Amortization Table.*

Main Menu Options

The Main Menu of the Loan Amortization Template offers the following options (see Menu Tree, Figure 2.3):

```
Data Recalc Print File Title Lock-screen
```

The **Data**, **Recalc**, and **Print** options are discussed below. See Chapter 1 for details of the File (save/quit) option, which includes two means for saving your work.

Data

To begin using the template, select the **Data** option. **Data** branches into a submenu that offers two options:

`Input Edit`

Input

Input invokes an auto-entry macro that moves the cell pointer through the following sequence of cells and prompts you to enter appropriate data:

```
Loan Amount (N) → Loan Term (N) → Annual Interest
Rate (N) → Loan Date (N) → Description (T) → Source (T)
T = Text field
N = Numeric field
```

When the cell pointer is in a text cell, you can stop the macro by pressing **CTRL-BREAK.** or **ESC.** If the current request is for numerical data (e.g., payment amount), only **CTRL-BREAK** will end the macro. (Note: If you are using Release 2.0 or 2.01, "Error" will be displayed in the mode indicator cell after you press **CTRL-BREAK**. You can clear the error message by pressing **ESC.**)

After pressing **‹RETURN›** in the *Source* cell, the template will ask whether you want to calculate a loan table or just the payment portion. **Payment** recalculates how much combined interest and principal you will have to pay each month and displays the result in the *Monthly Payment* cell. If you select the **Table** command, the template will calculate the entire amortization schedule for your loan, which will then be displayed on your screen. Once you select **Payment** or **Table**, the Main Menu will be redisplayed.

If you choose the **Payment** option, the template will display the following message:

`* * * Table Needs To Be Recalculated * * *`

This is to remind you that the recalculated figure does not correspond to the table below. The message is removed from the screen the next time the table is recalculated either by choosing Table during auto-entry or by using the **Recalc** option during manual entry. **Recalc** will be explained shortly.

Note: When the template is in auto-entry **Input** mode, you cannot enter a blank or leave the current value in a cell from a previous calculation. If you wish to retain the current value in a cell unchanged, use the **Edit** function. Also, once an item is input through the auto-entry macro and you have pressed **‹RETURN›**, you cannot alter it without exiting the macro and editing the cell in question.

Edit

The **Edit** option allows you to move the cursor freely between the input cells using the cursor control keys. The edit mode will continue until you press the **ESC** key or press **‹RETURN›** in a cell that you have not changed. At that time the Main Menu will be redisplayed. For example, to change the interest rate to 9.75 percent,

1. Select **Data/Edit** from the Main Menu.
2. Press **‹DOWN›** twice to move the cell pointer to the Annual Interest Rate cell.
3. Enter 9.75.
4. Press **ESC**, then select **Payment** or **Table**.

Sample Data Entry

Suppose that you wish to use the template to determine the monthly table for a two-year, $20,000 loan at 10.5 percent. The loan will be used to purchase a computer system, and will be secured from First National Bank on May 12, 1987. Here are the steps that would be taken to make the determination (press **‹RETURN›** after each step):

1. Select the **Data/Input** options from the Main Menu.
2. Enter the amount of the loan—$20,000.
3. Enter "24," the term of the loan in months.
4. Enter "10.5," the annual interest rate.
5. Enter "5" when prompted for the month, "12" when prompted for the date, and "87" when prompted for the year.

6. Type "Computer" as a notation of the loan type.
7. Type "First Natl." in the *Loan Source* cell.
8. Select **P**ayment or **T**able (refer to Figure 2.1). **Hint:** If you are using the template to compare various rates and principal amounts, you are best off selecting **P**ayment, since the calculation time is much quicker than that required to generate a new table, especially if the term is lengthy.

Manual Data Entry

To input data without using the auto-entry feature, escape from the Main Menu by pressing **ESC**. You can now move to whatever cell you wish by using the cursor keys. At any time you can call up the Main Menu by pressing **ALT-M**, and run any of the menu functions. After manually changing the data, be sure to recalculate the payment and table using the menu's **R**ecalc option (see next item).

Recalc

Each time you manually enter data into the template, you must select the **R**ecalc option from the Main Menu to compute the new monthly payment and amortization table. Note that the **R**ecalc function of the template is different from 1-2-3's Calc Function (**F9** key). If you merely press **F9**, the amortization table will not be correctly calculated. When you select **R**ecalc, a submenu will be displayed on your screen above the top of the worksheet, with the following options:

Payment **T**able

These options are the same as those described earlier in the section on auto-entry. The same reminder message will also be displayed if you only recalc the payment portion. The message will disappear when the table is recalculated.

Print

When you select the **Print** option from the Main Menu, the template will determine the print range for the table you have generated, and print the report. The report is designed to show four years to a page using condensed print—see Figure 2.1.

As with all Ready-to-Run templates, it is important to have your printer online before you invoke the Print command. If the printer is not online an error message will flash in the upper-right corner of the screen. In that case, press **ESC** and repeat the command.

File

The **File** menu choice provides three options: save and return to the worksheet (**Save**); save and leave 1-2-3 (**Put away**), and quit without saving (**Quit**).

Lock-Screen

Lock-Screen freezes the control panel and the screen during macro execution. It can only be used with 1-2-3 Release 2 and 2.01.

Common Questions and Problems

Auto-entry macro works improperly. This problem can occur because the Edit option uses an unrestricted input format to permit you to maintain the current value for a cell by pressing the **‹RETURN›** key. This input format also allows the use of the cursor and other control keys, which can accidentally move the cell pointer off of the intended input cell causing unpredictable results, including potential damage to the formulas and macros of the template.

If the macro should work improperly, you must stop and restart it using the **CTRL-BREAK** key combination. (Note: You will also have to press the **ESC** key to clear the resulting error message if you are using Release 2 or 2.01). You can restart the auto entry macro by pressing **ALT-M** and selecting the **Data** option again.

Data input overwrites existing data. The Amortization template provides two macros for data entry: Input and Edit. The Input option provides prompts and editing of the data as you input it. Unfortunately, the function used to provide this level of user assistance also overwrites the current contents of the cell. If you want to change only a few elements, you should select the Edit option, since it allows you to maintain the current values simply by pressing **<RETURN>**. Be careful, however, since the Edit option provides no error protection.

3 | DEPRECIATION SCHEDULE

CONTENTS

SPECIFICATIONS

Filename **DEPREC.WKS**

Function

- Calculates depreciation using nine methods:

  Straight Line
  Sum of the Year's Digits (SYD)
  200 percent declining balance
  150 percent declining balance
  ACRS-3 year (1981–1986)
  ACRS-5 year (1981–1986)
  MACRS-3 year (1987+)
  MACRS-5 year (1987+)
  MACRS-7 year (1987+)

Usage

- Generates depreciation schedules for book value or tax use.
- Creates reports for investment analysis.

Features

- Auto-entry.
- Quick calculation of depreciation schedules.
- Provides calculation under the 1981–1986 ACRS or the 1987 MACRS tables.
- Uses the half-year convention.
- Automatically converts from accelerated to straight line depreciation at optimal point.

Introduction

The Depreciation Schedule Template enables you to calculate and compare results from nine methods of depreciating business equipment. It also gives you the opportunity to conduct "what-if" calculations, varying the purchase amount and depreciation life, so that you can easily determine which method of depreciation is most advantageous for a given piece of equipment.

The depreciation tables can be used for determining book value and for tax purposes. In many cases, these calculations may be different. The book value depreciation is calculated by the template using four common methods: Straight Line, 200 percent Declining Balance, 150 percent Declining Balance, and Sum of The Year's Digits.

The tax tables are calculated using the published tables for the Accelerated Cost Recovery System (ACRS) for assets placed in service between January 1, 1981 and December 31, 1986. Tables are also calculated using the Modified Accelerated Cost Recovery System (MACRS) for assets placed in service after January 1, 1987 for several Asset Depreciation Ranges (ADRs) appropriate for non-real estate assets.

> **Important Note!** The Depreciation Template is not intended to provide tax advice. It is your responsibility to determine the appropriateness of a particular tax table for your company. The template is simply an easy method for calculating the annual depreciation values, given the correct data.

When you input data into the template, you will be asked to enter both the Useful Life for calculation of the Book depreciations and the Depreciation Method to use for the Tax calculation. The selection of the appropriate depreciation method for tax purposes depends on the midpoint life of the Asset Depreciation Range (ADR) as defined by the IRS and the year the asset was put into service. Table 3.1 shows a brief extract of the ADR guidelines for 1981–1986 as modified for 1987. Use it to determine the appropriate ADR class for some common business assets.

Table 3.1 *A brief extract of the ADR guidelines for 1981–1986 as modified for 1987.*

Asset Description	1981–1986 Class Life	1987 Class Life
Computers	5	5
Office Furniture/Fixtures	5	7
Office Equipment	5	7
Manufacturing Equipment	5	7
Telephone Equipment (nonutility)	5	5
Cars/Light trucks	3	5

Again, this is intended for information only. Please refer to your tax adviser for specific guidance on the ADR life of a particular asset.

Table 3.2 lists the tax methods available in the Depreciation Template:

Table 3.2 *Tax methods available in the Depreciation Template.*

Method	Description
1	ACRS - 3 year (1981–1986)
2	ACRS - 5 year (1981–1986)
3	MACRS - 3 year (1987+)
4	MACRS - 5 year (1987+)
5	MACRS - 7 year (1987+)

The tables of the Depreciation Template use the Half Year Convention, (i.e., the asset is assumed to have been placed in service six months into the year in which it was purchased). Therefore, the first year's depreciation is calculated for only the remaining six months of the year of purchase. This convention also produces a half year's depreciation in the calender year after the life of the asset. Also, all tables assume conversion to Straight Line Depreciation as soon as it is advantageous to do so.

Figure 3.1 shows a depreciation schedule calculated by the template.

DEPRECIATION SCHEDULE

```
==================================================================================================
Taxpayer Name:              Your name        1= ACRS 3 Year (1981-1986)
Description of Asset:        IBM AT           2= ACRS 5 Year (1981-1986)
Cost of Asset:              4235              3= MACRS 3 Year (1987+)
Useful Life (BOOK):            5              4= MACRS 5 Year (1987+)
Depreciation Method (TAX):     2              5= MACRS 7 Year (1987+)
Year Acquired:              1986              6= PRE-1981, Assume already fully
                                                 depreciated or use book method
==================================================================================================
```

			BOOK			TAX
Year		Straight Line	Sum of Year's Digits	200% Declining Balance	150% Declining Balance	ACRS or MACRS
1986	1	423.50	705.85	847.00	635.25	635.25
1987	2	847.00	1,270.50	1,355.20	1,079.93	931.70
1988	3	847.00	988.15	813.12	755.95	889.35
1989	4	847.00	705.85	487.87	705.55	889.35
1990	5	847.00	423.50	487.87	705.55	889.35
1991	6	423.50	141.15	243.94	352.78	0.00
1992	7	0.00	0.00	0.00	0.00	0.00
1993	8	0.00	0.00	0.00	0.00	0.00
1994	9	0.00	0.00	0.00	0.00	0.00
1995	10	0.00	0.00	0.00	0.00	0.00
		4,235.00	4,235.00	4,235.00	4,235.00	4,235.00

```
* Note all tables assume a half year convention, i.e. the asset is only depreciated
  for six month of the first tax year.
```

Figure 3.1 *Sample Depreciation Schedule*

Template Layout

The Depreciation Schedule Template is divided into three sections (see Figure 3.2):

1. *Depreciation Data.* This is where you enter the purchase data, and indicate the useful life of the asset, the depreciation method, and the year acquired.
2. *Depreciation Schedule.* This section is where the actual depreciation figures will be generated. (see Figure 3.1 for a completed table.)
3. *Macros.* This section contains the various macros that drive the menu and recalculation functions of the template.

Main Menu Options

The depreciation template offers the following menu options (see Menu Tree, Figure 3.3):

```
Data   Recalc   File   Lockscreen
```

Purchase Data
A1..G10

Macros
A107..J57

Tax Tables
A40..J106

Depreciation Schedule
A12..K35

Figure 3.2 *Layout of the Depreciation Schedule Template.*

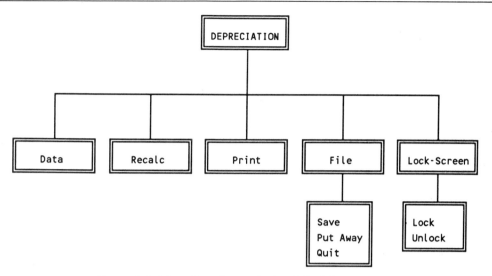

Figure 3.3 *Menu Tree, Depreciation Schedule Template.*

Data

The **Data** option branches into a submenu with two options:

```
Input   Edit
```

Input begins an auto-entry macro that prompts you to enter appropriate data as it moves the pointer through the cells of the Depreciation section in the following sequence:

```
Taxpayer Name (T) → Description of Asset (T) →
Cost of Asset (N) → Useful Life (N) → Depreciation
Method (N) → Year Acquired (N)
T = Text cell
N = Numeric cell
```

After pressing **<RETURN>** in the *Year Acquired* cell, the template will automatically calculate the depreciation values, and the Main Menu will reappear.

Note that when the cell pointer is in a text cell, you can stop the macro by pressing **ESC** or **CTRL-BREAK**. When the cell pointer is in a numeric cell, the macro can only be stopped by pressing **CTRL-BREAK**. If you are using Release 2.0 or 2.01, pressing **CTRL-**

BREAK will generate an error message. This can be cleared by pressing **ESC.**

To edit data already entered in the Depreciation Data section, select the **Data/Edit** option, which will allow you to freely move the cell pointer with the cursor keys. You can then change any data manually. As you enter new values, the depreciation table will be automatically updated.

Sample Data Entry

You paid $4,235 in 1986 for a computer and wish to determine the depreciation value using the ACRS-5 year method. Here's how the data would be entered:

1. Select the **Data/Input** option from the Main Menu. The cell pointer will move to the *Taxpayer Name* cell. Enter the appropriate information and press **<RETURN>**.
2. Enter a description of the asset, such as "Computer" or "IBM AT."
3. Enter the cost of the computer, "4235," without dollar signs or commas.
4. The next cell, *Useful life,* is for the book value. Select five years, which is the appropriate life from the matrix on page 30. This cell is programmed to only accept values of 3 to 9 years. If you enter a value above or below that range, the template will beep and again prompt you to enter a valid number.
5. Now input the depreciation method for tax purposes. You must enter a valid method number (1 through 6), otherwise the template will beep and prompt you to reenter a depreciation method.
6. Finally, enter the year of the acquisition. Do not use the Lotus date format—simply enter the date as a text item (e.g., 1985 would be entered as "1985"). When you press **<RETURN>**, the Main Menu will be redisplayed.

Print

The **Print** option generates hard copy of the table currently displayed on the screen. Make sure the printer is online before attempting to print a report.

File

When you select the **File** option, you will have the choice of saving and returning to the worksheet (**Save**); saving and leave 1-2-3 (**Put away**); and quitting without saving (**Quit**).

Updating the Tables

If you need to update the tables because of changes in the tax laws, use the following guides. Table 1 includes the Straight Line Sum of the Year's Digits and 150 and 200 percent declining balance. Table 1 is located in cells B41..J88. (Note: Table 1 also has the range name TABLE1, so you can press the **F5** (goto) key and type "TABLE1.") The Straight line section is contained in the first ten rows (48–57), the Sum of the Years section is the next ten rows (58–67), 200 Percent Declining Balance is the next ten rows (68–77), and 150 Percent Declining Balance is contained in the last ten rows (78–87). The "Life" fields run across columns D through columns J.

Table 2 contains the ACRS and MACRS data. It is located in cells B91..I105 (you can move the pointer to Table 2 by pressing **F5** and typing "TABLE2.") Columns D through I contain the table numbers 1–6, which refer to the different methods of depreciation, while the years are listed down the rows. Year one starts in row 96, year ten is in row 105, and so on.

Common Questions and Problems

The depreciation life or method is invalid for your use. The depreciation tables are provided for the most common terms for non-real estate assets. The ACRS and MACRS tax tables are provided for the same non-real estate assets. In many cases, you may be able to use a "Useful Life" for book purposes that is different than the life that must be used for tax purposes. If you try to enter a life that is not covered by the tables, the auto entry macro will alert you. If you manually enter an invalid life, the tables will show ERR.

In any case, the determination of the appropriate tax table must be made after consulting your tax adviser. The guidelines provided in this chapter are for information purposes only, and should not be relied on for tax advice.

The first year seems low. The first year may at first seem too low, since the table assumes a half-year convention. That is to say all assets are assumed to have been purchased half-way through the year, and therefore should all be depreciated for only six months during the first year. As a result, the first year's depreciation may appear lower than expected. The half-year convention also generates depreciation in the year following the life of the asset.

4 | CAPITAL ASSET INVENTORY

CONTENTS

SPECIFICATIONS

Filename **INVENT.WKS**

Function

- Tracks a business' capital assets, equipment, and/or personal possessions.

Usage

- Tracks capital assets for insurance purposes.
- Determines current book value of depreciable assets.

Features

- Auto-entry.
- Calculates depreciation using nine methods.
- Automatically converts from accelerated depreciation to straight line at optimal point.
- Assigns category codes for each piece of equipment.
- Extracts and subtotals groups of equipment by assigned code.
- Uses standard half-year convention for first and last years' depreciation.
- Screen lock for Release 2.

Introduction

The Capital Asset Inventory Template is designed to keep track of your business or home purchases. It can extract these purchases by code as well as depreciation life, method, and year. This can be helpful for insurance purposes, as well as for tracking your assets for tax purposes and financial statements. The template has fields for description/serial numbers, purchase date, purchase price, purchase source, depreciation life, and depreciated value.

Depreciated value can be determined for book or tax purposes. The book value depreciation is calculated by using four common methods: Straight Line, 200 percent Declining Balance, 150 percent Declining Balance, and Sum of The Year's Digits (see Depreciation Template, Chapter 3, for more details). The tax tables are calculated using the published tables for the Accelerated Cost Recovery System (ACRS) for assets placed in service between January 1, 1981 and December 31, 1986. Tables are also calculated using the Modified Accelerated Cost Recovery System (MACRS) for assets placed in service after January 1, 1987 for several Asset Depreciation Ranges (ADRs) appropriate for non-real estate assets.

The template automatically converts from the accelerated depreciation method to straight line depreciation at the most advantageous point. All depreciation methods use a standard half-year convention for the first and last year.

The selection of the appropriate depreciation method for tax purposes depends on the midpoint life of the Asset Depreciation Range (ADR) as defined by the IRS and the year the asset was put into service. The following matrix is a brief extract of the ADR guidelines for 1981–1986 as modified for 1987. Use it to determine the appropriate ADR class for some common business assets.

> **Important Note!** The depreciation function of the capital assets template is not intended as tax advice. It is your responsibility to determine the appropriateness of a particular tax table for your company. The template simply provides an easy method for calculating the annual depreciation values, given the correct data.

Table 4.1 *A brief extract of the ADR guidelines for 1981–1986 as modified for 1987.*

Asset Description	1981–1986 Class Life	1987 Class Life
Computers	5	5
Office Furniture & Fixtures	5	7
Office Equipment	5	7
Manufacturing Equipment	5	7
Telephone Equipment (non-utility)	5	5
Cars & Light Trucks	3	5

To begin using the Capital Assets Template, you will need to list each piece of equipment and provide the appropriate information for its valuation. It is not necessary to alphabetize the list, since the template will allow you to sort alphabetically by asset name as well as by category at any time. Figure 4.1 shows a completed inventory template.

Template Layout

The Capital Asset Inventory Template is divided into four sections (see Figure 4.2):

1. *Asset Entry.* This is where you list the pieces of equipment and the serial number, purchase date, purchase source, purchase price, depreciation life, depreciation method, and item code.
2. *Selection Screen.* The selection screen allows you to enter the code that you want to use to group entries. (See Extract function.)
3. *Selected Records.* Once you have indicated what kinds of records you want to Extract, they will appear in this area of the template for viewing or printing.
4. *Macros.* This section contains the macros that drive the menu operations and carry out extracting, printing, and saving functions.

CAPITAL ASSET INVENTORY Valuation Date:12-May-87

Item Number	Description and Serial Number	Purchase Date	Source	Purchase Price	Life	Deprec. Method	Deprec. Year	Depreciated Value	Item Code
			Totals:	$47,133.00				$14,763.32	
83001	Copier SX531 SN 343FRE	05-Apr-83	ACE Copy	3,670.00	5	2	5	0.00	1
83002	Desk	09-May-83	Al's Office	654.00	5	2	5	0.00	2
83003	Typewriter	12-Jun-83	Essex Office	687.00	5	2	5	0.00	1
83004	Filing cabinets--10	18-Jun-83	Al's Office	765.00	5	2	5	0.00	2
83005	Chairs 3	18-Aug-83	Al's Office	184.00	5	2	5	0.00	2
83006	IBM PC	22-Nov-83	Comp House	4,123.00	5	2	5	0.00	1
83007	NEC 3550 Printer	12-Jun-83	Comp House	2,032.00	5	2	5	0.00	1
83008	Chairs 4	12-Jun-83	Al's Office	321.00	5	2	5	0.00	2
84001	Hayes 1200b modem 4	01-Feb-84	Dynamic	421.00	5	2	4	88.41	1
84002	Computer tables 3	23-Mar-84	SyTek	279.00	5	2	4	58.59	2
84003	Desk	16-May-84	Al's Office	312.00	5	2	4	65.52	2
84004	Filing cabinets 4	24-Jun-84	Al's Office	246.00	5	2	4	51.66	2
84005	IBM XT SN4564563533	24-Jun-84	SyTek	4,712.00	5	2	4	989.52	1
85001	FAX 2000 SN B7654	29-Jul-85	ACE Copy	1,298.00	5	2	3	545.16	1
85002	BINDING MACHINE SN8912-09098	16-Aug-85	General	654.00	5	2	3	274.68	1
85003	SHREDDER SN QW2311	30-Sep-85	General	523.00	5	2	3	219.66	1
85004	Desk	07-Oct-85	Desks Unltd	543.00	5	2	3	228.06	2
85005	Bookcase 2	07-Oct-85	Desks Unltd	398.00	5	2	3	167.16	2
85006	Chevrolet Celebrity Wagon	07-Nov-85	JK Chevrolet	9,672.00	3	1	3	0.00	4
86001	Transciber SN 77900100	02-Feb-86	MCR Office	498.00	5	2	2	217.35	1
86002	Conference table	22-May-86	Al's Office	345.00	5	2	2	80.01	2
86003	Coffee table	22-May-86	Al's Office	127.00	5	2	2	102.06	2
86004	Secretarial chair 2	03-Jun-86	Al's Office	162.00	5	2	2	2,161.53	2
86005	AR 25 Phone system 5 phones	12-Jun-86	RJX Assoc	3,431.00	5	2	2	151.83	1
86006	Refrigerator	12-Jul-86	Big Top	241.00	5	2	2	3,560.13	3
87001	IBM AT SN 881514262	12-Jan-87	Sytek	5,651.00	5	5	1	2,560.28	1
87002	Laser printer plus SN 456 987	18-Feb-87	Micro Store	2,987.00	5	5	1	655.71	1
87003	EGA Monitor SN 2312222	23-Mar-87	Micro Store	765.00	5	5	1	765.00	1
87004	Partitions 6	11-Apr-83	Al's Office	1,432.00	5	5	5	1,821.00	2

Figure 4.1 *Sample Capital Assets Template.*

Asset Data
A10..J1000

Selection Screen
K1..P20

Selected Records
T10..AB1000

Macros
L21..S135

Tax Tables
L137..S195

Figure 4.2 *Layout of the Capital Assets Template.*

Main Menu Options

After pressing **‹RETURN›** at the title page, the Main Menu will automatically display the following options (see Figure 4.3, Menu Tree, for a view of the full menu structure.)

`Data Extract Print File Title Lock-Screen`

The File, Title, and Lock-Screen options are discussed in detail in Chapter 1. The Data, Extract, and Print options are described below.

Data

The Data option branches into five submenu choices:

`Continue Begin Edit Delete Valuation`

Continue and Begin

These two options start an auto-entry macro that moves the cursor through the following sequence of cells each time you enter data and press **‹RETURN›** (only use Begin the first time you enter data):

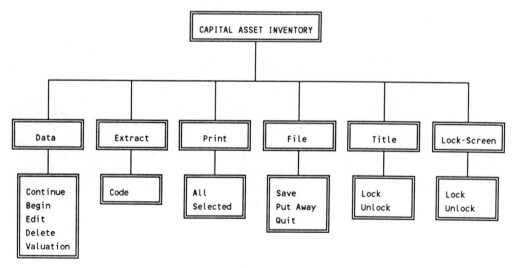

Figure 4.3 *Menu Tree, Capital Assets Template.*

```
Item # (T)→ Description/Serial Number (T) →
Purchase Date (N) → Source (N) → Purchase Price (N) →
Deprec. Life (N) → Deprec. Method (N) → Item Code (T)
T = Text cell
N = Numeric cell
```

When you enter an item code and press ‹RETURN›, the pointer will move to the *Item #* cell of the next row, and a menu will appear at the top of the control panel offering you the choice of continuing or stopping data entry. Press ‹RETURN› to continue, or select Stop to return to the Main Menu.

The auto-entry macro can be stopped at any time. To break the macro when the pointer is in a text cell, press **CTRL-BREAK** or **ESC**. When the pointer is in a numeric cell, only **CTRL-BREAK** will stop the macro. Note that with Release 2.0 and 2.01, pressing **CTRL-BREAK** will generate an error message. This can be cleared by pressing the **ESC** key.

Should you terminate the auto-entry macro in the middle of a line, you will have to manually enter data in the rest of the cells or erase the line entirely. This is necessary because the Extract function requires complete rows of data.

> **Caution!** Do NOT use the /Worksheet Delete Row function to erase a line of data, as this may damage the macros. Instead, erase the row cell-by-cell using the /Range Erase command.

Edit

The **Data/Edit** option allows you to use the cursor keys to move the pointer, so you can manually change data in cells of your choice. When you are done with your edits, press **ALT-M** to redisplay the Main Menu.

To edit a date, press **ALT-D**. You will then be prompted to enter the month, day, and year, pressing ‹RETURN› after each. If you do not wish to use the **ALT-D** edit function for editing dates, you must use the standard Lotus 1-2-3 date format, (@date(yy,mm,dd)).

Delete

This function replaces the Lotus 1-2-3 /Worksheet Delete Row function. See Chapter 1 for details.

Valuation

The Valuation option allows you to easily change the valuation date by prompting you for the day, month, and year. Press **‹RETURN›** after entering data at each prompt. The Main Menu will reappear when the date is complete. If you make a mistake and enter an invalid date, the template will prompt you for another one.

Sample Data Entry

You purchased a photocopier machine in 1983 for $3670, and wish to create an inventory record that will depreciate the item using the ACRS method. Here are the steps you'd take to include the item in your inventory.

1. Select the **Data/Begin** option. Enter a number in the *Item #* cell (Col A) as prompted. The number can be any alphanumeric combination. The item number is a unique identifier that should be assigned to each asset. Assume that our copier is item number 83001 (the first purchase in 1983). Press **‹RETURN›** when you have entered a code, and the cell pointer will move to the *description* cell.
2. Describe the copier model number and/or enter the serial number in the *Description* cell. In our example, that might be "SX531, SN 343FRE."
3. Enter the date the copier was bought in the *Purchase Date* cell. If the copier was bought April 4, 1987, you would enter the month, day, and last two digits of the year as prompted by the auto-entry macro.
4. Enter the company that sold you the copier, say "ACE Copy," in the *Source* cell (Col D).
5. The cell pointer should be in the *Purchase Price* cell (Col E). Enter the cost of the copier, "3670."
6. Now enter the depreciation life in Column "F." In the case of a copier, the depreciation life would be "5." Refer to the matrix of ADR lines in Figure 4.1 when determining an appropriate depreciation life for an item.
7. Select the appropriate depreciation method in Column "G" (refer to the Introduction of this chapter). In this case, we will use the accelerated method, ACRS-5 year, which is method #4 in the template. (See Table 4.2 for method numbers.)

Table 4.2 *Template depreciation methods.*

Method	Description
For tax purposes	
1	ACRS - 3 year (1981–1986)
2	ACRS - 5 year (1981–1986)
3	MACRS - 3 year (1987 +)
4	MACRS - 5 year (1987 +)
5	MACRS - 7 year (1987 +)
For book determination purposes	
6	straight line
7	sum of years digits
8	200% declining balance
9	150% declining balance

8. Next, the system will determine the depreciation year based on the purchase and valuation dates. The depreciation year is based on calendar year and is set to 1 if the purchase year equals the valuation year. Thereafter, it increased by 1 for each year's difference between the purchase year and the valuation year. Based on the depreciation year, the template will calculate the depreciated value of the item in Column "I" and move the pointer to the last column in the row, *Item Code*.

9. Enter an item code for the copier. This code is used with the extract function, so that you can group together all assets in the same category. For example, office equipment might be "01," furniture might be "02," processing equipment might be "03," and so on. Later, you could create a report consisting of all furniture owned by the company.

Once you fill in the *Item Code* cell and press **<RETURN>**, the pointer will move to the next row and display a continuation menu. You can continue adding data under macro control by pressing **<RETURN>**, or break the auto-entry macro by selecting the **S**top option, which will restart the Main Menu.

Extract

The Capital Asset Inventory Template allows you to extract all entries that have the same user-selected criteria. When you choose Extract from the Main Menu, a submenu with the following extract criteria will be displayed:

```
Code   Life   Method   Year
```

Select the criteria by which you would like records to be extracted. You will then see the Extract Selection Screen (see Figure 4.4).

Code

If you choose the Code option, enter a specific item code (e.g., "01") and all records with that code will be copied to the Selected Records area of the template. This operation will also give you a total for the extracted records, so at a glance you can view the depreciated value total for a specific category of assets.

Life

This extract option refers to depreciation life. When you select Life, the Selection Screen will prompt you to enter a number. If you entered "3," the template would then extract all assets with a deprecation life of three years. This enables you to extract all assets that have the same life.

Method

The Method option refers to the depreciation method used to depreciate an asset. Enter the desired method number in the Selection Screen, and the template will group together all assets that were depreciated by the method indicated.

Year

When you extract by Year, you will get all assets that are in the same year of depreciation. While this is similar in concept to the age

```
====================
     Enter
     selected
     Code
             1
====================
```

Figure 4.4 *Extract Selection Screen, Capital Assets Template.*

of the asset, the depreciation year differs in that it is based strictly on calendar year. If the purchase date and the valuation date are in the same calendar year, the depreciation year is set to 1. Thereafter, it is increased 1 for each year's difference between the purchase year and the valuation year.

Regardless of which extract criteria you chose, the records that met the criteria and were copied from the Data Entry section will remain in the Selected Records section until you use the Extract function again. At that time, the records will be overwritten by whatever records meet the new extract criteria.

After you're done viewing extracted records, you can press the **Home** key to return to the data entry area, or press **ALT-M** to restart the Main Menu. You can also print the extracted records with the **Print/Selected** option. When the printing is complete, the cell pointer will automatically be repositioned in the *Home* cell (A1). Figure 4.5, on page 48, shows a printout of the Selected Records section of the template following an extract.

Print

When you select the **Print** option from the Main Menu, you will see a submenu that gives you the following options:

`All Selected`

The **All** option prints out every entry in the template (see Figure 4.1 for a sample printout), including headings and rules. The Selected option prints out those entries that were most recently extracted through the Extract function. Make sure the printer is online before attempting to print.

File

The **File** menu choice provides three options: save and return to the worksheet (**Save**); save and leave 1-2-3 (**Put away**); and quit without saving (**Quit**).

```
CAPITAL ASSET INVENTORY  Valuation Date:12-May-87
                   Selection Criteria:Code                    1
=====================================================================================================
Item                              Purchase                  Purchase Deprec. Deprec. Deprec.  Depreciated  Item
Number   Description and Serial Number  Date     Source       Price Life  Method  Year         Value  Code
.....................................................................................................

                                           Totals:   $31,452.00                         $6,467.60

.....................................................................................................


83001 Copier SX531 SN 343FRE           05-Apr-83 ACE Copy      3,670.00   5     2     5          0.00    1
83003 Typewriter                       12-Jun-83 Essex Office    687.00   5     2     5          0.00    1
83006 IBM PC                           22-Nov-83 Comp House    4,123.00   5     2     5          0.00    1
83007 NEC 3550 Printer                 12-Jun-83 Comp House    2,032.00   5     2     5          0.00    1
84001 Hayes 1200b modem  4             01-Feb-84 Dynamic         421.00   5     2     4         88.41    1
84005 IBM XT    SN4564563533           24-Jun-84 SyTek        4,712.00   5     2     4        989.52    1
85001 FAX 2000  SN B7654               29-Jul-85 ACE Copy     1,298.00   5     2     3        545.16    1
85002 BINDING MACHINE    SN8912-09098  16-Aug-85 General        654.00   5     2     3        274.68    1
85003 SHREDDER    SN QW2311            30-Sep-85 General        523.00   5     2     3        219.66    1
86001 Transciber  SN 77900100          02-Feb-86 MCR Office     498.00   5     2     2        217.35    1
86005 AR 25 Phone system   5 phones    12-Jun-86 RJX Assoc    3,431.00   5     2     2        151.83    1
87001 IBM AT SN 881514262              12-Jan-87 Sytek        5,651.00   5     5     1      2,560.28    1
87002 Laser printer plus  SN 456 987   18-Feb-87 Micro Store  2,987.00   5     5     1        655.71    1
87003 EGA Monitor    SN 2312222        23-Mar-87 Micro Store    765.00   5     5     1        765.00    1
```

Figure 4.5 *Sample Extract, Capital Assets Template.*

Title

The title function locks the column headings so that they are visible even when you have scrolled down beyond 20 lines. The title function defaults to on, but can be removed by selecting the **Title/Unlock** option.

Lock-Screen

Lock-Screen freezes the control panel and the screen during macro execution. It can only be used with 1-2-3 Release 2 and 2.01.

Updating the Depreciation Tables

Refer to the Depreciation Schedule template in Chapter 3. (Note that the tables in the Capital Asset Inventory are cumulative.)

Common Questions and Problems

The depreciation year seems wrong. The depreciation year is determined on a calendar basis. If the valuation data is in the same calendar year as the purchase date, the depreciation year is set to "1." If the valuation date is in the next year, the depreciation year is set to "2." Therefore, if the asset was purchased on December 25, 1986, and the valuation date is December 30, 1986, the depreciation year is set to "1." If the valuation date is set to January 1, 1987, the depreciation year would be "2." Since the tables all assume a half-year convention, this calenderization of the depreciation year should be correct for most users.

5 | NET PRESENT VALUE:CONTINUOUS FLOW

CONTENTS

SPECIFICATIONS

Filename **NPV_C.WKS**

Function

- Calculates Net Present Value when payment intervals are regular and amounts are equal.

Usage

- Determines whether an equipment purchase is advantageous in terms of net present value of the investment cash flows.

Features

- Auto-entry makes it easy to enter payment amounts and intervals.
- Quick calculation of Net Present Value.

Introduction

The Net Present Value (NPV)—Continuous Flow Template allows you to evaluate a potential acquisition in light of cash flow. For example, you might be considering purchasing a computer that will cost $10,000 today, and will bring in an additional $200 a month in revenue or reduced overhead over its useful life. Over a given period of time, say five years, is that revenue (discounted for the time value of money) greater than the cost of the investment?

Simply adding the sum of the payments will not give you an accurate answer, since a dollar payment to be received a year from now is not as valuable today as cash already in hand—time really *is* money. This template gives you a better answer by taking the future payments and discounting them back to the current time period, indicating whether the purchase would represent a profit or loss (see sample Figure 5.1).

Note that the template assumes that benefits to cash flow will be regular and evenly spaced throughout the year. If the benefits and timing are irregular, you need to use the Net Present Value—Variable Cash Flow Template (Chapter 6), which requires that you indicate the amount and date of each payment.

Template Layout

The Net Present Value—Continuous Flow Template is divided into three sections (see Figure 5.2):

1. *Investment Data.* This is where you enter the details of the acquisition, including the cost, the payment amount per period, the life of the investment, the number of payments per year, and the annual interest rate.
2. *Calculations.* This section displays the calculated Net Present Value of the cash flow and the Profit or Loss.
3. *Macros.* This section contains the various macros that drive the menu and recalculation functions of the template.

Main Menu Options

This template offers three Main Menu options (see Menu Tree, Figure 5.3):

```
Data Print File
```

```
NET PRESENT VALUE                  Date:      12-May-87
CONTINUOUS FLOW             Investment:Computer


===========================================================

Cost of Acquisition:                        $10,000.00


Incremental Cash Flow per Period:            $200.00
Life of Investment (Years) :                    5
Cash Flow Payments Per Year:                   12
Annual Interest Rate:                        9.25 %



===========================================================

Present Value of Payments:                   $9,578.59


Net Present Value - Profit/(Loss)           ($421.41)


===========================================================
```

Figure 5.1 *Sample Net Present Value—Continuous Flow Calculation.*

Investment Data   *Macros*
A1..C12   **F1..J51**

Calculations
A14..C18

Figure 5.2 *Layout NPV—Continuous Flow Template.*

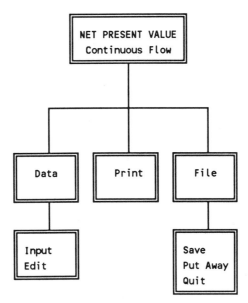

Figure 5.3 *Menu Tree for NPV—Continuous Flow template.*

Data

The **Data** option branches into a submenu offering two choices:

```
Input Edit
```

Input

The **Data/Input** option starts an auto-entry macro that moves the cursor through the following sequence of cells, prompting you for each entry:

```
Date (N) → Investment (T) → Cost of Acquisition (N) →
Incremented Cash Flow Per Period (N) → Life of Investment (N) →
Cash Flow Payments Per Year (N) → Annual Interest Rate (N)
T = text cell
N = numeric cell
```

Each time you input information into a cell and press **<RE-TURN>**, the pointer will move to the next cell in the sequence. When you press **<RETURN>** in the *Annual Interest Rate* cell, the pointer will return to the *Home* cell (A1) and the Main Menu will reappear.

If you press **<RETURN>** without entering data while the cell pointer is in a text cell, the cell will be left blank. If you attempt to leave a blank in a numeric cell, however, you will generate an error message. Press **<RETURN>** to clear the message.

To terminate the auto-entry macro, press **CTRL-BREAK**. This will cause an error message to be displayed if you are using Release 2.0 or 2.01. In that case, press **ESC**, and the template will return to READY status. If the cell pointer is in a text cell, you can also end the auto-entry macro by pressing **ESC**.

Edit

The **Data/Edit** option allows you to move the cursor freely between the input cells using the cursor control keys. The edit mode will continue until you press the **ESC** key or press **<RETURN>** in a cell that you have not changed. At that time the Main Menu will be redisplayed.

Sample Data Entry

We will now answer the question posed in the introduction regarding the proposed computer purchase. Consider a computer that would cost $10,000, and is expected to generate an additional $200 a month in revenue (or reduced overhead.) If the useful life is five years, and the current interest rate or cost of capital is 9.25 percent, would the additional income outweigh the cost of the purchase? To find out, enter the numbers in the template as follows:

1. Select the **Data/Input** option. The cell pointer will automatically move to the *Date* cell (C1). Enter the date of the acquisition, as prompted by the template (month, day, year). Press **<RETURN>** and the cursor will proceed to the *Investment* cell (C2).
2. Enter the type of equipment you are considering for purchase. In this case, type "Computer."
3. In the *Cost of Acquisition* cell (C6) enter the purchase price of the computer and press **<RETURN>**. (Do not enter dollar signs or commas).

4. The pointer should now be in the *Revenue Per Period* cell (C8). Enter "200," the amount that you expect the acquisition to add to your cash flow either as direct income or reduction in expenses.

5. Next, in the *Life of Investment* cell (C9), enter the number of years of cash flow over which you want to calculate Net Present Value and press **<RETURN>**. In this case, enter "5" (you must enter whole years.)

6. The cell cursor will next move to the *Revenue Periods Per Year* cell (C10). Enter the number of equal payments per year by which your cash flow will be affected by the acquisition and press **<RETURN>**. In our example, we want to calculate on the basis of 12 monthly payments per year, so we would enter "12." If the payments were quarterly, you would enter "4." You must enter whole numbers; otherwise, the system will round up or down.

7. The last cell in the data entry sequence is *Annual Interest Rate* (C11). Enter the percentage you wish to test. (Note: 9.25 percent would be entered as "9.25," not "0.0925.") Press **<RE-TURN>** and the Main Menu will again appear above the top row of the worksheet.

As you enter information in each cell, the template will automatically recalculate the Present Value of Payments (C16) and the Profit/Loss (C18) that the investment represents in terms of net present value. (Refer to Figure 5.1 for a printout of the numbers just input.) As you can see, cell C16 indicates a loss of $421.41. So you would be better off spending the money for the computer on another acquisition that offered a more significant increase to your cash flow.

Print

When you select the **Print** option from the Main Menu, the section of the template visible on the screen will be printed. Make sure your printer is online before selecting the option, or else you will generate an error message that must be cleared with the **ESC** key.

File

The File menu choice provides three options: save and return to the worksheet (**Save**); Save and leave 1-2-3 (**Put away**), and quit without saving (**Quit**).

Common Questions and Problems

Why can't I input the life in decimal form? The NPV calculation for continuous cash flow must assume a finite number of EQUAL payments EVENLY spaced over time. Fractional time periods violate this assumption. If you need to use a payment pattern other than the usual quarterly or monthly payments, you can alter the definition of the life to another time scale than years. Be sure to alter the interest rate to correspond to the life span definition.

Why do I have to enter the number of payments per period? The templates allows you to enter interest rates in the most common form (i.e., annual) even when the number payments may be monthly or quarterly. The formulas automatically convert the annual interest rate to the periodic interest rate.

How can I enter a number of periods other than even years? If you wanted to enter an uneven number of periods, such as 13 months, you can do so by redefining the default period years as months, so that the periodic interest rate must be expressed as the monthly interest rate. The number of periods would be 13 and the number of payments per period would be one. Another alternative is to use the variable cash flow NPV template (see Chapter 6).

6 | NET PRESENT VALUE: VARIABLE FLOW

CONTENTS

SPECIFICATIONS

Filename **NPV_V.WKS**

Function

- Calculates Net Present Value when payment intervals and amounts are irregular.

Usage

- Determines whether an equipment purchase is advantageous in terms of net present value of the future cash flow.

Features

- Auto-entry makes it easy to enter payment amounts and intervals.
- Quick calculation of Net Present Value.
- Accommodates both past and future payments.
- Compounds interest daily.

Introduction

This template has the same function as the Net Present Value (NPV)—Continuous Flow Template; it allows you to evaluate a potential acquisition in light of cash flow. (See the introduction to Chapter 5 for more details about the Net Present Value concept.) The difference is that the Variable (cash) Flow version in this chapter does not assume that the payments or timing are regular. Instead, it allows you to enter the date and the amount of the expected payment as a unique description of the resulting revenue stream.

The entry and functions of the Variable Flow version are also different from the Continuous Flow version, so even if you have familiarized yourself with the steps in Chapter 5, take a few moments to read the following instructions before attempting to perform a variable cash flow NPV calculation.

The variable flow NPV approach is used to evaluate a purchase that yields irregular cash flows. For example, suppose you were considering buying a piece of equipment that will not yield any cash benefits for a period of time after it is purchased because of a set up or testing period. Variable flow NPV would also be used in situations where the acquisition will be shut down for a period each year for maintenance, or for situations in which seasonal variations in demand are expected. In general, any situation in which the economic benefits of an acquisition are expected to vary over time will be amenable to analysis by variable flow NPV. Figure 6.1 shows a completed NPV calculation using the variable flow template.

Template Layout

The Net Present Value—Variable Flow Template is divided into three sections (see Figure 6.2):

1. *Acquisition Data.* This is where you enter the details of the acquisition, including the cost, the date of acquisition, and the annual interest rate.
2. *Payment Data.* This section is where you enter the payment data—amount and date.

```
======================================================================
Date of Acquisition:        01-Mar-87  Description:  Processing eq
Annual Interest Rate:            9.50 %
Cost of Acquisition:      $250,000.00  Total Payments   $321,000.00
Profit/(Loss):             $33,806.68  PV of Payments   $283,806.68
======================================================================
```

Payment Number	Payment Amount	Payment Date	Present Value	Cummulative P.V.
1	5,000.00	01-Apr-87	4,959.83	4,959.83
2	10,000.00	01-May-87	9,842.51	14,802.33
3	1,000.00	01-Jun-87	976.34	15,778.67
4	1,000.00	01-Jul-87	968.75	16,747.42
5	1,000.00	01-Aug-87	960.97	17,708.39
6	5,000.00	01-Sep-87	4,766.22	22,474.61
7	10,000.00	01-Oct-87	9,458.31	31,932.92
8	15,000.00	01-Nov-87	14,073.47	46,006.39
9	20,000.00	01-Dec-87	18,618.70	64,625.08
10	25,000.00	01-Jan-88	23,086.37	87,711.45
11	25,000.00	01-Feb-88	22,900.87	110,612.32
12	25,000.00	01-Apr-88	22,546.06	133,158.39
13	25,000.00	01-May-88	22,370.73	155,529.12
14	1,000.00	01-Jun-88	887.64	156,416.75
15	1,000.00	01-Jul-88	880.74	157,297.49
16	1,000.00	01-Aug-88	873.66	158,171.15
17	5,000.00	01-Sep-88	4,333.20	162,504.35
18	10,000.00	01-Oct-88	8,599.00	171,103.35
19	15,000.00	01-Nov-88	12,794.86	183,898.21
20	20,000.00	01-Dec-88	16,927.14	200,825.35
21	25,000.00	01-Jan-89	20,988.92	221,814.26
22	25,000.00	01-Feb-89	20,820.27	242,634.53
23	25,000.00	01-Mar-89	20,669.11	263,303.64
24	25,000.00	01-Apr-89	20,503.03	283,806.68

Figure 6.1 *Sample Net Present Value, Continuous Flow Calculation.*

3. *Macros.* This section contains the various macros that drive the menu and recalculation functions of the template.

Acquisition Date
A1..E7

Macros
F1..L64

Payment Data
A14..E1000

Figure 6.2 *Layout of NPV—Continuous Flow Template.*

Main Menu Options

The Variable Flow version of the NPV template (see Figure 6.3) offers these Main Menu options:

```
Data What if Print File Titles Zap
```

Data

The **Data** option offers three submenu options:

```
Continue Begin Edit
```

Begin

Begin moves the cell pointer through the following sequence of header cells:

```
Date of Acquisition (N) → Annual Interest Rate (N) →
Description (T) →
T = text cell
N = numeric cell
```

Once the description is entered, the pointer moves to the first row in the payment data section (refer to Figure 6.2). It then moves the pointer through these cells:

```
Payment Amount (N) → Payment Date (N)
```

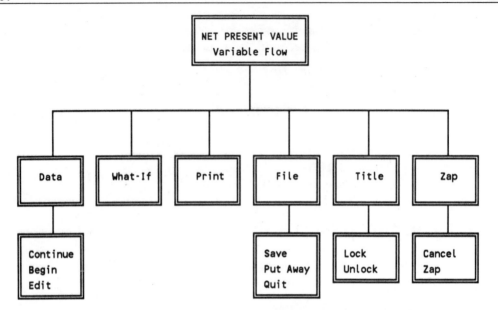

Figure 6.3 *Menu Tree for NPV—Continuous Flow Template.*

When you press **<RETURN>** in the *Payment Date* cell, the pointer moves down to the next row, assigns a new row number, and then displays a continuation menu in the control panel. Press **<RE-TURN>** to accept the Continue option. Press **Stop** to break the macro and return to the Main Menu. (Note: You can break the macro at any time by pressing **CTRL-BREAK** when you are working in a numeric cell, and **CTRL-BREAK** or **ESC** when working in a text cell. Release 2 and 2.01 users must press **ESC** following **CTRL-BREAK** to clear the resulting error message.)

Continue

The **Data/Continue** option skips the Acquisition Data section and proceeds directly to the next available row in the Payment Data section, where it prompts you to enter data in the *Payment Amount* and *Payment Date* cells. The same rules for breaking the macro and continuing data entry apply to the **Continue** option. (Note: If you want to vary any of the Acquisition Data cells, use the **What-If** option described later in this chapter.)

Edit

The **Data/Edit** option allows you to freely move the cursor in the Payment Data section. When you are done editing the data, press **ALT-M** to restart the Main Menu.

To edit a date, press **ALT-D**. You will then be prompted to enter the month, day, and year, pressing **‹RETURN›** after each. If you do not wish to use the **ALT-D** edit function for editing dates, you must enter in the standard Lotus 1-2-3 date format (@date(yy,mm,dd)).

Sample Data Entry

Consider the purchase of a piece of processing equipment that costs $250,000. For the first three months after its purchase, (March 3, 1987), you will not derive any economic benefit because it must be installed and tested. Each month you expect to increase production by $5,000 per month, up to a maximum of $25,000. In the summer months (June–August), however, production will fall because of decreased seasonal demand. In September, production will again resume, with a cap of $25,000 per month. Given an annual interest rate of 9.50 percent, what is the Net Present Value of the investment in this equipment after two years? Input the payment figures into the template, and you'll find out the answer.

1. After selecting **Begin**, the cell pointer will be in the *Date of Acquisition* cell. Enter the date according to the prompts (month, day, last two digits of the year). Press **‹RETURN›**.
2. The cell pointer will now be in the *Annual Interest Rate*, cell. Enter "9.50".
3. Enter the *Cost of Acquisition* amount, "250000."
4. The cell pointer should now be in the *Description* cell. Enter "Processing eq." This cell is optional, and is merely a memo to yourself. You can press **‹RETURN›** without entering any data and leave the cell blank if you wish.

5. Once the acquisition data section is completed, the cell pointer moves on to the *Payment Amount* cell in the first row in the payment section. Enter the payment amount, "5000," which is the amount this equipment will contribute to your cash flow as of April 1, 1987. Enter "04" **<RETURN>** "01" **<RETURN>** "87" **<RETURN>**when prompted to enter the date in the *Payment Date* cell. The pointer will automatically move to the next row. Press **<RETURN>** to continue data entry. Input the following payment amounts and dates, which accommodate the $25,000 ceiling stipulated in the example and the seasonal adjustments (if you don't want to enter all 24 payments, and understand the template, refer to Figure 6.1).

1	5,000.00	01-Apr-87
2	10,000.00	01-May-87
3	1,000.00	01-Jun-87
4	1,000.00	01-Jul-87
5	1,000.00	01-Aug-87
6	5,000.00	01-Sep-87
7	10,000.00	01-Oct-87
8	15,000.00	01-Nov-87
9	20,000.00	01-Dec-87
10	25,000.00	01-Jan-88
11	25,000.00	01-Feb-88
12	25,000.00	01-Apr-88
13	25,000.00	01-May-88
14	1,000.00	01-Jun-88
15	1,000.00	01-Jul-88
16	1,000.00	01-Aug-88
17	5,000.00	01-Sep-88
18	10,000.00	01-Oct-88
19	15,000.00	01-Nov-88
20	20,000.00	01-Dec-88
21	25,000.00	01-Jan-89
22	25,000.00	01-Feb-89
23	25,000.00	01-Mar-89
24	25,000.00	01-Apr-89

Notice the calculation in the *Profit/Loss* cell (C7): $33,806.68. That is the amount that the investment would yield over two years if the payments were considered on a Net Present Value basis.

What-If

The **What-If** option provides a quick method for changing acquisition data. The **What-If** option cycles though the *Date of Acquisition*, *Annual Interest Rate*, and *Cost of Acquisition* cells, returning to the Main Menu after each round.

Print

When you select the **Print** option from the Main Menu, the template will determine the print range for the schedule you have generated, and print the report. Refer to Figure 6.1 for a sample report.

File

The **File** menu choice provides three options: save and return to the worksheet (**Save**); Save and leave 1-2-3 (**Put away**); and quit without saving (**Quit**).

Title

The Title function locks the column headings so that they are visible even when you have scrolled down beyond 20 lines. The title function defaults to on, but can be removed by selecting the Title/Unlock option.

Zap

When you are done entering payment data and calculating NPV, you may wish to clear the payment area and examine another set of data. You can quickly accomplish this by selecting **Zap** from the Main Menu. You will immediately be asked to confirm that you want to erase the payment area. Once the area is cleared, you can enter another set of data for NPV computation. Be sure to use the **Begin** option rather than the **Continue** option.

Common Questions and Problems

Profit or loss appears to be inordinately high or low. Payments may have been entered as negative numbers. The template assumes all figures have been input as positive numbers, even though they represent cash flows in different directions. This is different than the logic used by some calculators, which require either the principal or the payments to be entered as negative numbers.

7 | TIME BILLING

CONTENTS

SPECIFICATIONS

Filename **TIMEBILL.WKS**

Function

- Tracks fee for service work.

Usage

- Logs hours for project work.
- Computes charge amounts.
- Analyzes workload by client.

Features

- Auto-entry.
- Automatically calculates time spent on projects and appropriate charges.
- Auto numbering of tasks.
- Sorts tasks by client, project, employee, or task code.
- Subgroups tasks by client, project, employee, or task code.
- Prints out entire worksheet or selected records.

Introduction

For a small consulting, accounting, law, or other professional firm, keeping track of the time spent is vitally important. This template makes it easy to log the start and stop times of various members of the firm on various tasks. The template automatically computes the time spent and the amount to be billed for the time.

The power of the template derives from the sorting and extracting functions, which allow you to reorganize the worksheet and to subgroup selected entries. For example, at any time you can group together all of client A's hours. You could also group together all of consultant A's jobs, or group together all work to date on a particular project. While the template is not meant as a substitute for a comprehensive time billing package, it provides an easy-to-use and effective means for logging time and computing bills. Figure 7.1 shows a sample page from the Time Billing Template.

Template Layout

The Time Billing Template has four sections (see Figure 7.2):

1. *Data Entry.* This is where you enter the description, project date, start and stop time, hourly rate, and the client, project, employee, and task identifiers.
2. *Selection Screen.* The selection screen allows you to enter the client, project, employee, or task codes to be extracted. (See Extract function, later in this chapter.)
3. *Selected Records.* Once you've indicated what kinds of records you want to Extract, they will appear in this area of the template for viewing or printing.
4. *Macros.* The macros that drive the menu operations and carry out sorting, extracting, printing, and saving functions are here.

Main Menu Options

The following Main Menu options are available:

```
Data Extract Sort Print File Title Lock-Screen
```

The complete menu structure is shown in Figure 7.3. Each option is described separately.

TIME BILLING

```
========================================================================================================
Task                                      Times    Hourly|--------- Codes ---------|    Total
Number     Description       Date    Start    Stop  Rate  Client Project    Emp   Task   Time    Charge
========================================================================================================


                                                                              Tota   33 :10  $2,861.25
........................................................................................................


7001 Presentation              02-Apr-87   8 :30   12 :30  90.00 MPS85  MPS-870114   102 PP1    4 : 0    360.00
7002 Conference call           02-Apr-87  13 :30   14 : 0  90.00 HJS83  HJS-870118   102 TEL    0 :30     45.00
7003 Meeting with B.Smith      02-Apr-87  15 :30   17 :30  90.00 GHD84  GHC-861114   102 MET    2 : 0    180.00
7004 Consulting                03-Apr-87   9 :15   12 :15  90.00 GHD84  GHC-861114   102 CON    3 : 0    270.00
7005 Copy writing              03-Apr-87  14 :30   16 :30  90.00 GHD84  GHC-861114   102 WRT    2 : 0    180.00
7006 Tel call--B. Smith        03-Apr-87  16 :30   17 :15  90.00 GHD84  GHC-861114   102 TEL    0 :45     67.50
7007 Travel to client          06-Apr-87   8 : 0    9 : 0  45.00 ALC86  ALC-870201   102 TRV    1 : 0     45.00
7008 Meeting with A. Lothrup   06-Apr-87   9 : 0   11 : 0  90.00 ALC86  ALC-870201   102 MET    2 : 0    180.00
7009 Travel from client        06-Apr-87  11 :30   12 :30  45.00 ALC86  ALC-870201   102 TRV    1 : 0     45.00
7010 Presentation              06-Apr-87  13 :45   16 :45  90.00 RJX86  RJX-871012   102 PP2    3 : 0    270.00
7011 Conference call           07-Apr-87   9 :30   10 :15  90.00 MPS85  MPS-870114   102 TEL    0 :45     67.50
7012 Meeting with H. Thurston  07-Apr-87  13 : 0   15 :15  90.00 THE82  THE-860501   102 MET    2 :15    202.50
7013 Tel call--H. Thurston     07-Apr-87  17 : 0   17 :25  90.00 THE82  THE-860501   102 TEL    0 :25     37.50
7014 Travel time to client     08-Apr-87   8 :45    9 :30  45.00 BGR85  BGR-861202   102 TRV    0 :45     33.75
7015 Presentation              08-Apr-87   9 :45   12 : 0  90.00 BGR85  BGR-861202   102 PP1    2 :15    202.50
7016 Copy writing              09-Apr-87   9 : 0   12 :15  90.00 THE82  JBS-870114   102 WRT    3 :15    292.50
7017 Copy writing              09-Apr-87  13 :30   17 :45  90.00 BGR85  MPS-870114   102 WRT    4 :15    382.50
```

Figure 7.1 *Sample Time Billing Template.*

Data Entry

A11...R1000

*Selection
Screen*

T1..Y20

*Selected
Data*

AB11..AS1000

Macros
T21..Z150

Figure 7.2 *Layout of the Time Billing Template.*

Data

The **Data** option offers two auto-entry macros, **Begin** and **Continue**, as well as an **Edit** and **Delete** function (Note: Only use **Begin** the first time you enter data.) The auto-entry macros move the pointer through the following sequence of cells each time **‹RETURN›** is pressed:

```
Task (N) →
Description (T) → Date (N) → Time Start (N) →
Time Stop (N)→ Hourly Rate (N)→ Client [Code] (T) →
Project [Code] (T)→ Employee [Code] (T)→ Task [Code] (T)
T = text cell
N = numeric cell
```

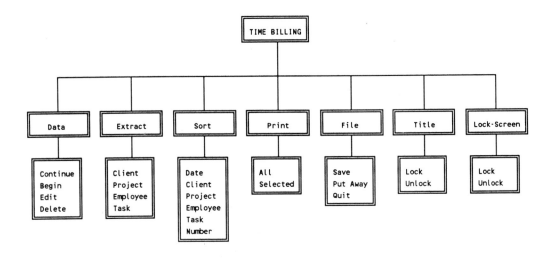

Figure 7.3 *Menu Tree, Time Billing Template.*

As soon as you input data in the *Task Code* cell, which is the last data entry cell in a row, the auto-entry macros calculate the time spent and charge, and then returns the pointer to the *Description* cell of the next row. The template will then ask if you want to **Continue** or **Stop**. Press **‹RETURN›** to continue and add another row. **Stop** ends the auto-entry macro and redisplays the Main Menu.

If you want to break the macro in the middle of a line, press **CTRL-BREAK**. If the current cell is formatted for text, you can also end the macro by pressing **ESC**. (Note: If you are using Release 2.0 or 2.01, pressing **CTRL-BREAK** will generate an error message. Just press **ESC** to resume normal operation.)

If you end the auto-entry macro in the middle of a line, you must complete the line manually or erase it entirely since the Extract and Sort routines require complete rows of data.

> **Caution!** Do not use the /Worksheet Delete Row function to erase a line of data, as this may damage the macros. Instead, erase the row cell-by-cell using the /Range Erase command.

Sample Data Entry

In the following example, the template will be used to log the four hours of consulting time you spent on April 2, 1987 with client M&P Systems on a new marketing campaign. Your firm bills your time at $100 per hour, and has assigned M&P the client code "MPS8503." The project you are working on is coded "MPS-870114." Your employee code is "SJB," and the task being logged is coded "PP1," (which stands for preliminary presentation.) We'll talk more about developing a coding system when we enter data into the various code cells.

1. Select **Data/Begin** (unless you've already entered some data, in which case you should use **Continue**. Otherwise, you will overwrite your entries.) The cell pointer will automatically move to the *Task #* cell (Column A) in row 11. You can begin entering numbers sequentially, or according to a coding scheme that provides some additional information about the task. You might, for example, want to start the task code with the last digit of the year, so that the task codes would begin with "7001," and progress in sequence. Press ‹RETURN› when you are done, and the pointer will move to the *Description* cell.
2. In the *Description* cell (Col B), either indicate the nature of the time spent, the name of the individual with whom you met, or some other appropriate notation. This cell is primarily intended to be used as a memo to yourself and is not used in Extracting or Sorting records.
3. Enter the date of the consultation (Col C), following the prompts at the top of the screen. April 2, 1987 would be entered as "4" ‹RETURN› "2" ‹RETURN› "87" ‹RETURN›.

When you press ‹**RETURN**› after the date, the cell pointer will move to the *Time Start* cell (Col G). First enter time when you "turned the meter on."

You can use either a 12-hour AM/PM format or a 24-hour format. Since the template does not indicate whether a time is AM or PM, however, we recommend using the 24-hour format. For your convenience, 12-hour to 24-hour clock conversions are shown in Table 7.1.

Table 7.1 *AM/PM Conversion Chart*

24-hour format	
12:00 am = 0:00	12:00 pm = 12:00
1:00 am = 1:00	1:00 pm = 13:00
2:00 am = 2:00	2:00 pm = 14:00
3:00 am = 3:00	3:00 pm = 15:00
4:00 am = 4:00	4:00 pm = 16:00
5:00 am = 5:00	5:00 pm = 17:00
6:00 am = 6:00	6:00 pm = 18:00
7:00 am = 7:00	7:00 pm = 19:00
8:00 am = 8:00	8:00 pm = 20:00
9:00 am = 9:00	9:00 pm = 21:00
10:00 am = 10:00	10:00 pm = 22:00
11:00 am = 11:00	11:00 pm = 23:00

(Another technique is simply to add the hour past noon to 12, so that 7PM = 12 + 7, or 19:00 hours)

Once you enter the hours and press ‹**RETURN**›, the template automatically inserts a colon and the cell pointer steps in the minutes section (Col I). Enter the minutes and press ‹**RETURN**›, and the cell pointer will move right to the Hourly Rate cell.

4. Enter the hourly rate (Col J), without a dollar sign. In our example, that would be "100." Press ‹**RETURN**›.

5. You are now ready to enter four codes: *Client* (Col K), *Project* (Col L), *Employee* (Col N), and *Task* (Col M) in their appropriate cells. Before entering any codes, take some time to think about how you will structure them. Each code should contain as much useful information as possible. The client code "MPS85," for example, keys the code into a logical abbreviation of the client's name (M&P Systems), which serves as a link to your alphabetic files. The "85" indicates that M&P Sys-

tems was acquired in 1985, giving you some historical information about your dealings with the client.

The project code should in some way be keyed into the client code. In our example, the project code used was "MPS701," indicating that the project in question was for M&P Systems, and that it was begun in January 1987. Again, the code contains useful historical information.

The employee code can be based on the employee's last name, initials, or whatever alphanumeric system corresponds to your payroll records. In our example, we simply use (one of the author's) initials. As you'll see in a moment, using full last names or abbreviations is not advisable, because of the likelihood of inconsistent entries that will render the Extract and Sort routines less effective.

The task code is the final code of a record. In our example, we use a simple code that corresponds to the consulting activity. "PP1" stands for "preliminary presentation to client, first round." The key to developing useful task codes is to first identify all the generic activities that are performed on the job, and then to refine them by whatever gradations are needed.

Note that there is a tradeoff between very simple and very sophisticated coding systems. Simple systems may not provide a great deal of information, but they may be easier to remember and less likely to be entered incorrectly. If you have many different people inputting information, a simple system may make more sense. A sophisticated system, on the other hand, can provide a good deal of useful information, but it can require more work on the part of the computer operators. You should achieve a balance that is most likely to succeed in your business setting.

Finally, whatever coding schemes you devise, you must be consistent in the way you enter the code information; otherwise the Extract and Sort routines will not yield the expected results. The client code "MPS85" will not be extracted or sorted with records coded "MPS 85" (space between the "S" and the "5."). Likewise, employee "SJB" will be treated differently than employee "S.J.B." (with periods). As you can see, punctuation marks and spaces count as valid characters.

For users of Release 1A, case sensitivity is also an issue, so that "PP1" is considered to be different from "pp1." Releases

2.0 and 2.01 are not case sensitive, so that entries differing only in case are treated the same. Nevertheless, to-the-letter consistency is to be encouraged with everyone who uses the template, regardless of what Release of 1-2-3 is being used. To this end, a master list that contains all "legal" codes and rules and grammar for forming new codes should be established and placed near the computer. The list will greatly reduce the chances of different operators creating their own hybrid codes and diminishing the effectiveness of the template.

6. When you are finished entering the employee code, press **<RETURN>**. The last two cells, *Total Time*(Col O) and *Charge* (Col P) will be computed for you. The pointer will then move to the *Task #* of the next row, and ask whether you wish to continue.

Edit

The **Data/Edit** option frees the pointer from macro control, so that you use the cursor keys to make any cell in the data section the current cell. Use the **F2** key to edit any entries, or overwrite existing cells with new information. If you turn off the worksheet protection feature, make sure you do not unintentionally change any formulas or macros; otherwise, the template may not work properly.

To edit a date, press **ALT-D**. You will be prompted to enter the month, day, and year, pressing **<RETURN>** after each. If you do not wish to use the **ALT-D** edit function for editing dates, you will have to use standard Lotus 1-2-3 date format @date(yy,mm,dd).

Delete

The **Data/Delete** option is fully explained in Chapter 1. It is intended to be a substitute for 1-2-3's /Worksheet Delete Row command, which should never be used with Ready-to-Run templates, since it can accidentally erase the template macros.

Extract

The Time Billing Template allows you to group together or extract all records that share a particular characteristic. The Extract function gives you choices for subgrouping records according to the following codes:

```
Client Project Employee Task
```

Select the option by which you would like to extract your Time Billing data, and press **<RETURN>**. The cell pointer will then move to the Selection Screen area of the template, and you will be prompted to enter a selection. (See Figure 7.4.)

Make sure your entry in the selection screen is consistent with the entries in the Task Entry Area. Suppose you wish to Extract all the work done on project MPS-870114. If that code has been entered in the selection screen as "MPS 870114," (with a space instead of a hyphen), you will not find the records you are seeking. Again, absolute consistency is required.

Records subgrouped through the Extract option are not actually removed from the Data Entry section of the template, but are copied into an "output range" located in the Selected Data Section (refer to Template Layout, Figure 7.2). The cell pointer will automatically move to the top of the output range after the extract, so you can view the records (see Figure 7.5).

To print the extracted records, use the **Print/Selected** command. When you're done viewing the extracted records, either press **Home** to move the cell pointer back to the Data Entry Section or press **ALT-M** to invoke the Main Menu and carry out another function. If you print the records, the cell pointer will be returned to the *Home* cell and the Main Menu will automatically be displayed.

(Note: The extracted records will remain in the Selected Data Section until you use Extract again, at which time the old records will be overwritten by whatever records are copied into the output range.)

```
==============================
            Enter
            selected
            Client


==============================
```

Figure 7.4 *Extract Selection Screen, Time Billing Template.*

```
TIME BILLING
          Selection Criteria: Client      = GHD84
===================================================================================================
Task                                        Times   Hourly|··········· Codes ··········|   Total
Number        Description        Date    Start   Stop  Rate  Client Project Emp    Task     Time    Charge
===================================================================================================

                                                                          Totals:    7 :45   $697.50
· · · · · · · · · · · · · · · · · · · · · · · · · · · · · · · · · · · · · · · · · · · · · · · · · · ·

7003  Meeting with B.Smith   02-Apr-87  15 :30   17 :30  90.00 GHD84  GHC-8611   102 MET    2 : 0    180.00
7004  Consulting             03-Apr-87   9 :15   12 :15  90.00 GHD84  GHC-8611   102 CON    3 : 0    270.00
7005  Copy writing           03-Apr-87  14 :30   16 :30  90.00 GHD84  GHC-8611   102 WRT    2 : 0    180.00
7006  Tel call--B. Smith     03-Apr-87  16 :30   17 :15  90.00 GHD84  GHC-8611   102 TEL    0 :45     67.50
```

Figure 7.5 *Sample Extract, Time Billing Template.*

Sort

You can reorganize the Time Billing Template by selecting the **Sort** option from the Main Menu. **Sort** offers the following choices (all choices but **Date** refer to codes):

```
Date Client Project Employee Task
```

Select the option by which you want the records in the Time Billing Template sorted. The sort options reorganize all records in the Record Entry Area of the worksheet. Alphabetic entries sort alphabetically, in ascending order (A to Z). Entries made up of numbers and alphabetic characters will also be sorted, but records starting with numbers will appear *before* those with characters.

The **Sort** options can be used to give you different views of the worksheet. It is a useful way to group together like codes without extracting them. This "Big Picture" will quickly show you how time is being distributed on various clients and projects.

If you wish to create a multilevel sort, you can do so by using the **Sort** option several times sequentially. For example, suppose you wanted to create a list of projects sorted alphabetically by employee for each client. You could do this by first selecting the **Employee** option, and then selecting the **Client** option. The rule is, the highest order of sorting should be the last sort you perform.

Print

When you select the **Print** option from the Main Menu, you will see a submenu that gives you the following options:

`All Selected`

The **All** option prints out every record in the template (see Figure 7.1 for sample printout), including headings and rules. The **Se**lected option prints out those records that were most recently extracted through the Extract function.

File

The File menu choice provides three options: save and return to the worksheet (**Save**); Save and leave 1-2-3 (**Put away**); and quit without saving (**Quit**).

Title

The Title function locks the column headings so that they are visible even when you have scrolled down beyond 20 lines. The **Title** function defaults to on, but can be removed by selecting the Title/Unlock option.

Lock-Screen

Lock-Screen freezes the control panel and the screen during macro execution. It can only be used with 1-2-3 Release 2 and 2.01.

Common Questions and Problems

The template does not compute tasks that run beyond midnight. There is no facility to handle projects that run over multiple dates. The user must split the task into separate tasks for each date.

8 | AUTO MILEAGE REIMBURSEMENT TEMPLATE

CONTENTS

Specifications

Filename **MILEAGE.WKS**

Function

- Logs business automobile use.

Usage

- Creates documentation of auto use for tax and other reporting purposes.
- Generates lists of mileage use by client or task, for billing purposes.

Features

- Auto-entry of data.
- Automatically calculates trip distance based on odometer start and end.
- Includes tolls and parking expense reimbursements.
- Automatically computes reimbursement amount.
- Extract trips by client or code.
- Prints out entire mileage log or selected trips.

Introduction

The Mileage template allows you to keep a log of your business auto use. You input the starting and ending odometer readings, as well as tolls and parking, and the template computes the distance and the reimbursement. The template automatically updates your cumulative mileage and reimbursement amounts, and displays them on the top of the screen as well as on reports.

In addition to providing space for a description and client, the template allows you to input a code for each trip. You can use the codes to further analyze your auto travel. A sample mileage log is shown in Figure 8.1.

```
AUTOMOBILE MILEAGE              Reimbursement Rate:     $0.22
          Traveller:                      Month:        Mar-87
===================================================================================================
                                       Code    Odometer              Tolls &
                                       Flag   Start   Stop   Distance Parking Reimbursement
Date       Destination    Client
===================================================================================================

                                                      Totals:    658    $22.55      $167.31
...................................................................................................


02-Mar-87 Westville      M&P Systems           2    32,456  32,487      31     2.50         9.32
02-Mar-87 Centerville    TekBiochem            2    32,487  32,492       5     4.35         5.45
03-Mar-87 Winter         Thurston Enterprises  2    32,499  32,532      33     0.00         7.26
03-Mar-87 Baxter         Daisyco               2    32,532  32,543      11     0.35         2.77
03-Mar-87 Centerville    TekBiochem            3    32,453  32,587     134     7.00        36.48
04-Mar-87 Ratherton      A.L. Lothrup & Co     2    32,602  32,752     150     0.00        33.00
05-Mar-87 Trower         MaxLite               3    32,764  32,786      22     0.25         5.09
05-Mar-87 Winter         Thurston Enterprises  2    32,786  32,791       5     0.00         1.10
06-Mar-87 Westville      M&P Systems           3    32,807  32,848      41     3.00        12.02
06-Mar-87 Wexley         World Food            3    32,860  32,887      27     0.00         5.94
09-Mar-87 Westville      M&P Systems           3    32,802  32,833      31     2.50         9.32
09-Mar-87 Centerville    TekBiochem            2    32,833  32,838       5     0.00         1.10
10-Mar-87 Winter         Thurston Enterprises  2    32,848  32,882      34     0.00         7.48
10-Mar-87 Baxter         Daisyco               2    32,882  32,893      11     1.25         3.67
11-Mar-87 Wexley         World Food            2    32,903  32,945      42     0.35         9.59
11-Mar-87 Trower         MaxLite               2    32,945  32,987      42     0.00         9.24
12-Mar-87 Winter         Thurston Enterprises  2    32,997  33,031      34     1.00         8.48
```

Figure 8.1 *Sample Mileage Log.*

Mileage Data   Selection   Selected Records
                      Screen
A11..I1000   L1..R20   U11..AE1000

                      Macros
                      M21..S143

Figure 8.2 *Layout of the Mileage Reimbursement Template.*

Template Layout

The Auto Mileage Template consists of four sections (see Figure 8.2):

1. *Data Entry.* This is where you enter the date, destination, client, code, and odometer start and stop.
2. *Selection Screen.* The selection screen allows you to enter the client, date, or code by which you want to sort the worksheet or extract entries. (See Extract and Sort functions, later in this chapter).
3. *Selected Records.* Once you've indicated what kinds of entries you want to Extract, they will appear in this area of the template for viewing or printing.
4. *Macros.* This section contains the macros that drive the menu operations and carry out auto-entry, sorting, extracting, printing, and saving functions.

Main Menu Options

The Main Menu of the Mileage template offers the following options:

```
Data Extract Sort Print File Title Lock-Screen
```

The File, Title, and Lock-Screen function are explained in depth in Chapter 1. The **Data**, **Extract**, **Sort**, and **Print** options are discussed in this chapter. See the Menu Tree (Figure 8.3), for a view of the entire menu structure used in the template.

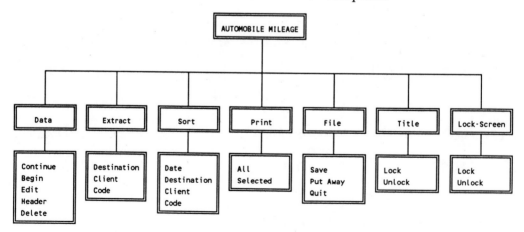

Figure 8.3 *Menu Tree, Mileage Reimbursement Template.*

Preliminary: Setting the Header Information

Before entering data, you need to set up the template. This involves entering three types of information.

1. Select **Data** from the Main Menu, then select **Header**. The template will prompt you to enter the traveler's name. Input any alphanumeric combination and press **‹RETURN›**.
2. The template will prompt you to enter the reimbursement rate. Enter the rate in decimal form, so that ".22" would represent 22 cents per mile.
3. At the prompts, enter the appropriate date for the log in "mm dd yy" format.

Data

The **Data/Continue** and **Data/Begin** options execute auto-entry macros that move the cell pointer through the following sequence of cells each time you enter data and press **‹RETURN›** (Do not use **Begin** other than the first time you enter data):

```
Date (N) → Client (T) → Destination (T) →
Code (T) → Odometer Start (N) → Odometer Stop (N) →
Tolls & Parking (N)
T = Text cell
N = Numeric cell
```

With text cells, you can enter a blank. You can also break the macro by pressing the **ESC** key. Numeric cells require a numeric input. If you attempt to enter a blank or letter in a numeric cell, 1-2-3 will beep and the bottom left corner of the screen will display the message:

```
"Invalid number input"
```

The mode indicator in the upper right corner will also display a flashing error message. If that should occur, either press **‹RE-TURN›** or **ESC** and the error message will clear. The information prompt will remain, so you can reenter numeric data.

To stop the auto-entry process when you are working in a numeric cell, press **CTRL-END**. With Release 2.0 or 2.01, "ERROR" will be displayed in the mode indicator cell after you press **CTRL-BREAK**. The error message can be cleared by pressing the **ESC** key.

Note: Since the Extract and Sort routines require complete rows of data, if you end the auto-entry macro in the middle of a line you must manually enter data in the rest of the cells or erase the line entirely. If you decide to erase the line, do NOT use the /Worksheet **D**elete **R**ow function—you might delete key macro code in other parts of the worksheet, and the template may be permanently damaged. Instead, erase the row cell-by-cell using the /**R**ange **E**rase command.

Once you've entered data in the *Parking/Tolls* cell, the template will compute the reimbursement amount and move the pointer to the *Date* cell, Column A, of the next row. A menu will then be displayed giving you the choice of continuing data entry, or returning to the Main Menu. Since **C**ontinue is the first choice, simply press **<RETURN>** to add another row of data.

Edit

The **D**ata/**E**dit option frees the pointer from macro control, so that you use the cursor keys to make any cell in the data section the current cell. Use the **F2** key to edit any entries, or overwrite existing cells with new information. If you turn off the worksheet protection feature, make sure you do not unintentionally change any formulas or macros; otherwise, the template may not work properly.

To edit a date, press **ALT-D**. You will then be prompted to enter the month, day, and year, pressing **<RETURN>** after each. If you do not wish to use the **ALT-D** edit function for editing dates, use standard Lotus 1-2-3 date format (@date(yy,mm,dd)).

Delete

The **D**ata/**D**elete option is fully explained in Chapter 1. It is intended to be a substitute for 1-2-3's /**W**orksheet **D**elete **R**ow command, which should never be used with Ready-to-Run templates since it can accidentally erase the macros.

Sample Data Entry

This example assumes that you have set up the template as just described. The record we will enter is for a meeting at the ABC Company in Westville, MA on April 3, 1987. The starting odometer reading is 27,198, and the ending odometer reading (round trip) is 27, 244. Here is how you would input this mileage record:

1. After selecting **Data/Begin**, the cell pointer will move to the *Date* cell. Enter the date according to the prompts that appear in the control panels. Our sample trip would be entered as "04" **‹RETURN›**, "03" **‹RETURN›**, and "87" **‹RETURN›**. Upon entering the year, the cell pointer will move to the *Destination* column.

2. Fill in the city, town, or other identifier. In the case of our example, you would input "Westville, MA" and press **‹RETURN›**. Note: You could also use the *Destination* cell to indicate a plant, office building, or any other location.

3. Next, enter the client's or customer's name or abbreviation. Be consistent in the way you abbreviate a client's name, otherwise the **Extract** and **Sort** routines will not work properly. The client name, "A.B.C. Company" (with periods) will not be extracted or sorted with "ABC Company" (no periods). Also, if you are using Release 1A, make sure you are consistent with your use of upper- and lowercase letters. (Releases 2 and 2.01 are not case sensitive; nevertheless, it is generally a good idea to be as consistent as possible will all entries.

4. Now enter the code for the trip into the *Code* column and press **‹RETURN›**. The code, which is optional, can be a valuable analysis tool. For example, you might use "00" for personal travel, "01" for deliveries, "02" for meetings, and so on. You can also use a code to identify a specific contact at client. "02DW," for example, might indicate a meeting with Dave Wilcox. Whatever scheme you devise, the key is to be consistent. If you want to leave Code blank, press **‹RETURN›** without making an entry, and the cell pointer will move onto the *Odometer/Start* cell

5. Enter the odometer reading at the start of the trip in the *Odometer Start* cell. Do not input commas—1-2-3 will do that for you. Press **‹RETURN›**.

6. The pointer will now be in the *Odometer End* cell. Enter the odometer reading at the end of the trip. When you press ⟨RE-TURN⟩, the trip mileage will be automatically calculated in the *Distance* cell (Col G). The cell pointer will also automatically move to the *Parking/Tolls* cell.

7. In the *Parking/Tolls* cell, enter any highway expenses you incurred. When you press ⟨RETURN⟩, the total reimbursement, based on mileage and tolls, will be computed in the *Reimbursement* cell (Col I), and the cell pointer will return to the *Date* cell (Col A) of the next row. Press ⟨RETURN⟩ from the menu to continue, or select Stop to return to the Main Menu.

Extract

The Mileage Template allows you to group together or extract all entries with similar attributes. To use this function, select Extract from the Main Menu. You will then see a submenu with the following options:

```
Client Code Destination
```

Select the option by which you would like to group the entries, and press ⟨RETURN⟩. The cell pointer will then move to the Selection Screen area of the template, and you will be prompted to enter a selection (see Figure 8.4). Make sure your entry is consistent with the data in the records; entering "ABC Company" in the selection screen will not extract records entered as "A.B.C Company" (periods) or "A B C Company" (spaces). Punctuation and spaces count as full characters. Case sensitivity with Release 1A also applies to the Extract function.

Extracted records are copied from the Mileage Data section into the Selected Records section of the template (see Template Layout, Figure 8.2). The pointer automatically moves to the cell at the top left corner cell of the Selected Records section, so you can view the extracted records. If you want to print the extracted records, select the Print/Selected option later. Otherwise, to return to the Data Entry section, press **HOME** or restart the Main Menu with **ALT-M**. (See Figure 8.5 for a sample extract.)

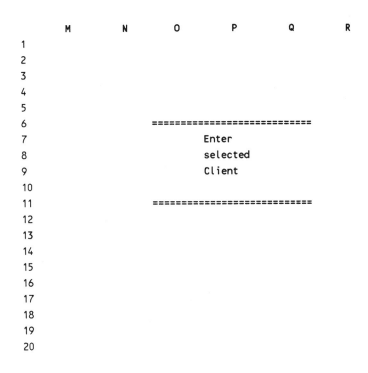

```
          M        N        O        P        Q        R
 1
 2
 3
 4
 5
 6                          ============================
 7                                  Enter
 8                                  selected
 9                                  Client
10
11                          ============================
12
13
14
15
16
17
18
19
20
```

Figure 8.4 *Extract Selection Screen, Mileage Reimbursement Template.*

```
AUTOMOBILE MILEAGE              Reimbursement Rate:      $0.22      Client
        Traveller:              Month:                   Mar-87     Thurston Enterprises
=========================================================================================================
                                                Code     Odometer              Tolls &
                                                Flag     Start    Stop    Distance Parking  Reimbursement
Date     Destination    Client
=========================================================================================================

                                                                 Totals:     106    $1.00       $24.32
- - - - - - - - - - - - - - - - - - - - - - - - - - - - - - - - - - - - - - - - - - - - - - - - - - - - -


03-Mar-87 Winter         Thurston Enterprises      2    32,499   32,532      33    0.00         7.26
05-Mar-87 Winter         Thurston Enterprises      2    32,786   32,791       5    0.00         1.10
10-Mar-87 Winter         Thurston Enterprises      2    32,848   32,882      34    0.00         7.48
12-Mar-87 Winter         Thurston Enterprises      2    32,997   33,031      34    1.00         8.48
```

Figure 8.5 *Sample Extract, Mileage Reimbursement Template.*

Sort

The Mileage Template can be sorted in four different ways:

`Date Client Code Destination`

These options are selected from the Sort function of the Main Menu. The Sort options reorganize all records in the Data Entry Area of the worksheet. Alphabetic entries sort alphabetically, in ascending order (A to Z). Entries made up of numbers and alphabetic characters will also be sorted, but entries starting with numbers will appear before those starting with characters. The Client, Code, and Destination options are alphanumeric. The Date cell is numeric, and sorted in ascending order from earliest to latest entry.

To create a multilevel sort, you can use the Sort option several times sequentially. For example, suppose you wanted to create a list of all codes in sequential order organized within a list of destinations. You could do this by first selecting the Code option, and then selecting the Client option. As a general principle, the highest order of sorting should be the last sort you perform.

Print

When you select the Print option from the Main Menu, you will see a submenu that gives you the following options:

`All Selected`

The All option prints out every record in the template (see Figure 8.1 for a sample printout). The Selected option prints out those records that were most recently selected through the Extract function.

File

The File menu choice provides three options: save and return to the worksheet (Save); save and leave 1-2-3 (Put away); and quit without saving (Quit).

Title

The **Title** function locks the column headings so that they are visible even when you have scrolled down beyond 20 lines. The Title function defaults to on, but can be removed by selecting the Title/Unlock option.

Lock-Screen

Lock-Screen freezes the control panel and the screen during macro execution. It can only be used with 1-2-3 Release 2 and 2.01.

Common Questions and Problems

You cannot extract records. The most probable cause for extraction problems is inconsistent client names and/or codes. Lotus Release 1-A is case and spacing sensitive. You must enter the criteria exactly as you entered the data. Alternatively, you may have accidentally introduced a blank cell into the data. Depending on which column the blank cell is located in, you may or may not get correct results. All cells in the data must contain at least a label prefix (e.g., ', ", or ^).

The template doesn't sort as expected. Lotus 1-2-3 evaluates a number in a text field the same as it would any text, one character at a time, starting at the left. As a result, "10" will sort before "2", in the same way that "Bill" will sort before "Bob," even though 10 has more digits than 2 and Bill has more characters than Bob. Therefore, if you want to use numerical entries in text fields such as Code, you must include leading zeroes (e.g., "01", "02", "03" if there are two-digit entries, and "001", "002", and "003" if there are three-digit entries) to ensure correct numerical as well as alphabetical sorting.

9 | TRAVEL EXPENSE RECORDER

CONTENTS

Specifications

Filename **TRAVEL.WKS**

Functions

- Logs travel expense items.
- Computes expense.

Usage

- Reports travel expenses for business and tax purposes.
- Tracks and reconciles travel advances.

Features

- Auto entry.
- Automatically computes amount due traveler/due company from advance.

Introduction

The Travel Expense Template helps you organize and present your travel expenses. In addition to providing space for the date, purpose, and location of travel, the template breaks down expenses into transportation, local travel, lodging, meals, and miscellaneous expenses. Each category is further broken down into personally paid and company-paid expenses, so that you can separate your out-of-pocket expenses from prepaid company expenses, or expenses paid for by a company credit card. If you receive travel advances, you can indicate the amount in the template, and the balance due to you or due to the company will be computed.

The travel reports can be printed on two 8.5 by 11 inch sheets using condensed print with an 80 column printer. A sample two-page 80-column report is shown in Figure 9.1.

Template Layout

The Travel Expense Template is divided into three sections (see Figure 9.2):

1. *Travel Data.* This section is where you enter the travel expenses and descriptions. It is divided into five subsections for various kinds of expenses.
2. *Calculations.* This section contains the formulas for computing the totals, and displays the amount due the traveler and due the company.
3. *Macros.* This section contains the various macros that drive the menu and recalculation functions of the template.

Main Menu Options

The Main Menu offers the following choices (see Figure 9.3 for full menu structure):

```
Data Express Print File Title
```

TRAVEL EXPENSE RECORDER   Report Date: 28-Feb-87
Traveler: S. West   Description: Feb Travel

Date	Purpose	Location	Transport Mode	Company	Personal	Local Travel Mode	Company	Personal	Lodging Company	Personal
		Totals ->		818.00	0.00		0.00	253.00	640.00	0.00
02-Feb-87	Alpha Biomedical	New York City	A	135.00				45.00	164.00	
02-Feb-87	Thurston Hotels	New York City	A			!		34.00		
12-Feb-87	Maxlite	New York City	A	135.00				54.00	175.00	
12-Feb-87	Appleton	New York City	A					35.00		
13-Feb-87	TekBiochem	Elizabeth, NJ	A	130.00				26.00		
23-Feb-87	TekBiochem	Elizabeth, NJ	A	130.00				26.00		
25-Feb-87	Trident Running Shoe	San Fran, CA	A	423.00				78.00	465.00	

Advance Amount: $500.00   Total Company: $2,534.00
Advance Date: 01-Feb-87   Total Personal: $296.00
Check Number: 81243   Total Travel: $2,830.00

TRAVEL EXPENSE RECORDER   Report Date: 28-Feb-87
Traveler: S. West   Description: Feb Travel

Date	Purpose	Location	Meals Meal	Company	Personal	Misc. Des	Company	Personal	Total Company	Personal
		Totals ->		823.00	0.00		0.00	43.00	2,534.00	296.00
02-Feb-87	Alpha Biomedical	New York City	D	134.00					188.00	77.00
02-Feb-87	Thurston Hotels	New York City	ALL	154.00		Ent		43.00	440.00	54.00
12-Feb-87	Maxlite	New York City	L,D	76.00					211.00	35.00
12-Feb-87	Appleton	New York City	ALL	176.00					176.00	35.00
13-Feb-87	TekBiochem	Elizabeth, NJ	L	34.00					190.00	26.00
23-Feb-87	TekBiochem	Elizabeth, NJ	L	29.00					185.00	26.00
25-Feb-87	Trident Running Shoe	San Fran, CA	ALL	354.00					1,320.00	78.00
									0.00	0.00
									0.00	0.00
									0.00	0.00

Advance Amount: ****   Date Paid:
Total Personal: ****   Check #:   Applied
Due to Employee: ****   to next month
Due to Company: ****

Figure 9.1 *Sample Travel Expense Report.*

Travel Data
A11..O42

Macros
AC1..AH77

Calculations
A46..W53

Figure 9.2 *Layout of Travel Expense Recorder Template.*

Data

The **Data** option allows you to select six submenu choices:

```
Continue Begin Edit Advance Header Delete
```

Continue and Begin

Continue and **Begin** automatically move the cell pointer through the *Travel Data* section each time you make an entry and press **<RETURN>**. Only use **Begin** the first time you enter data—otherwise you will overwrite existing data entries. The pointer moves through the following sequence of cells:

```
Date (N) → Purpose (T) → Location (T) →
Mode [Transport] (N)→ Company [Transport](N) → Personal
[Transport] (N) → Mode [Local Travel] (N) → Company
[Local] (N) → Personal [Local] (N) → Company [Lodging] (N)
→ Personal [Lodging] (N) → Meal [Meal] (N) → Company
[Meal] (N) → Personal [Meal] (N) → Description [Misc] (N)
→ Company [Misc] (N) → Personal [Misc] (N)
T = text cell
N = numeric cell
```

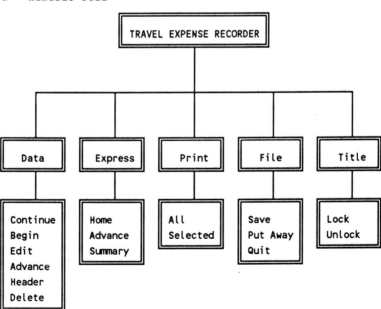

Figure 9.3 *Menu Tree, Travel Expense Recorder Template.*

After inputting information in the *Personal [Misc]* cell, the template will automatically calculate the totals for company-paid expenses, personally paid expenses, and total trip cost. The auto-entry macros return the cell pointer to the *Date* cell of the next row, then displays a menu with two choices: Continue and Stop. Press <RETURN> to accept continue, so you can enter another row of data, or select Stop to return to the Main Menu.

To stop the auto-entry macro before you reach the end of a line, press **CTRL-BREAK.** If the pointer is currently in a text formatted cell, you can also press **ESC** to break the macro. When using Release 2.0 and 2.01, pressing **CTRL-BREAK** will result in an error message. This can be cleared by pressing **ESC**.

One other difference between text cells and numeric cells should be mentioned: text cells can be left blank during auto-entry, whereas numeric cells cannot. If you do not want to enter data into a numeric cell during auto-entry, enter zero.

Edit

Data/Edit allows you to use the cursors to move the pointer to any cell in the Travel Data section and manually change your inputs. When you are done with your edits, press **ALT-M** to redisplay the Main Menu.

To edit a date, press **ALT-D.** You will then be prompted to enter the month, day, and year, pressing <RETURN>after each. If you do not wish to use the **ALT-D** edit function for editing dates, you will have to use the standard Lotus 1-2-3 date format @date (yy,mm, dd).

Advance

This option moves the cursor through three cells each time you press return:

```
Advance Amt (N) → Advance Date (N) → Check # (T)
T = text cell
N = numeric cell
```

The coordinates of the advance information cells are as follows:

```
Advance Amt:  G47
```

```
Advance Date: G49
Check #:      G51
```

After you press **<RETURN>** in the *Check #* cell, the cell pointer moves to the *Home* cell, and the Main Menu appears in the control panel.

Header

Data/Header moves the cell pointer through the following cells:

```
Traveler [name] (T) → Date (N) → Comment (T)
Cell coordinates:
Traveler: B2
Date:     F1
Comment:  F2
```

When you press **<RETURN>** in the *Comment* cell, the Main Menu is redisplayed.

Reimbursement

The **Reimbursement** option moves the cursor through two cells.

```
Date Paid (N) → Check # (T)
Cell coordinates:
Date Paid: x47
Check #:x49
```

Use this function to indicate when a reimbursement check was cut (either from the company to the traveler, or vice versa.)

Delete

The **Data/Delete** function is used as a substitute for the 1-2-3 /Worksheet **Row** Delete function. The **Data/Delete** function enables you to remove entire rows of data without damaging the macros. The 1-2-3 /**WDR** command, on the other hand, may eliminate portions of the macros and render the template nonfunctional. Follow the prompts that appear when you invoke the **Data/Delete** option.

Sample Data Entry

The Travel Expense Template can be used to record individual trips or monthly data—it depends on how fine a break out you need. For instance, if you use the template for individual trips, you can use a separate line for each meal or entertainment event. If a month's worth of travel data is logged, you might have to aggregate the meals. Also, if more than one travel advance has been given to the traveler, the amounts will have to be aggregated into one lump sum.

In the following example, we will log in expenses for a one-day excursion to New York City on behalf of your client, Alpha Biomedical. You were issued a $200 advance, which you largely used for taxis. Plane fare was already paid for by the company, and you charged your meals and entertainment on your company credit card. Here is how the day's expenses would be entered. (Refer to Figure 9.1 to orient yourself with the template.)

1. Select the **Data/Header** option. The pointer will move to the *Traveler* cell. Enter your name and press **<RETURN>**.
2. The cell pointer will now be in the *Date* cell. Enter the date of the travel report, following the day, month, and year prompts at the top of the screen.
3. The next field, *Comment,* can be used in a variety of ways. You might use it to indicate that the report is for a month's total travel, as in "March 1986 Travel." You could also use it for the time span of a specific trip, such as "London, Apr. 14-23, 1987." In our example, enter "NYC 2/2/87." After you press **<RETURN>**, the Main Menu will reappear. (You may extend your comment beyond the boundaries of the cell if you wish; no other cells will be affected by the overlapping data.)
4. Select the **Data/Advance** option. The cell pointer will move to the *Advance Amount* cell (see Figure 9.4). Enter the $200 advance issued for this trip as "200." Press **<RETURN>** and the pointer will move to the *Advance Date* cell—follow the prompts at the top of the screen to enter the appropriate date. Finally, the pointer will move to the *Check #* cell. You can enter both alphabetic and numeric characters. When you press **<RE-TURN>**, in the *Check #* cell, the Main Menu will be displayed.

5. You are now ready to enter expense data. Select the **Data/B**egin option, and the pointer will move to the *Date* cell. Enter the date, "02/02/87," as prompted, and the pointer will move to the *Purpose* cell. Indicate "Alpha meeting," since Alpha Biomedical was your Feb. 2 meeting. For the next cell, *Location*, you can either repeat "NYC" or the street address. The field is optional.

3. You are now ready to enter some expenses. The first category is Transport. Notice that the cell is divided into three columns: *Mode* (Col E), *Company* (Col F), and *Personal* (Col G). You can use mode to indicate whether you went by Air "A," Train "T," or Rental Car "R." (You can devise any coding scheme of your choosing; "A", "T", and "R" are just suggestions.) Mode can also be left blank. If the company paid for the transportation, either directly or by credit card, indicate the amount in the company column ($135.00 in this case). If you paid in cash or with your own credit card, the fare would be listed in the

```
K50: (C2) [W10]                                                    READY


                  C       D   E     F       G     H   I    J      K
        41
        42
        43  ========================================================================
        44
        45
        46
        47                  Advance Amount:   $0.00    Total Company:   $0.00
        48
        49                  Advance Date:              Total Personal:  $0.00
        50
        51                  Check Number:              Total Travel:    $0.00
        52
        53
        54  ========================================================================
        55
        56
        57
        58
        59
        60
```

Figure 9.4 *Advance Section, Travel Expense Template.*

personal column. This distinction is important for calculating the amount that you should be reimbursed, or the amount that you owe the company for unspent travel advance funds.

5. The preceding pattern of Company/Personal expenses applies to the following categories:

Local Travel

Mode = Col I (Taxi, Limo, etc.)

Company = Col J

Personal = Col K

In our example, say that you spent $74 on taxis. Enter that number in the *Personal* column. (Note: You can use the plus (+) key to combine your individual receipts.) When you press **<RETURN>**, the total amount will be displayed in the cell.

Lodging

Company = Col M

Personal = Col N

These columns will be entered as zero in our sample since the excursion was a day trip. (Remember, numeric fields cannot be left blank when entering data through the **Begin** or **Continue** macros. Enter "0" instead.) If you were to use the template for single day entries of a trip lasting several days, you would enter each night's total; if each row is used per excursion, enter the total bill in the appropriate column.

Meals

Meal = Col P (e.g., Breakfast Lunch Dinner)

Company = Col Q

Personal = Col R

Since this trip will be logged on one line, aggregate your meals: lunch, $47.20 and dinner $123.10. Use the plus (+) key to aggregate (i.e., enter "47.20 + 123.10" at the prompt.)

Misc.

Descript(ion) = Col T

Company = U

Personal = V

Use this column for any expenses that don't fit in the other categories. You can also use it for business entertainment, if you wish to isolate entertainment as a separate category.

6. When you finish entering data into the miscellaneous columns (or leave them blank and press **<RETURN>**, the Company and Personal expenses will be totaled in columns X and Y,

respectively. The cell pointer will then move to the next row, and a menu will offer you the choice of continuing data entry or stopping and returning to the Main Menu.

7. In addition to calculating company and personal expense totals, the template applies the amounts against the advance, and indicates the additional amounts due to the traveler, or the amount that the traveler owes the company. To view these computations, select the Express/ **A**dvance option to view the trip totals. Select the Express/**S**ummary option to view the reimbursement calculations (see Figure 9.5).

This summary section appears on the bottom of reports (refer to Figure 9.1). Since the advance was not fully used, you owe the company the balance ($26.00).

Use the **D**ata/**R**eimburse option to move the cursor to the *Date Paid* cell. Fill in the date you reimbursed the company, and then enter the *Check #*.

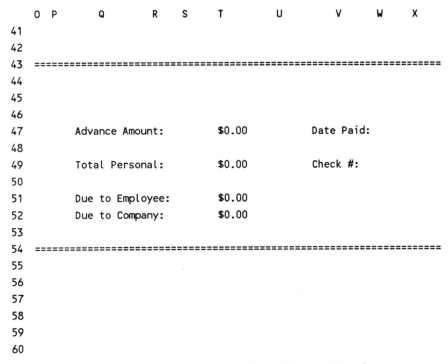

Figure 9.5 *Expense Reimbursement Summary, Travel Expense Template.*

Express

The Express option moves the pointer to one of three sections of the spreadsheet:

```
Home Advance Summary
```

Advance moves the pointer to the cells associated with the advance amount and date. Summary allows you to view the trip total and reimbursement calculations, while Home returns you to the top-left-hand corner of the expense data.

Print

The Print function is automatically set up to print the template on two pages (see Figure 9.1). Both pages print the *Date/Destination/Purpose* columns. Page one also prints the transportation, local travel, and lodging expenses, while the second page includes meals, miscellaneous, and expense totals. As soon as you select the Print option, output will be directed to your printer—make sure your printer is online, or else 1-2-3 will display an error message. Press **ESC** to clear the message.

File

The File menu choice provides three options: save and return to the worksheet (Save); Save and leave 1-2-3 (Put away); and quit without saving (Quit).

Title

The Title function locks the column headings so that they are visible even when you have scrolled down beyond 20 lines. The Title function defaults to on, but can be removed by selecting the Title/Unlock option.

Common Questions and Problems

The travel expense reimbursement amount appears to be in error. This is most likely caused by incorrect entry of personal and company expenses. Check and make sure that the expenses were entered in the correct column.

10 | 1099 MISCELLANEOUS INCOME RECORDER

CONTENTS

Specifications

Filename **1099.WKS**

Function

- Tracks miscellaneous income

Usage

- Simplifies end-of-year record keeping and totals miscellaneous income paid to consultants.
- Tracks amount paid to various vendors for historical purposes.

Features

- Easy-to-use menus.
- Auto entry.
- Sorts and extracts entries by vendor, date of payment, or user-defined code.
- Prints out entire worksheet or selected entries.
- Lock-Screen for Release 2.

Introduction

The 1099 Income Recorder makes it easy to keep accurate records of the fees paid to consultants, casual laborers, and other vendors. You can use the information for internal accounting purposes, or for filling out 1099 forms at the end of the calendar year.

The template is designed to allow you to easily input significant information, and to assign a code to each vendor. The code can be used to designate a particular category of service or goods that have been provided. Later, you can sort the worksheet by those codes or extract entries with like codes. When you perform an extract, the total amount paid to a particular vendor will be calculated and listed on the top of the worksheet. The total will also appear on printed reports. The total amount of all monies paid to all vendors in the worksheet is automatically calculated and displayed under the column headers as you enter new data. A sample 1099 template is shown in Figure 10.1.

Template Layout

The 1099 Miscellaneous Income template (see Figure 10.2) consists of four sections:

1. *1099 Data.* This is where you enter the payment date, the vendor, vendor's social security or tax ID number, the vendor code, and the amount of payment. Each row constitutes one payment to the vendor.
2. *Selection Screen.* The selection screen allows you to indicate which vendor, code, or payment date you wish to use as criteria for extracting entries. (See Extract function, later in this chapter).
3. *Selected Records.* Once you have indicated what kinds of entries you want to Extract, they will appear in this area of the template for viewing or printing.
4. *Macros.* This section contains the macros that drive the menu operations and carry out sorting, extracting, printing, and saving functions.

```
Federal Tax ID Number:    123-456-7890

========================================================================
          Social                                    Payment
Date      Security      Vendor              Code     Amount
========================================================================


                                                     $9,536.00
........................................................................


23-Jan-86 999-999-9999  Becksworth, R.        1        250.00
26-Jan-86 111-111-1111  Bulfinch, M.          2         60.00
04-Feb-86 222-222-2222  Parnette, J.          2         45.00
07-Feb-86 333-333-3333  McGuire, L.           1         55.00
19-Feb-86 444-444-4444  Hopewell, B.          4        250.00
01-Mar-86 999-999-9999  Becksworth, R.        1        150.00
07-Mar-86 999-999-9999  Becksworth, R.        1         75.00
23-Mar-86 999-999-9999  Becksworth, R.        1         75.00
01-Apr-86 111-111-1111  Bulfinch, M.          2        155.00
04-Apr-86 444-444-4444  Hopewell, B.          4        130.00
06-Apr-86 222-222-2222  Parnette, J.          2        200.00
26-Apr-86 333-333-3333  McGuire, L.           1        385.00
01-May-86 999-999-9999  Becksworth, R.        1        225.00
03-May-86 999-999-9999  Becksworth, R.        1         75.00
22-May-86 111-111-1111  Bulfinch, M.          2         55.00
29-May-86 333-333-3333  McGuire, L.           1         75.00
04-Jun-86 333-333-3333  McGuire, L.           1         85.00
04-Jun-86 222-222-2222  Parnette, J.          2        256.00
09-Jun-86 999-999-9999  Becksworth, R.        1         75.00
10-Jun-86 999-999-9999  Becksworth, R.        1      1,150.00
12-Jun-86 444-444-4444  Hopewell, B.          4         45.00
22-Jun-86 999-999-9999  Becksworth, R.        1        350.00
02-Jul-86 222-222-2222  Parnette, J.          2        220.00
02-Jul-86 999-999-9999  Becksworth, R.        1      1,135.00
08-Jul-86 333-333-3333  McGuire, L.           1        600.00
22-Jul-86 333-333-3333  McGuire, L.           1         35.00
24-Jul-86 999-999-9999  Becksworth, R.        1        150.00
16-Aug-86 222-222-2222  Parnette, J.          2        145.00
16-Aug-86 333-333-3333  McGuire, L.           1         45.00
06-Sep-86 999-999-9999  Becksworth, R.        1        750.00
06-Sep-86 222-222-2222  Parnette, J.          2        145.00
29-Sep-86 333-333-3333  McGuire, L.           1        130.00
29-Sep-86 111-111-1111  Bulfinch, M.          2        120.00
02-Oct-86 999-999-9999  Becksworth, R.        1         55.00
05-Oct-86 111-111-1111  Bulfinch, M.          2         80.00
17-Oct-86 444-444-4444  Hopewell, B.          4        155.00
19-Oct-86 999-999-9999  Becksworth, R.        1        450.00
18-Nov-86 999-999-9999  Becksworth, R.        1        250.00
18-Dec-86 999-999-9999  Becksworth, R.        1        850.00
```

Figure 10.1 *Sample 1099 Miscellaneous Income Template.*

1099 Data   *Selection*   *Selected*
                     Screen   *Records*
All...E1000   **Fl..L20**   **Oll...S1000**

Macros
G21..M138

Figure 10.2 *Layout of 1099 Miscellaneous Income Template.*

Main Menu Options

The 1099 template offers the following Main Menu options (see Menu Tree, Figure 10.3):

`Data Extract Sort Print File Title Lock-Screen`

Data

The **Data** option offers two auto-entry macros (**Continue** and **Begin**), as well as **Edit** and **Delete**. Refer to Chapter 1 for a detailed

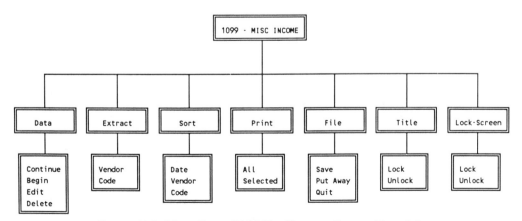

Figure 10.3 *Menu Tree, 1099 Miscellaneous Income Template.*

discussion of how these functions are used. When you select **Con-tinue** or **Begin**, the macro moves the template through the follow-ing sequence of cells each time you enter data and press **⟨RETURN⟩**:

```
Date (N) → Social Security (T) →Vendor (T) →
Code → (T) →Payment Amount (N)
T = text cell
N = numeric cell
```

You can stop the auto-entry process at any time by pressing **CTRL-END**. If the current input request is for text data (e.g., *Description*), pressing **ESC** will work as well. If the current request is for numerical data (e.g., *Payment amount*), only **CTRL-BREAK** will end the macro. (Note: If you are using Release 2.0 or 2.01, "Error" will be displayed in the mode indicator cell after you press **CTRL-BREAK**. You can clear the error message by pressing **ESC**.)

If you end the auto-entry macro in the middle of a line, you must complete the line manually or erase it entirely since the Extract and Sort routines require complete rows of data. Caution: Do not use the /Worksheet **D**elete **R**ow function to erase a line of data, as this may damage the macros. Instead, erase the row cell-by-cell using the /Range Erase command.

After inputting information in the *Payment Amount* cell, which is the last data entry cell in a record, the auto-entry macro returns the cell pointer to the *Date* cell of the next row, and asks whether you wish to continue data entry.

Sample Data Entry

Your company has a number of consultants in areas such as graphic design, PR, marketing, accounting, and finance, as well as several people who perform casual clerical labor. Tax laws require you to issue a 1099 form, Miscellaneous Income, to anyone who earned more than $600 and is not incorporated. This template makes it easy to keep track of 1099 wages, and to generate lists of all dis-bursements made to 1099 payment recipients. Here are the steps you need to enter 1099 records:

1. The first step is to assign a vendor code. The code can be used in one of two ways. First you can assign each vendor a unique code, which will be used during Extract and Sort operations.

While the template allows you to Extract and Sort vendors by name, you must be very careful to enter names with to-the-letter consistency; 1-2-3 treats "Becksworth, R." differently from "Becksworth R." (no comma after Becksworth). If you wanted to extract all "Becksworth, R." entries, your list would not include those without a comma (or space or period after R), and your total would be incorrect. In contrast, a code of "101" for Richard Becksworth is less likely to be inconsistently entered, and might therefore be more appropriate for your business, especially if numerous people are going to be entering data.

A second use for the vendor code is to identify a category of activity. Marketing consultants might, for example, be assigned code "101", graphic designers might be "103", accountants might be "104", and so on. This approach allows you to Find and Sort entries by category of activity. If you are not using a general ledger program, this capability might be useful for analyzing your consulting expenses. If you choose this approach, however, you will only be able to extract consultants by name, so you will have to be especially careful about consistent data entry.

2. Once you've assigned vendor codes, you can begin to input individual transactions. Select the Data/Begin option, and follow the prompts at the top of the screen. At the beginning of each line you have the option of continuing with the data entry or breaking the auto-entry macro and returning to the Main Menu. Notice that each time you enter a transaction, the amount is added to the running total at the top of the spreadsheet (refer to Figure 10.1).

3. Break the macro when you are done entering data. (Remember to select the Continue option the next time you use the auto-entry macro).

4. Once you've entered data into the template, you can use the Edit or Delete function or the Extract, Sort, or Print functions.

Extract

The Extract function of the 1099 Miscellaneous Income template allows you to create a list of all payments made to a particular

consultant. When you select Extract from the Main Menu, the following submenu options will be displayed:

Vendor Code

Select the option by which you would like to group records, and
press **<RETURN>**. The cell pointer will then move to the Selection
Screen area of the template, and you will be prompted to enter an
extract criterion (see Figure 10.4).

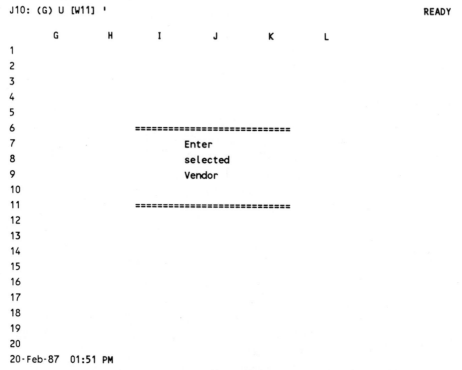

```
J10: (G) U [W11] '                                               READY

         G        H        I        J        K        L
 1
 2
 3
 4
 5
 6                    =============================
 7                          Enter
 8                          selected
 9                          Vendor
10
11                    =============================
12
13
14
15
16
17
18
19
20
20-Feb-87  01:51 PM
```

Figure 10.4 *Extract Selection Screen, Miscellaneous Income Template.*

Make sure your entry in the selection screen is identical to the
entries in the 1099 Data section, including punctuation. If you want
to extract "Becksworth R." records, but you enter "Becksworth R"
(no period) in the selection screen, you will not find the records
you're seeking. Again, to-the-letter consistency is required for the
template function to work properly.

Records grouped together through the Extract option are copied
into an "output range" located in the Selected Data Section (refer to

template layout, Figure 10.2.) The cell pointer will automatically move to the output range after the extract, so you can view the entries. (See sample extract, Figure 10.5.)

To print the extracted entries, use the **Print/Selected** function. When you're done viewing the extracted entries, either press **Home** to move the cell pointer back to the Record Entry Area or press **ALT-M** to invoke the Main Menu and carry out another function. If you **Print** the extracted records, the cell pointer will automatically return to the **Home** cell. (Note: The extracted records will remain in the Selected Entries section until you use the Extract function again. Old extracted records will be overwritten by new ones.)

```
Federal Tax ID Number:     123-456-7890              Vendor   Becksworth,
========================================================================
               Social                                        Payment
Date           Security      Vendor               Code       Amount
========================================================================


                                                             $6,065.00
. . . . . . . . . . . . . . . . . . . . . . . . . . . . . . . . . . . . . .

    23-Jan-86 999-999-9999   Becksworth, R.          1          250.00
    01-Mar-86 999-999-9999   Becksworth, R.          1          150.00
    07-Mar-86 999-999-9999   Becksworth, R.          1           75.00
    23-Mar-86 999-999-9999   Becksworth, R.          1           75.00
    01-May-86 999-999-9999   Becksworth, R.          1          225.00
    03-May-86 999-999-9999   Becksworth, R.          1           75.00
    09-Jun-86 999-999-9999   Becksworth, R.          1           75.00
    10-Jun-86 999-999-9999   Becksworth, R.          1        1,150.00
    22-Jun-86 999-999-9999   Becksworth, R.          1          350.00
    02-Jul-86 999-999-9999   Becksworth, R.          1        1,135.00
    24-Jul-86 999-999-9999   Becksworth, R.          1          150.00
    06-Sep-86 999-999-9999   Becksworth, R.          1          750.00
    02-Oct-86 999-999-9999   Becksworth, R.          1           55.00
    19-Oct-86 999-999-9999   Becksworth, R.          1          450.00
    18-Nov-86 999-999-9999   Becksworth, R.          1          250.00
    18-Dec-86 999-999-9999   Becksworth, R.          1          850.00
```

Figure 10.5 *Sample Extract, Miscellaneous Income Template.*

Sort

You can reorganize the 1099 Miscellaneous Income Template by selecting the Sort option from the Main Menu. Sort offers you the following options:

`Date Vendor Code`

Select the option by which you want the records in the worksheet sorted. The Date option sorts the records in ascending order by date. Vendor sorts records alphabetically by name, in ascending order (A to Z). Code sorts on the vendor code field, which can be made up of alphabetical and numeric characters (e.g., A01). Entries starting with numbers (e.g., "10-B") will appear *before* those starting with characters ("B-10").

If you wish to create a multilevel sort, you can do so by using the Sort option several times sequentially. For example, say you have the code to designate certain types of vendors, so that "01" is used for all consultants and companies involved with printing. You could create a list of all "01" vendors sorted alphabetically by first selecting the Vendor option, and then selecting the Code option. The rule is, the highest order of sorting should be the last sort you perform.

Sort can be extremely useful for reorganizing your data base. The Date sort can be used to provide a chronological list of payments to consultants, which can be easily compared to your checkbook register. Sorting by Vendor name or Code is also a good way to generate a list that can be used to cross-check payments against ledgers and other sources.

Print

When you select the Print option from the Main Menu, you will see a submenu that gives you the following options:

`All Selected`

The All option prints out every record in the template, including headings and rules. Use the Selected option to print those records that were most recently extracted into the output range of the template. Printouts of selected records can be valuable back-up materials for your tax files. You can also send them to your consultants before issuing 1099s, to make sure that your records agree with theirs.

File

The **File** menu choice provides three options: save and return to the worksheet (**Save**); save and leave 1-2-3 (**Put away**); and quit without saving (**Quit**).

Title

The **Title** function locks the column headings so that they are visible even when you have scrolled down beyond 20 lines. The **Title** function defaults to on, but can be removed by selecting the Title/Unlock option.

Lock-Screen

Lock-Screen freezes the control panel and the screen during macro execution. It can only be used with 1-2-3 Release 2 and 2.01.

Common Questions and Problems

You cannot extract records. The most probable cause for extraction problems is inconsistent Vendor names and/or codes. Lotus Release 1-A is case and spacing sensitive. You must enter the criteria exactly as you entered the data. Alternatively, you may have accidentally introduced a blank cell into the data. Depending on which column the blank cell is located in, you may or may not get correct results. All cells in the data must contain at least a label prefix (e.g, ' " or ^).

The template does not sort as expected. Lotus 1-2-3 evaluates a number in a text field the same as it would any text, one character at a time, starting at the left. As a result, "10" will sort before "2," in the same way that "Bill" will sort before "Bob," even though 10 has more digits than 2 and Bill has more characters than Bob.

Therefore, if you want to use numerical entries in text fields such as Code, you must include leading zeroes (e.g., "01," "02," "03" if there are two digit entries, and "001," "002," and "003" if there are three digit entries) to ensure correct numerical as well as alphabetical sorting.

11 | COMMISSION CALCULATOR

CONTENTS

SPECIFICATIONS

Filename **COMMIS.WKS**

Function

- Calculates commission payments for four different levels of reward, three different commission rates.

Usage

- Determines commission payments for commission-based sales personnel.
- Determines whether group performance bonus has been earned.

Features

- Quick calculation of commission base from various sources at differing sales factor levels.
- Automatically calculates base salary and two levels of individual commission rates.
- Automatically includes group performance bonuses when earned.
- Easy addition of new employees into the worksheet.
- Permits the use of a draw system for calculating net pay due.

Introduction

The Commission Calculator template makes it easy to determine the commission payments when you have more than one product, and when the commission rates differ for each one. For example, with some product lines, 75 percent of the net revenues might be applied to the calculation of the commission base, while for others, only 25 percent is used. This facilitates your focusing your commission compensation system more heavily toward certain product lines.

In addition to computing the commission base for various product factors, the template determines commission payments for three different brackets of sales performance. You might, for example, establish a base compensation with two differing rates of commission for various sales levels. The sample compensation plan shown in Figure 11.1 pays sales people a base commission of $500 regardless of sales level, 25 percent of net sales for sales between $2,000 and $5,000 per month, and 35 percent for sales exceeding $5,000 per month. In addition, a group bonus is earned when the entire sales force achieves more than $25,000 in sales for the month.

The bottom section of the template computes net pay after deductions and draw payments already made have been subtracted from the gross. Finally, the template computes period pay by dividing the net due by the number of pay periods per month (see Figure 11.1).

Template Layout

The Commission Calculator Template (see Figure 11.2) is divided into three sections:

1. *Sales Data.* This is where you enter the gross sales amount and cost of goods sold, as well as the commission rate on various items.
2. *Commission Calculation.* This is where the actual commission figures are computed. In order for the calculations to be made, you will have to input the base salary and commission rates

COMMISSION CALCULATION

```
=====================================================================================================
                 Month:    Oct-87
       # of Pay Periods:       4
=====================================================================================================
```

Employee:		Bill	Mary	Joe	Jane	Alan	Steve	Total
Status: (1=Active, 0=In-Active)		1	1	1	1	0	1	

		Bill	Mary	Joe	Jane	Alan	Steve	Total
Gross Sales		1,000.00	7,000.00	10,000.00	500.00	0.00	5,000.00	23,500.00
Cost of Goods Sold		500.00	2,000.00	5,000.00	250.00	0.00	4,000.00	11,750.00
	Factor:	········	········	········	········	········	········	········
Net Sales Revenue	100%	500.00	5,000.00	5,000.00	250.00	0.00	1,000.00	11,750.00
Misc. Revenue 1	75%	2,000.00	3,000.00	2,000.00	3,000.00	0.00	1,000.00	11,000.00
Misc. Revenue 2	50%	4,000.00	1,000.00	1,000.00	1,000.00	0.00	0.00	7,000.00
Misc. Revenue 3	25%	100.00	0.00	4,000.00	1,000.00	0.00	0.00	5,100.00
		········	········	········	········	········	········	········
Total Revenue		6,600.00	9,000.00	12,000.00	5,250.00	0.00	2,000.00	34,850.00
Commission Base		4,025.00	7,750.00	8,000.00	3,250.00	0.00	1,750.00	24,775.00

```
=====================================================================================================
```

COMMISSION CALCULATION
....

			Bill	Mary	Joe	Jane	Alan	Steve	Total
Base Salary									
	For Sales								
$500	Below $	2,000	500.00	500.00	500.00	500.00	0.00	500.00	2,500.00
Level 1 Commission									
25.00%	Above $	2,000	506.25	750.00	750.00	312.50	0.00	0.00	2,318.75
Level 2 Commission									
35.00%	Above $	5,000	0.00	962.50	1,050.00	0.00	0.00	0.00	2,012.50
Group Bonus									
	If Revenue								
$250 is Above $		25,000	250.00	250.00	250.00	250.00	0.00	0.00	1,000.00

```
=====================================================================================================
```

	Bill	Mary	Joe	Jane	Alan	Steve	Total
Gross Pay	1,256.25	2,462.50	2,550.00	1,062.50	0.00	500.00	7,831.25

```
=====================================================================================================
```

	Bill	Mary	Joe	Jane	Alan	Steve	Total
Less Deductions	0.00	0.00	0.00	0.00	0.00	0.00	0.00
	········	········	········	········	········	········	········
Net Pay	1,256.25	2,462.50	2,550.00	1,062.50	0.00	500.00	7,831.25

```
=====================================================================================================
```

	Bill	Mary	Joe	Jane	Alan	Steve	Total
Less Draw	0.00	0.00	0.00	0.00	0.00	0.00	0.00
	········	········	········	········	········	········	········
Net Due	1,256.25	2,462.50	2,550.00	1,062.50	0.00	500.00	7,831.25

```
=====================================================================================================
```

	Bill	Mary	Joe	Jane	Alan	Steve	Total
Period Pay	314.06	615.63	637.50	265.63	0.00	125.00	1,957.81

Figure 11.1 *Sample Commission Plan.*

for various performance levels, and the level at which a group bonus will be earned.

3. *Macros.* This section contains the various macros that drive the menu and recalculation functions of the template.

Sales/Commission Data   *Macros*
A1..J18   **N1..V84**

Commision Calculation
A20..J56

Figure 11.2 *Layout of Commission Calculator.*

Main Menu Options

The Main Menu of the Commission Calculator Template offers the following menu options:

Data Print File New Initialize Title

(The Menu Tree shown in Figure 11.3 shows the full structure of the menu and submenu options.) Before you use any menu options, you should first create a "master template" that you can call up each month. This is done by means of the Initialize function.

Initializing the Template

In most cases, you will only change your commission rates and levels once, after which you will enter sales figures on a regular basis. For this reason, you need to create a separate Master Template that has the correct commission figures embedded in it. You can call up the Master Template, enter the current monthly data, and then save the current month under a new name, thereby preserving the Master Template. (Alternately, you can enter data into the Master, print it out, and then quit 1-2-3 without saving the data, so the Master remains clear of data. This can be done with the File/Quit option. See later in this chapter.) Here's how you create a

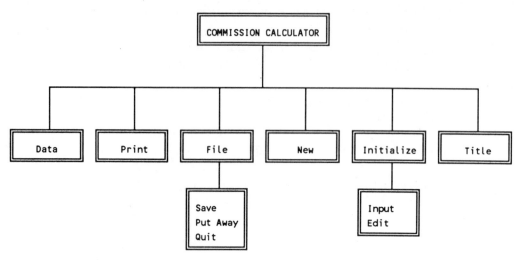

Figure 11.3 *Menu Tree, Commission Calculator.*

Master Template (refer to Figure 11.1 to orient yourself to the worksheet):

To set up the template, select the Initialize option, which offers two choices:

Input Edit

Input

Input invokes an auto-entry macro that moves the cell pointer through the data sections each time you make an entry and press **<RETURN>**, and prompts you for appropriate information. The pointer moves through the following sequence.

Month (N) → # of Pay Periods (N) Net Sales Revenue Factor
(N) → Misc Revenue 1 (T)→ [Misc Revenue 1] Factor (N)→
Misc Revenue 2 (T)→ [Misc Revenue 2] Factor (N)→Misc Reve-
nue 3 (T)→ [Misc Revenue 3] Factor (N)→Base Salary (N)
→Level I Commission (N)→ Level I Commission Start Point
(N) →Level II Commission (N) → Level II Commission Start
Point (N) →Group Bonus Amount (N) → Group Bonus Target (N)
T= text cell
N= numeric cell

Most of the cells entered during the initialization of the template require numeric input, so the best way to break the auto-entry initialization macro is to press **CTRL-BREAK**. This action will cause an error message with Release 2 and 2.01. Press **ESC** to clear the error display. You can break the input while working in the text cells by pressing **ESC**. No error message will be generated.

Edit

The Initialize/Edit option allows you to scan through the same cell sequence as just described. The difference, however, is that Edit allows you to retain the current value in a cell by pressing ‹RE-TURN› or to overwrite existing cells with new data. Press **Alt-M** to return to the Main Menu.

Sample Initialization

In this example, (refer to Figure 11.4) we will create a Master Template for a company that offers its sales force a commission based on 100 percent of general net sales revenue, plus 75 percent of revenue from Model A, 50 percent of revenue from Model B, and 25 percent of revenue from Model C. The base salary is $500 a month, which is guaranteed if sales are below $2,000. The lower tier commission (Level I) is 25 percent for gross sales above $2,000, but less than $5,000. If gross sales exceed $5,000 the commission rises to 35 percent (Level II). Finally, a group bonus of $250 is offered if monthly gross sales for the entire group exceeds $25,000. Here is how these numbers would be entered into the Master Template.

1. Select Initialize. The cell pointer will move to the *Month* cell. For convenience, enter "1" when prompted for the day, month, and year. This will enter a date of Jan-80. Each month when you call up the Master template, you will overwrite the Jan-80 designation with the correct date. (Note: Because of the structure of the Lotus date function, you will be prompted to enter the day even though the cell only displays the month and year.) Press ‹RETURN› to continue.
2. Enter "4" for the number of pay periods. For months that have five pay periods, you can overwrite this entry.
3. The cell pointer will now be in the *Net Sales Revenue Factor* cell. Since the company is calculating the commission on 100

COMMISSION CALCULATION

```
===================================
                 Month:
     # of Pay Periods:          4
===================================
Employee:
Status: (1=Active, 0=In-Active)
. . . . . . . . . . . . . . . . . . . . . . . . . . . . . . .

Gross Sales
Cost of Goods Sold
                              Factor:
Net Sales Revenue              100 %

Misc. Revenue 1                 75 %
Misc. Revenue 2                 50 %
Misc. Revenue 3                 25 %

Total Revenue

Commission Base
=================================

COMMISSION CALCULATION
. . . . . . . . . . . . . . . . . . . . . . .

Base Salary
             For Sales
      $500      Below $    2,000

Level 1 Commission
        25.00 %  Above $    2,000

Level 2 Commission
        35.00 %  Above $    5,000

Group Bonus
             If Revenue
      $250  is Above $   25,000
===============================
```

Figure 11.4 *Sample Initialization, Commission Calculator.*

percent of general net sales revenue, enter "100" (no percent sign). If the company wanted to count general net sales revenue less than one of the specific product lines entered below, this percentage would be set for less than 100 percent.

4. The template will now prompt you to enter a title that will replace the words "Misc Revenue 1." In our example, this revenue source is Model A, so you would input those words after the prompt.

5. Next, enter the revenue factor that will be used for sales of Model A. This amount is 75 percent. The idea behind the revenue factor is to establish the percentage of the revenue that will be added to the commission base. By varying the relative percentages, you can weight the various revenue sources differently. In the example, general net sales revenue is weighted four times greater at 100 percent than revenue from Model C at 25 percent.

6. Repeat this procedure of entering new titles and commission levels for Model B, at 50 percent, and Model C, at 25 percent. Note: If you do not need all (or any) of the additional revenue sources, enter a blank for the revenue source title. The related percentage cells, however, will not accept a blank, as they are numeric cells. Enter zero for these cells.

7. Once you have finished entering the revenue factors for the various revenue sources, the cell pointer will move to the *Base Salary* cell. Enter "500" (no dollar signs), the base amount offered in our example.

8. Now enter the "Level I Commission" as prompted. Level I is the lower tier commission. In our example, the Level I percentage is 25 percent. Enter "25," press **‹RETURN›**, and the cell pointer will move to the *Level I Commission Start Point* cell, which is the gross sales level at which the lower tier commission will be awarded. (Note: The Level I start point amount is the same as the base salary cutoff amount. When you enter the Level I start point amount, it is automatically copied to cell C30, which is the base salary cutoff point.

9. The cell pointer next moves on to the Level II commission level. Enter "35" and press **‹RETURN›**. As prompted, input the level at which the Level II commission will be awarded.

10. The last step is to enter the flat bonus amount that will be awarded if the sales force as a whole achieves a target level.

The flat amount is entered in the *Group Bonus* cell, and the target level is entered in the *Group Target Amount* cell.

Editing the Master Template

Once you've pressed **‹RETURN›** in the *Group Target Amount* cell, the cell pointer will return to the *Month* cell at the top of the worksheet and restart the Main Menu. Select the Data/Edit option and you will be free to maneuver the pointer and manually edit cells.

Saving the Master Template

When you are done entering employees and/or making your changes, redisplay the Main Menu, and save the file as "Master" (or any other generic name) with the File/Save option. If the percentages change in the future, you can recall the Master template, make your edits, then resave as "Master."

Data Entry: Monthly Use

The procedure for using the Commission Template each month is as follows:

1. Load the Master Form file you created.
2. Select the **Data** option from the Main Menu. This will automatically move the pointer to the *Month* cell. Enter the appropriate month as prompted. Once you press **‹RETURN›**, the cursor will no longer be under macro control, so you can use the cursor keys to move the pointer through the Sales Data Section (Refer to Figures 11.1 and 11.2).
3. Next, move the cell pointer down and change the number of pay periods in the month if it differs from the number you entered in the Master Template.
4. Enter the employees' names across the top of the worksheet, adjacent to the label "Employee." Enter one employee per column. If you need to add more employees than there are blank columns, see **New Employee** option. On the row under the employee's name, indicate whether they were active ("1") or

inactive ("0"). If you indicate an employee was inactive for the month, the minimum salary calculation will be eliminated from his or her gross pay figures. If you do not enter any status number, the template assumes that employee was *inactive*. It is therefore important to enter the status number to ensure proper compensation.

5. Enter the various revenues and cost of goods sold. The worksheet will automatically compute all totals, commissions, and pay figures as you enter new data.

Print

When you select the **Print** option from the Main Menu, the template will determine the print range for the commission schedule you have generated, and print the report. See Figure 11.1 for a sample report.

File

The **File** menu choice provides three options: save and return to the worksheet (**Save**); save and leave 1-2-3 (**Put away**); and quit without saving (**Quit**). These function are described more fully in Chapter 1.

New (Employee)

The **New** option of the Main Menu inserts a column in the worksheet, so that you can enter a new employee. Note that this is considerably more sophisticated than 1-2-3's /Insert Column command. If you use the /Insert Column command, you will misalign the totaling ranges and the calculations will be incorrect. The **New** option readjusts the ranges to accommodate the new column.

When you invoke the **New** option from the Main Menu, you will be prompted to press **‹RETURN›**, position the cell pointer where you want the new column to be inserted, and then press **‹RETURN›** again for the column insert to take place. For example, if you wanted to insert a column between the employees in columns E and F, select **New**, press **‹RETURN›**, then move the pointer to column F and press **<RETURN>** again. A new column will be inserted, so that Column F will become column G. You can then type in the salesperson's name and status.

Title

The Title function locks the column headings so that they are visible even when you have scrolled down beyond 20 lines. The Title function defaults to on, but can be removed by selecting the Title/Unlock option.

Common Questions and Problems

You can't change labels. The only labels that can be easily changed are those that can be edited via the Initialize option from the main menu. If you need to edit other labels, you must first set the data protection off using the Lotus command /Worksheet Global Protection Disable. After you are finished editing, be sure to reset the protection via the command /Worksheet Global Protection Enable command. Also, when you are changing the labels, be careful not to accidentally edit any of the macro fields or formulas.

The wrong period pay is calculated. The period pay is simply the net pay divided by the number of pay periods per month. You can edit the number of pay periods per month manually to insert the correct number.

Group performance bonus kicks in too soon. The group performance bonus is based on total revenue, not on the commission base. If necessary, you can edit the formulas in line 40 to use line 22 commission base, instead of line 20, total revenue, for determining eligibility. The formula in E40, for example, is:

```
@IF($K$20>$C$40)#AND#(E33>0),$A$40,1)
```

Substitute "$22" for "$20" to calculate the group performance on commission base rather than total revenue.

You can't turn off base salary. The base salary calculation can only be turned off by setting the employee status to inactive.

You can't add new employee. New employees can only be added via the **New** employee option from the main menu. Any attempt to add employees manually is likely to produce errors.

You can't delete an employee. There is no easy way to delete employees. You can delete or edit the employees' names to remove them from the printout and you can set the status of the now blank column to INACTIVE to remove it from the calculations. In general it is best simply to reuse columns for other new employees.

12 | DIRECT MAIL RESPONSE CALCULATOR

CONTENTS

SPECIFICATIONS

Filename **DIRECT.WKS**

Functions

- Calculates expenses, gross revenues, and net revenues for a direct mail solicitation.

Usage

- Evaluates feasibility of direct mail solicitation for profit and nonprofit fundraising campaigns.
- Compares effect on net revenues of size and cost of mailings and computes solicitation amounts against response range.
- Determines breakeven point of direct mail campaigns.

Features

- Allows easy what-if analysis with different cost, mailing size, and mailing response variables.
- Allows you to simultaneously compare four different solicitation amounts and ten different response rates.
- Lookup function automatically links mailing costs and mailing sizes for determination of gross and net profit.
- Prints gross and net revenue reports.
- Graphs the net profit for various combinations of solicitation price and rate of return.

Introduction

Direct mail is an increasingly popular approach to sales. Magazine or newsletter subscriptions are usually sold by direct mail, and the range of other goods and services marketed in this fashion has grown rapidly over the past decade. With direct mail, it is particularly important to know the breakeven point; small changes in the rate of return on the mailing can lead to great differences in gross and net revenue.

This template facilitates your analysis of the revenue and expense projections of a direct mail campaign. It can also be used to analyze fundraising or donation campaigns. In either case, all you need to do is enter your expenses, decide the mailing sizes you would like to test, and enter the solicitation prices or donation amount you want to analyze. The template will do the rest. You will be able to see the cost of your mailing, the gross revenues for different rates of return and different prices, and the corresponding net revenues. See Figure 12.1 for a sample response calculation.

Template Layout

The Direct Mail Response Calculator Template is divided into four sections (see Figure 12.2):

1. *Mailing Cost Data.* This is where you enter the various costs that constitute the mailing (artwork, printing, lists, postage, and so on).
2. *Gross Revenue.* This section shows you the gross revenue generated for mailings of a specified size at a specified cost for various solicitation amounts.
3. *Net Revenue.* This section subtracts the cost of the mailing and the cost of fulfillment from the gross revenue figures to show the net revenue. It can be used to find the breakeven point.
4. *Macros.* This section contains the various macros that drive the menu and recalculation functions of the template.

Main Menu Options

The Direct Mail Response Calculator Template has four Main Menu choices (see Figure 12.3, Menu Tree).

```
Express Print Graph File
```

II. Projected Revenue

                                              Date: 03-Feb-87
A. Gross Revenue

        Mailing Size: 100,000 pieces

                    --------------------Solicitation Amount--------------------
Response $32.00 $37.00 $46.00 $49.00 $59.00
----------   -------   -------   --------   -------   -------
   0.25 %   8,000.00   9,250.00   11,500.00   12,250.00   14,750.00
   0.50 %   16,000.00   18,500.00   23,000.00   24,500.00   29,500.00
   0.75 %   24,000.00   27,750.00   34,500.00   36,750.00   44,250.00
   1.00 %   32,000.00   37,000.00   46,000.00   49,000.00   59,000.00
   1.25 %   40,000.00   46,250.00   57,500.00   61,250.00   73,750.00
   1.50 %   48,000.00   55,500.00   69,000.00   73,500.00   88,500.00
   1.75 %   56,000.00   64,750.00   80,500.00   85,750.00   103,250.00
   2.00 %   64,000.00   74,000.00   92,000.00   98,000.00   118,000.00
   2.25 %   72,000.00   83,250.00   103,500.00   110,250.00   132,750.00
   2.50 %   80,000.00   92,500.00   115,000.00   122,500.00   147,500.00
   2.75 %   88,000.00   101,750.00   126,500.00   134,750.00   162,250.00
   3.00 %   96,000.00   111,000.00   138,000.00   147,000.00   177,000.00
   3.25 %   104,000.00   120,250.00   149,500.00   159,250.00   191,750.00
   3.50 %   112,000.00   129,500.00   161,000.00   171,500.00   206,500.00
   3.75 %   120,000.00   138,750.00   172,500.00   183,750.00   221,250.00
   4.00 %   128,000.00   148,000.00   184,000.00   196,000.00   236,000.00
   4.25 %   136,000.00   157,250.00   195,500.00   208,250.00   250,750.00
   4.50 %   144,000.00   166,500.00   207,000.00   220,500.00   265,500.00
   4.75 %   152,000.00   175,750.00   218,500.00   232,750.00   280,250.00
   5.00 %   160,000.00   185,000.00   230,000.00   245,000.00   295,000.00

B. Net Revenue

        Mailing Size: 100,000 pieces   Fulfillment
        Mailing Cost: $21,155.00   Cost: $11.00

                    ------------------Solicitation Amount----------------
Response $27.00 $36.00 $48.00 $52.00 $59.00
----------   -------   -------   -------   -------   -------
   0.25 %   (14,416.00)   (12,166.00)   (9,166.00)   (8,166.00)   (6,416.00)
   0.50 %   (7,666.00)   (3,166.00)   2,834.00   4,834.00   8,334.00
   0.75 %   (916.00)   5,834.00   14,834.00   17,834.00   23,084.00
   1.00 %   5,834.00   14,834.00   26,834.00   30,834.00   37,834.00
   1.25 %   12,584.00   23,834.00   38,834.00   43,834.00   52,584.00
   1.50 %   19,334.00   32,834.00   50,834.00   56,834.00   67,334.00
   1.75 %   26,084.00   41,834.00   62,834.00   69,834.00   82,084.00
   2.00 %   32,834.00   50,834.00   74,834.00   82,834.00   96,834.00
   2.25 %   39,584.00   59,834.00   86,834.00   95,834.00   111,584.00
   2.50 %   46,334.00   68,834.00   98,834.00   108,834.00   126,334.00
   2.75 %   53,084.00   77,834.00   110,834.00   121,834.00   141,084.00
   3.00 %   59,834.00   86,834.00   122,834.00   134,834.00   155,834.00
   3.25 %   66,584.00   95,834.00   134,834.00   147,834.00   170,584.00
   3.50 %   73,334.00   104,834.00   146,834.00   160,834.00   185,334.00
   3.75 %   80,084.00   113,834.00   158,834.00   173,834.00   200,084.00
   4.00 %   86,834.00   122,834.00   170,834.00   186,834.00   214,834.00
   4.25 %   93,584.00   131,834.00   182,834.00   199,834.00   229,584.00
   4.50 %   100,334.00   140,834.00   194,834.00   212,834.00   244,334.00
   4.75 %   107,084.00   149,834.00   206,834.00   225,834.00   259,084.00
   5.00 %   113,834.00   158,834.00   218,834.00   238,834.00   273,834.00

Figure 12.1 *Sample Direct Mail Response Analysis.*

Express

To begin using the template, select the Express option. You will then be presented with the following submenu:

```
Costs Gross revenues Net Revenues
```

Each option represents an area of the worksheet.

Mailing Costs (Refer to Figure 12.4)

1. When you select the Express/Cost option, the pointer moves immediately to the *Date* cell (F7) of the Costs, where you can enter the date of the mailing. The template will prompt you to enter the day, month, and last two digits of the year.
2. Underneath the cell labeled *Date* you will see two cells labeled *Other* (E8 and E9). You can overwrite "Other" with labels of your own choosing (e.g., "Code" or "Description"). If you plan to use these labels on each analysis, you should stop and save this template as a master that you can call up each time you want to analyze a direct mail campaign.

   In cells F8 and F9, opposite the *Other* cells, enter corresponding comments if you wish—these are optional and do not effect the functioning of the worksheet.
3. Move the cell pointer to C15 and begin entering the costs of the items listed in column B. The items included with the template are universally used in direct mail (artwork, printing, postage, handling, mailing lists); however, you can edit or overwrite any item, and can enter additional ones of your own

Mailing Costs
A1..G29

Macros
A105..L142

Gross Revenue
A31..G59

Net Revenue
A62..G89

Figure 12.2 *Layout of Direct Mail Response Calculator.*

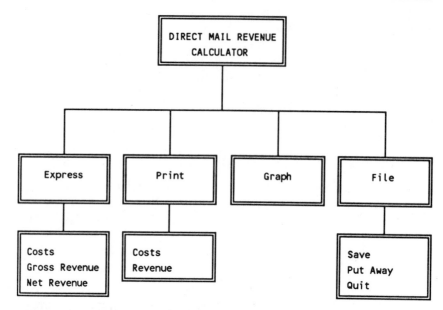

Figure 12.3 *Menu Tree, Direct Mail Revenue Calculator.*

choosing. If you want to erase any items, use the /Range Erase
command by moving the pointer to the cell you wish to erase,
and then typing /**RE ‹RETURN›**. To erase more than one cell,
move to the top of the range that you want to erase and type
/**RE**. Press the period "." key to anchor the range, and use the
cursor keys to move the cell pointer to highlight each cell you
want to erase. Press **‹RETURN›** again, and the range will be
erased. Be careful!

> **Caution!** Do not use the /**Row Delete** function to elimi-
> nate rows. The macros will no longer work correctly if
> any rows have been deleted.

After you have edited or added the items in Column B, enter the
quantities you wish to price in row 13, beginning with cell C13.
Then enter the costs of the various items (printing, postage, etc.)
for each mailing quantity, without dollar signs or commas, in their
appropriate rows. The total cost for each mailing quantity will be
automatically calculated in row 25. (See Figure 12.4 for a sample.)
The cost per thousand (\M) is shown in cells C27 through F27.
Once you have entered the costs, you can test various size mailings
and solicitation amounts and compare the gross and net revenues.

I. Projected Costs

Specifications

Date   03-Feb-87
Mailing: Bus Comp

| | -------------------Quantity------------------- | | | |
Item	50,000	100,000	150,000	200,000
1. Artwork	1,423.00	1,423.00	1,423.00	1,423.00
2. Printing	8,634.00	10,432.00	12,434.00	14,563.00
3. Postage	5,500.00	1,100.00	16,500.00	22,000.00
4. Handling	1,050.00	1,700.00	2,250.00	2,400.00
5. Lists	3,250.00	6,500.00	9,750.00	13,000.00
6.				
7.				
8.				
9.				
TOTAL COST	$19,857.00	$21,155.00	$42,357.00	$53,386.00
COST/M	$397.14	$211.55	$282.38	$266.93

Figure 12.4 *Cost Record Section, Direct Mail Template.*

Gross Revenues (Refer to Figure 12.5)

1. When you select the Express/Gross Revenues option, the pointer will move to the *Mailing Size* cell (D35) of the Gross Revenues section. Enter the size of the mailing you would like to test. This number will be copied down to the Mailing Size cell of the Net Revenue section. The total costs associated with that number will also be derived from the Costs section and used in the net revenue calculations.

   Caution! You must input Mailing size numbers exactly as they were entered into the Mailing Cost section (Row 13). If you entered a quantity below your lowest entry, you will get an error message (e.g., if you entered the quantities "50,000," "100,000," "150,000," and "200,000," but asked the template to analyze a mailing size of only 30,000 in the Gross Revenues section, you will cause an error message to be displayed.) Press **ESC** to clear the message. If you input a number greater than the largest number in the cost section (in this example, greater than 200,000 pieces), an error message will not be displayed;

however, the template will use the total amount associated with the largest number in the cost section, so that
the computations will be incorrect.

2. Enter the *Solicitation Amounts* you want to test in cells C38
   through F38 (e.g., various subscription prices, retail prices,
   donation amounts, etc.). Do not enter dollar signs or commas.
   Note: Whatever solicitation prices you enter in the Gross Revenue section will be automatically copied down to the Net
   Revenue section.

3. If you want to change the response percentage range, overwrite the cells with the desired figures. (Note: The template

```
II.  Projected Revenue

                                       Date:     03-Feb-87

A.  Gross Revenue


         Mailing Size:          100,000 pieces


                  ------------------Solicitation Amount------------------
Response            $32.00      $37.00      $46.00      $49.00      $59.00
----------          -------     -------     -------     -------     -------
   0.25 % |        8,000.00    9,250.00   11,500.00   12,250.00   14,750.00
   0.50 % |       16,000.00   18,500.00   23,000.00   24,500.00   29,500.00
   0.75 % |       24,000.00   27,750.00   34,500.00   36,750.00   44,250.00
   1.00 % |       32,000.00   37,000.00   46,000.00   49,000.00   59,000.00
   1.25 % |       40,000.00   46,250.00   57,500.00   61,250.00   73,750.00
   1.50 % |       48,000.00   55,500.00   69,000.00   73,500.00   88,500.00
   1.75 % |       56,000.00   64,750.00   80,500.00   85,750.00  103,250.00
   2.00 % |       64,000.00   74,000.00   92,000.00   98,000.00  118,000.00
   2.25 % |       72,000.00   83,250.00  103,500.00  110,250.00  132,750.00
   2.50 % |       80,000.00   92,500.00  115,000.00  122,500.00  147,500.00
   2.75 % |       88,000.00  101,750.00  126,500.00  134,750.00  162,250.00
   3.00 % |       96,000.00  111,000.00  138,000.00  147,000.00  177,000.00
   3.25 % |      104,000.00  120,250.00  149,500.00  159,250.00  191,750.00
   3.50 % |      112,000.00  129,500.00  161,000.00  171,500.00  206,500.00
   3.75 % |      120,000.00  138,750.00  172,500.00  183,750.00  221,250.00
   4.00 % |      128,000.00  148,000.00  184,000.00  196,000.00  236,000.00
   4.25 % |      136,000.00  157,250.00  195,500.00  208,250.00  250,750.00
   4.50 % |      144,000.00  166,500.00  207,000.00  220,500.00  265,500.00
   4.75 % |      152,000.00  175,750.00  218,500.00  232,750.00  280,250.00
   5.00 % |      160,000.00  185,000.00  230,000.00  245,000.00  295,000.00
```

Figure 12.5 *Gross Record Section, Direct Mail Template.*

3. If you want to change the response percentage range, over-write the cells with the desired figures. (Note: The template converts all numbers into percentages, so that "25%" would be entered as "25." Do not enter percentage signs.) Any time you change a response rate in the Gross Revenue section, that number will automatically be copied down to the response rate in the Net Revenue section.

4. Press **F9** and the template will automatically calculate the gross revenues from the mailing for each response rate and each solicitation amount.

Net Revenue (Refer to Figure 12.6)

1. The **Express/Net** Revenue option takes you to the *Mailing Cost* cell (D65) of the Net Revenue section. Notice that the size of the mailing has been automatically carried down from the Gross Revenue section, and the cost of that size mailing has been derived from the cost section of the template.

2. Enter the amount it will cost you to fulfill your obligation in the *Fulfillment Cost* cell (G65). If you are selling a newsletter or magazine subscription, for example, you would enter the combined editorial, administrative, production, postal, and overhead costs that are required to fulfill a subscription. Enter the number in G65. The same applies if you are selling a prod-uct—what does it cost to make and deliver that item? If you are conducting a fundraiser and giving away a premium, enter the cost of the premium. If you are fundraising and do not plan on giving away a premium, enter "0." (As with all value entries, do not use a dollar sign or comma.)

3. If you decide to change the solicitation amounts or revenue, return to the Gross Revenue section; these numbers are auto-matically copied down from the Gross Revenue section to the Net Revenue section. If you overwrite the solicitation amounts and response percentages in the Net Revenue section, you will actually be overwriting formulas, and the template will not work properly in the future.

4. Press **F9** and the template will automatically calculate the gross revenues from the mailing for each response rate and

B. Net Revenue

| | Mailing Size: | 100,000 pieces | | Fulfillment | |
| | Mailing Cost: | $21,155.00 | | Cost: | $11.00 |

| | | | ----------------Solicitation Amount---------------- | | |
Response	$27.00	$36.00	$48.00	$52.00	$59.00
0.25 % |	(14,416.00)	(12,166.00)	(9,166.00)	(8,166.00)	(6,416.00)
0.50 % |	(7,666.00)	(3,166.00)	2,834.00	4,834.00	8,334.00
0.75 % |	(916.00)	5,834.00	14,834.00	17,834.00	23,084.00
1.00 % |	5,834.00	14,834.00	26,834.00	30,834.00	37,834.00
1.25 % |	12,584.00	23,834.00	38,834.00	43,834.00	52,584.00
1.50 % |	19,334.00	32,834.00	50,834.00	56,834.00	67,334.00
1.75 % |	26,084.00	41,834.00	62,834.00	69,834.00	82,084.00
2.00 % |	32,834.00	50,834.00	74,834.00	82,834.00	96,834.00
2.25 % |	39,584.00	59,834.00	86,834.00	95,834.00	111,584.00
2.50 % |	46,334.00	68,834.00	98,834.00	108,834.00	126,334.00
2.75 % |	53,084.00	77,834.00	110,834.00	121,834.00	141,084.00
3.00 % |	59,834.00	86,834.00	122,834.00	134,834.00	155,834.00
3.25 % |	66,584.00	95,834.00	134,834.00	147,834.00	170,584.00
3.50 % |	73,334.00	104,834.00	146,834.00	160,834.00	185,334.00
3.75 % |	80,084.00	113,834.00	158,834.00	173,834.00	200,084.00
4.00 % |	86,834.00	122,834.00	170,834.00	186,834.00	214,834.00
4.25 % |	93,584.00	131,834.00	182,834.00	199,834.00	229,584.00
4.50 % |	100,334.00	140,834.00	194,834.00	212,834.00	244,334.00
4.75 % |	107,084.00	149,834.00	206,834.00	225,834.00	259,084.00
5.00 % |	113,834.00	158,834.00	218,834.00	238,834.00	273,834.00

Figure 12.6 *Net Revenue Section, Direct Mail Template.*

each solicitation amount. Negative numbers will show up in
parentheses.

Conducting a Direct Mail Analysis

The net revenue analyses can be used to determine the feasibility
and potential profitability of a mailing. Notice in Figure 12.6 that
the response does not turn a profit until the mailing achieves at
least 0.75 percent at the lowest solicitation price ($27 per item). At a
solicitation price of $36 per item, however, the mailing begins to

show a profit at .50 percent, and at $48 per item the campaign inches into the black 0.25 percent. Also notice that as the response increases, profit rises sharply with an increase in solicitation price.

You can use this information one of two ways. First, if you do not expect to achieve a response higher than 0.75 percent, you cannot offer the item at a price of $27 and expect to make a profit. That means you must first determine whether the market will bear prices of $36 or more for the item in question. The profits at the high end are certainly impressive; but if no one is willing to pay those amounts, then the mailing will be a money loser.

The other way to use the net revenue information is to determine what profit level you need to justify the mailing and support your business plan. If that level is unrealistic in terms of the response or the amount you would need to charge for the item, then you should rethink the mailing. For example, if you need to double your money each mailing to meet your target revenue levels, than you will have to net approximately $21,000. As you can see in Figure 12.6, that means achieving between 1.50 percent and 1.75 percent at the $27 level, which would be a strong response. Although many promotions do achieve a 2.0 percent or better response, most do not. In fact, a response of 1.0 percent is considered excellent by many people. So again, it looks like it would be unrealistic to attempt to achieve your target number by selling the item at $27.

As you move across the net revenue section, the response needed to achieve the target figure of $21,000 drops considerably. But again, counterbalancing this favorable trend is the difficulty you may have in trying to sell the product at the higher prices.

In both cases, lowering the cost of the mailing or the fulfillment cost will have a positive effect on the numbers, and either may be the solution when a mailing appears to be marginal. While this discussion is not meant to be a substitute for a thorough explanation of direct mail theory, it should give you a basic understanding of the relationship between the cost of the mailing, the response rate, and the fulfillment cost of the item.

Print

When you select the **Print** option from the Main Menu, you will see a submenu that gives you the following options:

```
Costs Revenues
```

The **Costs** option prints out the cost analysis sections of the template (refer to Figure 12.4 for a sample printout), including headings and rules. The **Revenue** option prints out the Gross and Net Revenue sections (refer to Figures   12.5 and 12.6). Make sure your printer is online before using either print option. Otherwise, you will generate an error message.

Graph

The **Graph** option produces a graph of the net profit versus response for various solicitation amounts (see figure 12.7). The **Graph** option assumes that you have a graphics or color card and a graphics or color monitor.

To switch back to the worksheet after viewing the graph, press **ESC**. The template will then create a .PIC file that you can later print from the Lotus PrintGraph utility. To complete the .PIC file, the template will prompt you to enter a name. If you are planning on graphing several different sets of numbers, be sure to give each .PIC file a unique name. Otherwise, you will overwrite the same file.

File

The **File** menu choice provides three options: save and return to the worksheet (**Save**); save and leave 1-2-3 (**Put away**); and quit without saving (**Quit**).

Common Questions and Problems

The most likely problem you will encounter occurs during setup. The Direct Mail Revenue Calculator Template contains an "auto-burst" macro that copies the necessary formulas into place to save space on the distribution diskette. If you terminate the autoexec macro prior to completion, the necessary formulas will not be properly copied. The auto-burst macro is invoked the first time you run the template and press **<RETURN>** at the title screen. The macro would be interrupted if you pressed **CTRL-BREAK** before the Main Menu is displayed. Once the formulas are correctly copied to the right cells in the template, the auto-burst macro is no longer functional, and the template should perform calculations without any difficulties.

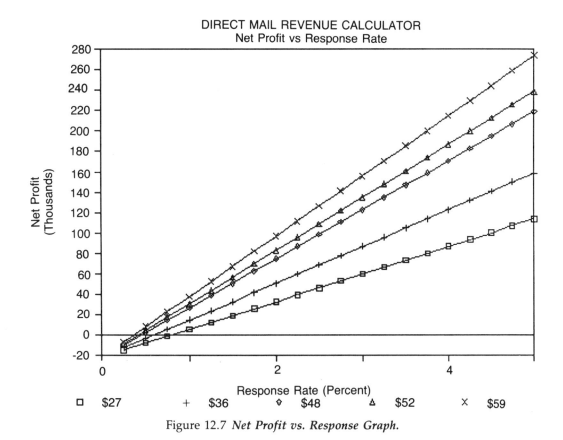

Figure 12.7 *Net Profit vs. Response Graph.*

13 | SALES FORECAST GENERATOR

CONTENTS

SPECIFICATIONS

Filename **SALEFORE.WKS**

Functions

- Generates sales forecast based on historical data.
- Plots graph using least squares line fit.

Usage

- Projects sales forecast.
- Determines marketing feasibility and break-even point.

Features

- Auto-entry.
- Generates Lotus 1-2-3 .PIC file for easy graph printing.
- Screen lock for Release 2.

Special Requirements

- Computer: graphics capability (graphics or RGB card and graphics or color monitor).
- Printer capable of generating graphs, or plotter.

Introduction

The Sales Forecast Template enables you to input historical sales data, and then project future sales growth using the least squares line fit method. The template provides a report showing the forecast, and generates graphs for the historical data as well as the forecast.

This Template represents a powerful addition to 1-2-3's capabilities. While Release 2 does have a regression function that calculates the slope and intercept of a line, Release 1A of 1-2-3 has no line fitting functions. That means when you have a series of data points, 1-2-3 will merely connect them. This provides little help in understanding the data or projecting the data into the future. The Sales Forecast Template draws the best fit line through the data points, then continues that line through a period twice as long as the data period that you input.

Because of the template's design, you do not need to input regular or equal sales periods. The template also allows you to put in the sales period in random sequence, and then sort the periods prior to making a projection. (Figure 13.1 shows the data input section of the template. Figure 13.2 shows a sample historical plot, and Figure 13.3 shows a corresponding sales projection using the forecast data.)

Before using the Sales Forecast template to analyze your business, be aware that any forecasting technique is dependant on the accuracy and consistency of the data that are being analyzed. Therefore, if the data are either cyclical, widely dispersed, or erratic, a straight line forecast will be less accurate.

Finally, although the template is set up to forecast sales, it can be used to project *any* data. If necessary, the format of the input cells can be altered to accommodate other types of data using more or fewer decimal places.

Template Layout

The Sales Forecast Template is divided into three sections (see Figure 13.4):

1. *Data/Forecast.* This is where you enter the historical data and view the forecast. In addition, the count (number of data points), the slope, and the intercept are displayed in the right hand panel.
2. *Calculation.* The line fit calculations are performed in this area.
3. *Macros.* This section contains the various macros that drive the menu and recalculation functions of the template.

SALES FORECAST GENERATOR

```
=================================================================================
       Sales History          |       Sales Forecast        |   Calculations
                              |                             |
                              |                             |
Period           Sales        | Period           Sales      |
.........................................................+.................
        1        345.00       |     1          366.95       | Count
        2        413.00       |     2          368.64       |            6.00
        3        312.00       |     3          370.32       |
        4        399.00       |     4          372.01       | Slope
        5        427.00       |     5          373.70       |            1.69
        6        331.00       |     6          375.38       |
                              |     7          377.07       | Intercept
                              |     8          378.75       |          365.27
                              |     9          380.44       |
                              |    10          382.12       |
                              |    11          383.81       |
                              |    12          385.50       |
```

Figure 13.1 *Data/Forecast Sections of the Sales Force Template.*

Main Menu Options

The Main Menu of the Sales Forecast Template offers the following options (see Menu Tree, Figure 13.5):

```
Data Sort Recalc Forecast Graph Print File Lock-Screen
```

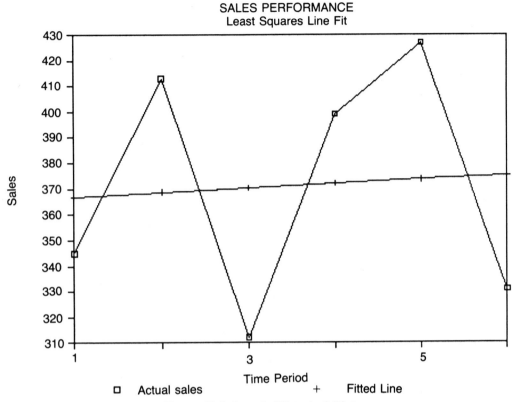

Figure 13.2 *Sample Historical Plot.*

Data

To begin using the template, select the **Data** option. You will then be presented with the following submenu:

```
Continue Begin Edit Zap
```

Here's how each option would be used to enter the following historical data:

Period	Sales (in thousands)
1	345
2	413
3	312
4	399
5	427
6	331

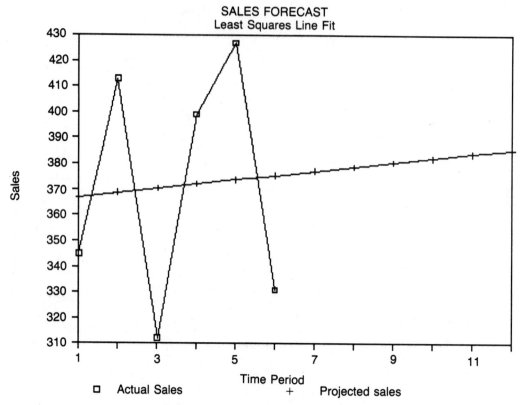

Figure 13.3 *Sample Sales Projection.*

Data Entry	Calculation	Macros
A8..B1000	D8..N1000	P1..X116

Figure 13.4 *Layout, Sales Forecast Template.*

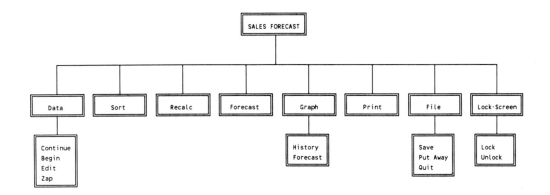

Figure 13.5 *Menu Tree, Sales Forecast Template.*

1. Select the **Data/Begin** option. The pointer will move to cell A8, which is the first *Period* cell in the first data row (refer to Figure 13.6). Note: Begin will overwrite any data in the worksheet, so you should only use it if you wish to do so. If you wish to add to existing data, use **Continue**.

2. When the pointer is in cell A8, enter the week, month, or whatever time period you wish to forecast. In the case of historical data, enter "1" for the first period. Press **<RETURN>** and the pointer will move into the adjacent cell under the *Sales* column. Enter "345," and press **<RETURN>**. The cell pointer

```
         SALES FORECAST GENERATOR


         ============================
           Sales History        |
                                 |
                                 |
         Period          Sales   |
         - - - - - - - - - - - - - - - - - - - - -
              1          345.00   |
              2          413.00   |
              3          312.00   |
              4          399.00   |
              5          427.00   |
```

Figure 13.6 *Data Entry Section, Sales Forecast Template.*

will move to the *Period* cell in the next line. Enter the next period, "2." press **<RETURN>**, and then enter the corresponding amount ("413"). Continue this process until you have entered all your historical data.

After each pair of data points has been entered, the macro will ask if you wish to continue or stop. Press **<RETURN>** to continue or select the **S**top option to end data entry and resume the Main Menu.

Continue

Unlike **Begin**, which starts the data entry process in the first row of the Data/Forecast section, **Continue** moves the cell pointer to the first column in the next available row, so you can add another period and sales amount. Note: You should *not* use **Continue** if you have not entered any data in the worksheet because it will not properly copy down the formulas in the first row. If you accidentally select **Continue** when you are first entering data, press **CTRL-BREAK** to stop the macro (with Release 2 you have to press **ESC** after **CTRL-BREAK**), and then **ALT-M**, to bring up the Main Menu. Select **Data/Begin** to add the first entry.

When you use **Continue** to add data, don't worry if it is not in sequential order. For example, if you had previously only entered sales periods 2, 4, and 6, you could add periods 1 and 3 after period 6. You would then use the **S**ort function to put the periods in their proper sequence.

Edit

When you select **Edit** from the **D**ata submenu, the pointer will move to cell A8, and the macro will stop. You can then use the cursor keys to browse through the periods and sales figures and make whatever changes you wish. The edit feature is especially useful for quickly performing "What-if" routines, where you want to compare a number of different sales figure scenarios.

For example, you might want to compare alternative growth models that anticipate seasonal changes in sales. You might also want to vary the historical periods by certain levels to account for unexpected factors that either increased or decreased normal sales.

In any case, once your editing is complete, press **ALT-M** to sort, recalculate, graph, or forecast the data.

Zap

The **Zap** function clears the historical and forecast data (except the first two periods) so that you can start reentering data from the beginning using the **Begin** option. It cannot erase the first two entries since the formulas used to calculate the line reference them. If the first two rows are deleted, the formulas will be damaged. The **Begin** option allows you to overwrite any values remaining in the first two rows.

Sort

The **Sort** option allows you to resequence the historical sales periods prior to generating a forecast or a graph. This is useful, because it allows you to add data that may be chronologically out of sequence with earlier periods. **Sort** orders the periods from lowest to highest.

Recalc

Each time you enter data into the template, you must select the **Recalc** option from the Main Menu to compute the count (number of data points), the slope (rate of change), and the intercept (base line sales). Note that the **Recalc** function of the template is different from 1-2-3's Calc Function (**F9** key); it "autosizes" the data range, then copies the correct number of formulas from the *Calculation* section. If you merely press **F9**, you will not generate correct line calculations.

Forecast

The **Forecast** option takes the historical data range, and doubles it, applying the best fit line between points. The results of the forecast are displayed in the Data/Forecast section of the template (middle panel—see Figure 13.1). Note that the sales figures associated with the historical sales period will be higher or lower than those you actually entered since the forecast represents the best approximation for all historical data points together, not just individually. The forecast can also be viewed in graph form.

Graph

When you select the **Graph** option, the following submenu will be displayed:

`Historical Forecast`

The **Historical** option gives you a plot of the actual sales data (see Figure 13.2 for a sample), while the **Forecast** option plots the results of the forecast function. To see the graphs, you must have graphics viewing capabilities (a graphics or color card and a graphics or color monitor.) Even if you don't have viewing capabilities for graphs, you can still print the historical or forecast graphs if your printer has graphics capabilities.

To switch back to the worksheet after viewing the graph, press **ESC**. The template will then create a .PIC file that you can later print from the Lotus PrintGraph utility. To complete the .PIC file, the template will prompt you to enter a name. If you are planning on graphing several different sets of numbers, be sure to give each .PIC file a unique name. Otherwise, you will simply overwrite the same file.

Print

When you select the **Print** option from the Main Menu, the template will print the historical data, the most current sales forecast, and the most current line fit calculations. See Figure 13.1 for a sample printout.

File

The **File** menu choice provides three options: save and return to the worksheet (**Save**); save and leave 1-2-3 (**Put away**); and quit without saving (**Quit**).

Lock-Screen

Lock-Screen freezes the control panel and the screen during macro execution. It can only be used with 1-2-3 Releases 2 and 2.01.

Common Questions and Problems

The forecast for the current period doesn't match the historical data. The data points in the forecast corresponding to the same periods as the historical data are generated according to the line calculated to fit the historical data. Therefore, they represent what the historical data *would* have been if they fit the line perfectly. The points generated are actually used to graph the forecasted line.

The forecast doesn't handle cyclical data. The model only generates a linear best fit. If the data are cyclical or erratic, the linear fit will produce less reliable results.

The graphs aren't displayed. You must have the proper hardware and drivers installed to view the graphs on your screen—see your 1-2-3 manual for assistance.

The graphs don't print. You must save the graph image in a .PIC file as prompted by the Graph menu option, and then print it using the PrintGraph utility provided with the 1-2-3 program. The graph macros will automatically prompt you to save your graphs for later printing or plotting. See your 1-2-3 manual for directions on printing graphs. (Note: if you do not want to save the graph data, press **ESC** when prompted for a graph file name. This will break the macro, and you will have to press **ALT-M** to return to the Main Menu. Alternately, you can assign the name "Temp," to the file, and the macro will automatically return you to the Main Menu. You can later delete the "Temp" file at your convenience.)

14 | BUDGET PLANNER

CONTENTS

Specifications

Filename **BUDGET.WKS**

Functions

- Compares projected vs. actual expenses and revenues.

Usage

- Plans cash flow.
- Calculates net revenue.
- Compares budget to actual performance and percent variance.

Features

- Auto-entry of data.
- Automatically calculates year-to-date and quarterly figures for projected/actual revenues, expenses, variance, and net profit.
- Graphs gross income, operating expenses, and net profit.

Introduction

The Budget Planner Template helps you with your financial planning by allowing you to compare projected and actual revenues and expenses. It then calculates the amount and percentage of variance, and shows you your net profit. The Template has space for six types of goods or services sold, as well as a miscellaneous category. The expense categories include those items common to most businesses and you can easily modify them to suit your needs.

The Template makes it easy to quickly move to the month for which you wish to enter or edit data, and to print out the month or months you wish to view. A sample budget plan is shown in Figure 14.1, and a summary version is shown in Figure 14.2.

First Time Use

The first time you use the Budget Template, you will be asked to enter the Release you are using. Input the number (1 for Release 1A, or 2 for Release 2 or 2.01). The Template will then "unfold" itself, a process that can take up to several minutes, depending on what kind of computer you are using. This is a one-time process. The next time you use the template, you will press **‹RETURN›** to move beyond the title screen into the actual worksheet. For more information about the macro that sets up the spreadsheet, and the rationale for including it, see Auto-burst macro in Appendix A.

Template Layout

The Budget Template is divided into four sections (see Figure 14.3):

1. *Categories.* This section lists the various revenue and budget categories used in the worksheet.
2. *Monthly Input.* This section is divided into 12 subsections, one for each month. Each monthly subsection is three columns wide (one for budgeted amount, one for actual amount, and one for variance).
3. *Combined calculations.* The combined year-to-date calculations and quarterly calculations are made in this section.

```
                                              JANUARY
SALES                              Budget      Actual    Variance
-----
        Model 100                 75,000.00   50,000.00   -33.33%
        Model 200                 50,000.00   60,000.00    20.00%
        Model 300                 35,000.00   25,000.00   -28.57%
        Model 400                      0.00        0.00     0.00%
        Product E                      0.00        0.00     0.00%
                                       0.00        0.00     0.00%
                                       0.00        0.00     0.00%
                                  ----------- -----------
        TOTAL SALES              160,000.00  135,000.00   -15.63%

COST OF GOODS SOLD
------------------
        Model 100                 60,000.00   40,000.00   -33.33%
        Model 200                 30,000.00   40,000.00    33.33%
        Product C                 20,000.00   10,000.00   -50.00%
        Product D                      0.00        0.00     0.00%
        Product E                      0.00        0.00     0.00%
        Product F                      0.00        0.00     0.00%
        Misc. Sales                    0.00        0.00     0.00%
                                  ----------- -----------
        TOTAL COST OF GOODS SOLD 110,000.00   90,000.00   -18.18%
================================================================
GROSS INCOME                      50,000.00   45,000.00   -10.00%
================================================================

OPERATING EXPENSES


                                             Page 1



--------------------
        Wages                      5,000.00    5,000.00     0.00%
        Contract Labor            15,000.00   10,000.00   -33.33%
        Rent                       2,500.00    2,500.00     0.00%
        Utilities                    450.00      543.00    20.67%
        Telephone Local              750.00      500.00   -33.33%
        Telephone Long Distance      600.00    1,100.00    83.33%
        Travel - Means               800.00      600.00   -25.00%
        Travel - Meals & Lodging   2,000.00    2,346.00    17.30%
        Advertizing                  850.00    1,025.00    20.59%
        Legal Expenses                 0.00    1,200.00  1200.00%
        Accounting                   350.00      425.00    21.43%
        Depreciation                 250.00      250.00     0.00%
        Repairs                       50.00       95.00    90.00%
        Postage                      150.00      151.00     0.67%
        Photocopies                   75.00       55.00   -26.67%
        Shipping                     235.00      200.00   -14.89%
        Office Supplies              225.00      258.00    14.67%
        Auto                         330.00      330.00     0.00%
        Insurance                    120.00      120.00     0.00%
        Subscriptions                 30.00       30.00     0.00%
        Interest Expense             120.00      120.00     0.00%
        Taxes                      1,250.00    1,250.00     0.00%
        Miscellaneous Expenses       175.00      112.00   -36.00%
                                  ----------- -----------
        TOTAL OPERATING EXPENSES  31,410.00   28,210.00   -10.19%
================================================================
NET PROFIT                        18,590.00   16,790.00    -9.68%
```

Figure 14.1 *Sample Budget Plan.*

4. *Macros.* This section contains the various macros that drive the menu and recalculation functions of the template.
5. *Selection Screen.* This section displays a selection screen that prompts you for the month you wish to enter, and the number of months you wish to print.

Main Menu Options

The Main Menu of the Budget Planner Template offers the following options:

```
Express Print File Title Lock-Screen
```

The Menu Tree (Figure 14.4) shows the complete menu structure of the template. The various options are described.

Setting Up the Template

Before you use the Budget Planner Template, you will want to customize the category labels. The expense categories provided with the template are shown in Table 14.1. You can change the name of a category by moving the cell pointer to it, and then overwriting it with a new name of your choice. You can also change the revenue categories. For example, if you want to change Product A to a specific item name, say, "Model 100," move the pointer to cell A10, and type "Model 100", then press **<RETURN>**. If Model 100 was your only product, you might also want to blank Products B (Cell B7) through Product F (Cell B12) by moving the pointer to those cells and using 1-2-3's erase feature (In this example, you would move the cursor to cell B7, type /RE., press the down arrow four times, then press **<RETURN>**.) You can adjust the expense column in the same way.

> **CAUTION!** Do not use the row or column insert or delete command to modify the worksheet. Also do not erase any of the formulas in the variance columns or the YTD or Quarterly total sections; otherwise, the macros or recalculation functions will not work properly and you will have to start with a clean copy from your master diskette!

BUDGET PLANNER SUMMARY

===

Month	Gross Income Budget	Actual	Varience	Operating Expenses Budget	Actual	Varience	Net Profits Budget	Actual	Varience
Jan	50,000.00	45,000.00	-10.00%	31,310.00	28,210.00	-9.90%	18,690.00	15,965.00	-14.58%
Feb	60,000.00	50,334.00	-16.11%	32,000.00	26,671.00	-16.65%	28,000.00	23,663.00	-15.49%
Mar	70,000.00	55,232.00	-21.10%	33,000.00	27,564.00	-16.47%	37,000.00	27,668.00	-25.22%
Apr	80,000.00	60,545.00	-24.32%	35,000.00	25,445.00	-27.30%	45,000.00	35,100.00	-22.00%
May	90,000.00	75,796.00	-15.78%	37,000.00	35,678.00	-3.57%	53,000.00	40,118.00	-24.31%
Jun	90,000.00	85,234.00	-5.30%	45,000.00	37,453.00	-16.77%	45,000.00	47,781.00	-6.18%
Jul	100,000.00	105,098.00	-5.10%	45,000.00	41,432.00	-7.93%	55,000.00	63,666.00	-15.76%
Aug	105,000.00	112,432.00	-7.08%	50,000.00	46,234.00	-7.53%	55,000.00	66,198.00	-20.36%
Sep	107,500.00	115,943.00	-7.85%	50,000.00	46,875.00	-6.25%	57,500.00	69,068.00	-20.12%
Oct	110,000.00	115,796.00	-5.27%	55,000.00	48,756.00	-11.35%	55,000.00	67,040.00	-21.89%
Nov	112,000.00	120,654.00	-7.73%	55,000.00	50,678.00	-7.86%	57,000.00	69,976.00	-22.76%
Dec	115,000.00	128,879.00	-12.07%	60,000.00	53,077.00	-11.54%	55,000.00	72,802.00	-32.37%
YTD	1,089,500.00	1,070,943.00	-1.70%	528,310.00	468,073.00	-11.40%	561,190.00	599,045.00	6.75%

Figure 14.2 *Sample Budget Summary.*

Categories	Monthly Input	Combined Calc	Macros	Selection Screen	Summary
A1..D60	F1..AZ60	BA1..BU60	BV1..CS100	CD1..CH37	CJ1..CS33

Figure 14.3 *Layout, Budget Planner Template.*

Entering/Editing Monthly Data

Once you've customized the category labels, you can enter, edit, or review data. To do so, select the Express option, and the cell pointer will move to the Selection Screen (Figure 14.5), which will ask you which month you want to input or edit. Alternatively, you can escape from the Main Menu and use the **Tab** key to move one month to the right or **Shift+Tab** to move one month to the left. Note: You must first lock the title for this method.

Table 14.1 *Expense Categories*

Wages
Contract Labor
Rent
Utilities
Telephone Local
Telephone Long Distance
Travel - Means
Travel - Meals & Lodging
Advertising
Legal Expenses
Accounting
Depreciation
Repairs
Postage
Photocopies
Shipping
Office Supplies
Auto
Insurance
Subscriptions
Interest Expense
Taxes
Miscellaneous Expenses

Type in the name of the month as prompted. You can also type "YTD" (year-to-date) or "QRT1", "QRT2", "QRT3", or QRT4 (for the quarters if the year) to review combined monthly data.

When you press **‹RETURN›**, the cell pointer will move to whatever month or period you indicated in the Selection Screen. The auto-entry macro now stops, and control of the cell pointer returns to the cursor keys. You can move freely about the worksheet, entering data as appropriate in the *Budget* and *Actual* columns.

Caution! Do not enter data in the *Variance* columns; they contain formulas, and the worksheet will not generate accurate results if the formulas are overwritten.

Print

When you select the **Print** option from the Main Menu, the following submenu options will be displayed:

```
Single Month Multiple [Months] Summary
```

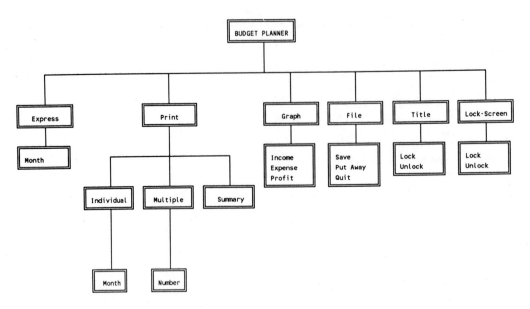

Figure 14.4 *Menu Tree, Budget Planner Template.*

Single Month

If you select **Single Month**, the cell pointer will move to the Selection Screen shown in Figure 14.5. Type in the character name of the month you wish to print, in UPPERCASE, letters and press **<RE-TURN>**. The printout will begin (see Figure 14.1 for a sample monthly printout). Note: If you type in "YTD" instead of a month, you will print the year-to-date summary; if you type "QRT1", you will print out the first quarter summary. Use "QRT2", "QRT3", and "QRT4" for the second through fourth quarters, respectively.

Multiple Months

If you choose **Multiple Months**, the cell pointer will move to a Selection Screen that asks you for the number of months you wish to

	CD	CE	CF	CG	CH
15					
16					
17					
18					
19					
20					
21		=======================================			
22		Enter the name of the month			
23		(eg JAN or AUG) or the period			
24		(eg YTD or QRT2). Must be			
25		all CAPS:			
26		=======================================			
27					
28					
29					
30					
31					
32					
33					
34					

Figure14.5 *Monthly Selector Screen, Budget Planner.*

print. If you type "5" in the Selection Screen, for example, the template will print the first five months. If you type "7" it will print out the first seven months, and so on. In addition, the Multiple Month option will print the YTD and appropriate quarterly reports as well.

Summary

The **Summary** option generates a report that shows the total budget and actual totals for each month, along with the variance and the net profit. (See Figure 14.2 for a sample summary report.)

Graph

The **Graph** option offers you three choices:
```
Income  Expenses  Profit
```

The Income option generates a bar graph of gross income over 12 months (Figure 14.6). The Expense option plots annual operating expenses in bar form (Figure 14.7), and the Profit option generates a bar graph of net income for each month of the year (Figure 14.8).

To switch back to the worksheet after viewing the graph, press **ESC**. The template will then create a .PIC file that you can later print using the Lotus PrintGraph utility. To complete the .PIC file, the template will prompt you to enter a name. If you are planning on graphing several different sets of numbers, be sure to give each .PIC file a unique name. Otherwise, you will simply overwrite the same file.

Note: To view graphs you must have a color monitor or a graphics card. You must also configure 1-2-3 for your equipment as detailed in the install booklet supplied by Lotus Development Corp.

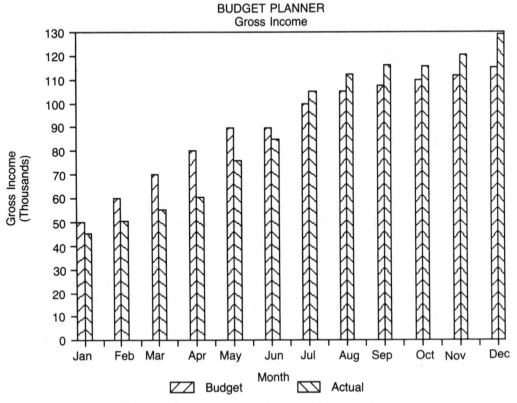

Figure 14.6 *Gross Income Graph, Budget Template.*

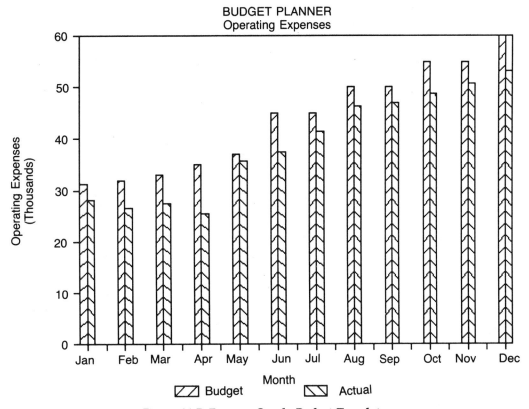

Figure 14.7 *Expense Graph, Budget Template.*

File

The **File** menu choice provides three options: save and return to the worksheet (**Save**); save and leave 1-2-3 (**Put away**); and quit without saving (**Quit**).

Title

The **Title** function locks the row headings so that they are visible even when you have scrolled to the right of the first screeen. The

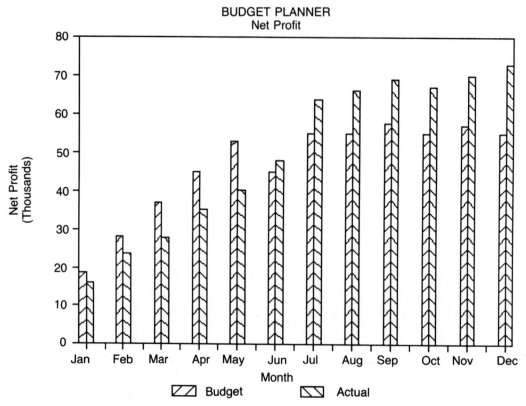

Figure 14.8 *Profit Bar Graph, Budget Template.*

Title function defaults to on, but can be removed by selecting the Title/Unlock option.

Lock-Screen

Lock-Screen freezes the control panel and the screen during macro execution. It can only be used with 1-2-3 Release 2 and 2.01.

Common Questions and Problems

The worksheet is blank. The template contains an "auto-burst" macro that copies the necessary formulas into place. This is used to conserve space on the distribution diskette. If you terminate the autoexec macro prior to completion, the necessary formulas will not be properly copied.

You cannot see the graphs. You must have the proper hardware and drivers installed to view the graphs on your screen. (See the Lotus 1-2-3 manual for your particular hardware configuration.)

You cannot print a graph. Lotus requires that you save the graph image in a .PIC file and then print it using the separate PrintGraph utility provided with the 1-2-3 program. The graph macros will automatically prompt you to save your graphs for later printing or plotting. See the 1-2-3 manual for directions on printing graphs.

The template prints too many months of data. The Multiple months print out assumes that you will want to print all months up to the month requested in the selection screen. In addition, it will automatically print the quarterly and YTD figures. If you wish to print only specific months, select the single month option.

You can't print out a specific month. The Individual month print routine requires that you input the month label exactly as it is defined (e.g., JAN must be entered as three letters with all caps).

You can't get to the labels to change them. You must first turn the Title lock off in order to move the cell pointer to the titles section of the template to edit the titles. You can either choose the Title/Unlock option from the template's main menu or use the Lotus **/WTC** command to accomplish this.

The calculations don't add up correctly. In order to improve the data input speed, the recalculation has been set off. You must recalculate the worksheet after making any changes by pressing the **F9** recalc key. This is especially important prior to manually printing or graphing the data since the CALC warning flag will not be displayed on the printout. The menu print and graph options automatically recalculate the worksheet prior to sending output to the printer.

15 | ACCOUNTS RECEIVABLE

CONTENTS

Specifications

Filename **AR.WKS**

Function

- Tracks accounts receivables.

Usage

- Logs invoices.
- Generates aging reports.
- Tracks cumulative income.

Features

- Auto-entry.
- Automatically calculates balance due on partial payments.
- Sorts invoices by client, number, invoice date.
- Extracts invoices by client and payment status.
- Generates aging reports for selected or all clients/customers.
- Generates aging graphs for selected or all clients/customers.
- Prints out entire invoice register or selected invoices.

Introduction

This template is designed to help small businesses and consulting operations track and age their accounts receivable. And while it is not designed as a substitute for a stand-alone AR package that generates invoices and integrates into a general ledger, it can be very effectively used to manage receivables for a small business or department.

The Accounts Receivable Template allows you to input basic invoice data, such as invoice number and date, the client or customer, a description of the work done or goods shipped, the total due, the amount paid, and the balance due. The template will also show you the age of each invoice and the total amount you have billed and received, and will generate aging reports for individual clients/customers or everyone in the template. The **Graph** option generates a bar graph of aged receivables.

In addition, the AR template allows you to extract all invoices for a particular client, and to extract all paid or unpaid invoices. At any time you can reorganize the template by client/customer, invoice number, or date by using the **Sort** function. A sample Accounts Receivable template is shown in Figure 15.1.

Template Layout

The Accounts Receivable Template (see Figure 15.2) consists of four sections:

1. *Invoice Data.* This is where you enter the invoice number, client/customer, description, invoice date, invoice amount, date paid, and amount paid.
2. *Selection Screen.* The selection screen allows you to enter a client you would like to subgroup in a separate report. (See Extract later in this chapter).
3. *Selected Records.* Once you have indicated what kinds of invoice records you want to Extract, they will appear in this area of the template for viewing or printing.
4. *Macros.* This section contains the macros that drive the menu operations and carry out sorting, extracting, printing, and saving functions.

ACCOUNTS RECEIVABLE   20-Feb-87

===

Invoice Number	Client	Description	Invoice Date	Invoice Total	Date of Payment	Payment Amount	Balance Due	Age	Status
									1=OPEN
			Totals:	$44,215.00		$11,500.00	$32,715.00		2=PAID
Number	Client	Description	Date	Total	Payment	Amount	Due	Age	Status
87001	US Pipe Co	Stationery	12-Jan-87	4,100.00		0.00	4,100.00	39	1
87002	ABC Truck	Cabinets	01-Dec-86	7,500.00	12-Feb-87	7,500.00	0.00	73	2
87003	Acme Finance	Forms	12-Feb-87	525.00		0.00	525.00	8	1
87004	Elgin Farms	Typewriters	30-Nov-86	1,700.00	15-Jan-87	1,700.00	0.00	46	2
87005	Jack's Bakery	Misc Supplies	04-Jan-87	745.00		0.00	745.00	47	1
87006	Excellco	Paper Products	02-Jan-87	1,200.00	05-Feb-87	1,200.00	0.00	34	2
87007	Carewell Ins	Stationery	20-Dec-86	3,135.00		0.00	3,135.00	62	1
87008	WISO Inc	Diskettes	22-Nov-86	450.00		0.00	450.00	90	1
87009	Zyrex	Desks	27-Jan-87	5,500.00		0.00	5,500.00	24	1
87010	Zyrex	Chairs	28-Jan-87	2,200.00		0.00	2,200.00	23	1
87011	ABC Truck	Misc Supplies	30-Dec-86	4,100.00		0.00	4,100.00	52	1
87012	US Pipe Co	Diskettes	14-Feb-87	235.00		0.00	235.00	6	1
87013	WISO Inc	Furniture	27-Nov-86	1,400.00		0.00	1,400.00	85	1
87014	Carewell Ins	Forms	23-Jan-87	1,100.00		0.00	1,100.00	28	1
87015	Excellco	Misc Supplies	15-Dec-86	1,100.00	31-Jan-87	1,100.00	0.00	47	2
87016	Acme Finance	Stationery	18-Feb-87	1,350.00		0.00	1,350.00	2	1
87017	US Pipe Co	Furniture	31-Jan-87	3,700.00		0.00	3,700.00	20	1
87018	US Pipe Co	Forms	02-Feb-87	1,475.00		0.00	1,475.00	18	1
87019	WISO Inc	Typewriters	01-Feb-87	2,300.00		0.00	2,300.00	19	1
87020	WISO Inc	Stationery	07-Feb-87	400.00		0.00	400.00	13	1

Figure 15.1 *Sample Accounts Receivable Template.*

Invoice Data	*Selection Screen*	*Selected Records*
A11..J1000	K1..O20	AA11..AJ1000

Macros

K21..Z141

Figure 15.2 *Layout of AR Template.*

Main Menu Options

The Main Menu of the Accounts Receivable Template offers the following options:

Data Extract Print Aging Sort File Title Lock-
Screen

Figure 15.3 shows the template's complete menu structure.

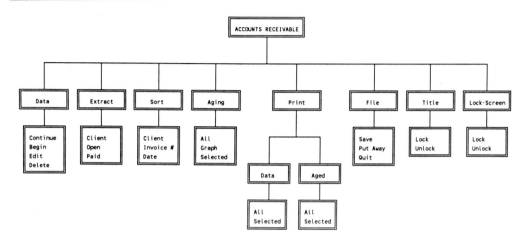

Figure 15.3 *Menu Tree, Accounts Receivable Template.*

Data

The **Data** option offers two auto-entry macros (**Continue** and **Begin**), as well as **Edit** and **Delete**. **Begin** is only used the first time you enter data, and **Continue** is used thereafter. **Edit** allows you to manually move the cursor, and **Delete** is a special substitute for the Lotus 1-2-3 /Worksheet **Delete Row** function, which can damage the template. Refer to Chapter 1 for a detailed discussion of how these functions are used.

When you select **Continue** or **Begin**, the macro moves the template through the following sequence of cells each time you enter data and press **<RETURN>**:

```
Invoice Number (N) → Client (T) → Description (T) →
Invoice Date (N) → Invoice Total (N) → Date of Pay-
ment (N) → Payment Amount (N)
T = text cell
N = numeric cell
```

You can stop the auto-entry process at any time by pressing **CTRL-BREAK**. If the current input request is for text data (e.g., *Client*), pressing **ESC** will work as well. If the current request is for numerical data (e.g., *Invoice amount*), only **CTRL-BREAK** will end the macro. (Note: If you are using Release 2.0 or 2.01, "Error" will be displayed in the mode indicator cell after you press **CTRL-BREAK**. You can clear the error message by pressing **ESC**.)

If you end the auto-entry macro in the middle of a line, you must complete the line manually or erase it entirely since the Extract and Sort routines require complete rows of data. Caution: do not use the /**Worksheet Delete Row** function to erase a line of data, as this may damage the macros. Instead, erase the row cell-by-cell using the /**Range Erase** command.

After inputting information in the *Amount Paid* cell, which is the last data entry cell in a record, the auto-entry macro returns the cell pointer to the *Date* cell of the next row, and asks whether you wish to continue data entry.

> **IMPORTANT NOTE:** The age of Open invoices and the Aging Reports are calculated by subtracting the invoice date from today's date. It is therefore necessary to make sure that you manually enter the current date at the DOS date prompt prior to starting 1-2-3 if you do not have a built-in clock in your computer or a multifunction board with a clock. If you do have a built-in clock, make sure the date is correct.

Edit

The **Data/Edit** option allows you to use the cursor keys to move the pointer, so you can manually change data in cells of your choice. When you are done with your edits, press **ALT-M** to redisplay the Main Menu.

To edit a date, press **ALT-D**. You will then be prompted to enter the month, day, and year, pressing **<RETURN>** after each. If you do not wish to use the **ALT-D** edit function for editing dates, you must use the standard Lotus 1-2-3 date format ((@date(yy,mm,dd)).

Delete

The **Data/Delete** option is fully explained in Chapter 1. It is intended to be a substitute for 1-2-3's /**Worksheet Delete Row** command, which should never be used with Ready-to-Run templates since it can accidentally erase the template macros.

Sample Data Entry

Here is how you would create a record for an invoice issued to the U.S. Pipe Co. on May 5, 1987, for $41.00:

1. Select **B**egin. Enter an invoice number in Column A. Many businesses find it useful to create invoice numbers that begin with the last two digits or last digit of the year. For example, 87001 or 7001. In any case, the *Invoice number* cell will accept any alphanumeric combination.

2. Enter the client's name or code (Col B). Be consistent in the way you abbreviate a client's name, otherwise the **E**xtract and **S**ort routines will not work properly. The client name or code, "U.S. Pipe Co." (with periods) is treated differently from "US Pipe Co" (no periods). The same with "U S Pipe Co" (with a space) and "US Pipe Co" (no space, no periods).

   If you are using Release 1A, you must also take case sensitivity into account, since the program will regard capital letters differently from lowercase letters during **E**xtract and **S**ort routines. If more than one person will be using the template, you should create a standards list that shows the proper form for entering each client's name or code.

3. Once you've input the client's name, enter in Column C a brief description of the goods or service purchased. If you have a wide carriage printer (132 columns), you can expand this column using the /**W**orksheet **C**olumn **S**et command. (Note: You must also expand the right margin using the /**PPOMR** command. Refer to your 1-2-3 manual for help.)

4. Enter the invoice date (May 5, 1987), as "05", **‹RETURN›** "06", **‹RETURN›** "87", **‹RETURN›** following the month, day, and year prompts at the top of the screen (Col D).

5. Enter the amount of the invoice in the *Invoice Total* cell (Col E). Four thousand one hundred dollars would be entered as "4100," without dollar signs or commas. If you accidentally press an alphabetic key, the 1-2-3 will beep and not accept the entry. Press **‹RETURN›** to clear the error, and reenter the amount correctly.

6. You will probably want to leave the *Date of Payment* cell (Col F) blank until the invoice is actually paid. Since the auto-entry

macro requires you to input a valid entry in all cells, the Accounts Receivable and Payable templates have been equipped with a special blank function. When prompted for the date, enter "1" for the month, day, and year (i.e., "1/1/1"). Lotus 1-2-3 will then insert a blank in the cell.

When you edit the date after payment is received, you must use the **ALT-D** function or the Lotus date format @date(yy,mm,dd) then press the **F9** (calc) key. Also in Edit mode, you cannot use "1/1/1" to create a blank record date. Instead, simply enter a label prefix.

7. Enter the amount paid in the *Payment Amount* cell (Col G) as zero. Remember, you cannot leave the cell blank. If you do press ‹RETURN› without entering a value, press ‹RETURN› once more to clear the "Error" message, then enter a value without dollar signs or commas, and press ‹RETURN›. When the invoice is paid, you can edit the *Payment Amount* cell. You must press the calc key (**F9**) after manually inputting the payment amount cell to see the correct calculation. When you print, the template will automatically recalcuate all formulas.

8. The Balance Due, Age, and Status will automatically be computed when you finish data entry. The Balance Due will be the difference of the Invoice Amount and the Amount Paid. If the Balance Due is greater than zero, the status is set to Open. Otherwise it is set to Paid.

The age of an invoice is determined either as the time difference between the invoice date and the payment date if the Status is open (i.e., balance due is greater than zero). Otherwise, it is determined between the invoice date and the current system date, showing the age of the invoice as of today. Therefore, if you create an illogical situation, such as a balance due of $0.00 with no date of payment, you may get an illogical aging display.

Once the calculations are completed, the cell pointer will move to Column A of the next row and prompt you to continue entering data or to abandon the data entry process.

Extract

The Accounts Receivable template allows you to create a list of all invoices issued to a selected client (see Figure 15.5). When you select Extract from the Main Menu, you will have the choice of extracting invoices according to the following options:

```
Client Paid Open Age
```

Client

After you've chosen an Extract option, the cell pointer will then move to the Selection Screen area of the template (Figure 15.4). If you choose the Client option, you will be prompted to enter the name of a client or customer.

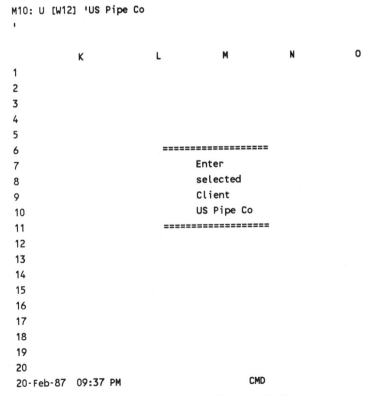

```
M10: U [W12] 'US Pipe Co                                    LABEL
  ¹
                K           L         M         N         O

  1
  2
  3
  4
  5
  6                                 ====================
  7                                 Enter
  8                                 selected
  9                                 Client
 10                                 US Pipe Co
 11                                 ====================
 12
 13
 14
 15
 16
 17
 18
 19
 20
 20-Feb-87  09:37 PM                           CMD
```

Figure 15.4 *Sample AR Report.*

If you entered client/customer names consistently, and your entry in the Selection Screen is also consistent with the invoice entries, you should extract all desired records. (If the extract does not yield the expected results, recheck the way you input your records. Remember, spaces and punctuation count as valid characters). The extracted records will be located in the "output range" of the Selected Record Section (refer to template layout, Figure 15.2).

After the extract is complete, the cell pointer will automatically move to the output range. You can maneuver the pointer with the cursor keys, or use **PgUp** or **PgDn** to view the extracted records. You can also print the extracted records by selecting the **Print/Selected** option later in this chapter. When you are done viewing the extracted records, either press **Home** to move the cell pointer back to the Record Entry Area or press **ALT-M** to invoke the Main Menu and carry out another function. If you **P**rint the extracted records, the cell pointer automatically returns to the *Home* cell when the print job is complete. (Note: The extracted records will remain in the Selected Records section until you use **Extract** function again, at which time they will be overwritten.)

Paid, Open

The **P**aid and **O**pen options are executed without input from the Selection Screen. All paid or open invoices are automatically extracted and copied to the Selected Records section when the **P**aid or **O**pen options are selected.

Age

When you select the **A**ge option, the Accounts Receivable template will offer you the following extract options:

0 – 30 31 – 60 61 – 90 91 +

Select the desired aging range and press **〈RETURN〉**. All invoices that fall within the specified range will be extracted. (See Figure 15.5 for sample extract.)

Sort

You can sort your Accounts Receivable template by the following options:

`Client Invoice Date`

Select the option by which you want the records in the worksheet sorted. **Client** sorts records alphabetically by name, in ascending order (A to Z). **Invoice** sorts by invoice number alphabetically, in ascending order. Since **Invoice** treats numbers as text characters, entries starting with numbers (e.g., "87001B") will appear *before* those starting with characters (e.g., "B87001"). The **Date** option sorts records in ascending order by invoice date.

If you wish to create a multilevel sort, you can do so by using the **Sort** option several times sequentially. For example, suppose you wanted to create a list of invoices organized chronologically within each client. You could do this by first selecting the **Date** option, and then selecting the **Client** option. The rule is, the highest order of sorting should be the last sort you perform.

The **Sort** options can be used to give you different views of the worksheet, which can be useful for scanning all of your invoices by specific clients. Also, you may wish to print your Accounts Receivable Template sorted by date or number for collection or follow up. See Figure 15.6 for a sample of a sorted template.

```
ACCOUNTS RECEIVABLE                        20-Feb-87
          Client:      US Pipe Co
==================================================================================================
Invoice                            Invoice     Invoice Date of     Payment    Balance
Number    Client     Description   Date        Total   Payment     Amount     Due          Age  Status
--------------------------------------------------------------------------------------------------
                                                                                           1=OPEN
                                   Totals:  $9,510.00             $0.00      $9,510.00      2=PAID
--------------------------------------------------------------------------------------------------
Number    Client     Description   Date        Total   Payment     Amount     Due          Age  Status
87001     US Pipe Co Stationery    12-Jan-87   4,100.00            0.00       4,100.00      39    1
87012     US Pipe Co Diskettes     14-Feb-87     235.00            0.00         235.00       6    1
87017     US Pipe Co Furniture     31-Jan-87   3,700.00            0.00       3,700.00      20    1
87018     US Pipe Co Forms         02-Feb-87   1,475.00            0.00       1,475.00      18    1
```

Figure 15.5 *Sample extract, AR Template.*

Aging

When you select the **Aging** option from the Main Menu, the following submenu will be displayed:

```
All Graph Selected
```

All

If you choose **All**, the template will display an Aged Receivables Report for all invoices in the template (see Figure 15.7).

Graph

The Graph option graphs all aged receivables by time category (0-30, 31-60, and so forth—Figure 15.8). The **Graph** option also as-

```
ACCOUNTS RECEIVABLE                          20-Feb-87
```

Invoice Number	Client	Description	Invoice Date	Invoice Total	Date of Payment	Payment Amount	Balance Due	Age	Status
									1=OPEN
			Totals:	$44,215.00		$11,500.00	$32,715.00		2=PAID
Number	Client	Description	Date	Total	Payment	Amount	Due	Age	Status
87011	ABC Truck	Misc Supplies	30-Dec-86	4,100.00		0.00	4,100.00	52	1
87002	ABC Truck	Cabinets	01-Dec-86	7,500.00	12-Feb-87	7,500.00	0.00	73	2
87003	Acme Finance	Forms	12-Feb-87	525.00		0.00	525.00	8	1
87016	Acme Finance	Stationery	18-Feb-87	1,350.00		0.00	1,350.00	2	1
87007	Carewell Ins	Stationery	20-Dec-86	3,135.00		0.00	3,135.00	62	1
87014	Carewell Ins	Forms	23-Jan-87	1,100.00		0.00	1,100.00	28	1
87004	Elgin Farms	Typewriters	30-Nov-86	1,700.00	15-Jan-87	1,700.00	0.00	46	2
87015	Excellco	Misc Supplies	15-Dec-86	1,100.00	31-Jan-87	1,100.00	0.00	47	2
87006	Excellco	Paper Products	02-Jan-87	1,200.00	05-Feb-87	1,200.00	0.00	34	2
87005	Jack's Bakery	Misc Supplies	04-Jan-87	745.00		0.00	745.00	47	1
87001	US Pipe Co	Stationery	12-Jan-87	4,100.00		0.00	4,100.00	39	1
87012	US Pipe Co	Diskettes	14-Feb-87	235.00		0.00	235.00	6	1
87018	US Pipe Co	Forms	02-Feb-87	1,475.00		0.00	1,475.00	18	1
87017	US Pipe Co	Furniture	31-Jan-87	3,700.00		0.00	3,700.00	20	1
87008	WISO Inc	Diskettes	22-Nov-86	450.00		0.00	450.00	90	1
87013	WISO Inc	Furniture	27-Nov-86	1,400.00		0.00	1,400.00	85	1
87019	WISO Inc	Typewriters	01-Feb-87	2,300.00		0.00	2,300.00	19	1
87020	WISO Inc	Stationery	07-Feb-87	400.00		0.00	400.00	13	1
87010	Zyrex	Chairs	28-Jan-87	2,200.00		0.00	2,200.00	23	1
87009	Zyrex	Desks	27-Jan-87	5,500.00		0.00	5,500.00	24	1

Figure 15.6 *Sample Sorted AR Template.*

```
T28: [W6]                                                        READY


        T       U         V         W         X       Y      Z
28
29   ================================================================
30   *                                                         *
31   *                                        20-Feb-87         *
32   *                                                         *
33   *                                                         *
34   *           Aged Accounts Receivable  -  US Pipe Co        *
35   *                                                         *
36   *                                                         *
37   *         0-30       31-60      61-90      91 +            *
38   *                                                         *
39   *                                                         *
40   *       5,410.00   4,100.00      0.00       0.00           *
41   *                                                         *
42   *                                                         *
43   *                                                         *
44   *                                                         *
45   *                                                         *
46   ================================================================
47
20-Feb-87  09:41 PM    HAL \
```

Figure 15.7 *Sample AR Aging Report.*

sumes that you have a graphics or color card and a graphics or color monitor.

To switch back to the worksheet after viewing the graph, press **ESC**. The template will then create a .PIC file that you can later print from the Lotus PrintGraph utility. To complete the .PIC file, the template will prompt you to enter a name. If you are planning on graphing several different sets of numbers, be sure to give each .PIC file a unique name. Otherwise, you will simply overwrite the same file.

Selected

If you choose the **Selected** option, the cursor will move to the Selection Screen and prompt you to enter the client's name (refer to Figure 15.4). Press **⟨RETURN⟩** and the aging report for that client will appear on the screen. Once the report is complete, the Main Menu will be displayed. You can either choose a menu option (such as **Print**) or escape by pressing **ESC**, after which you can press **⟨Home⟩** to reposition the cell pointer in the Invoice Data section.

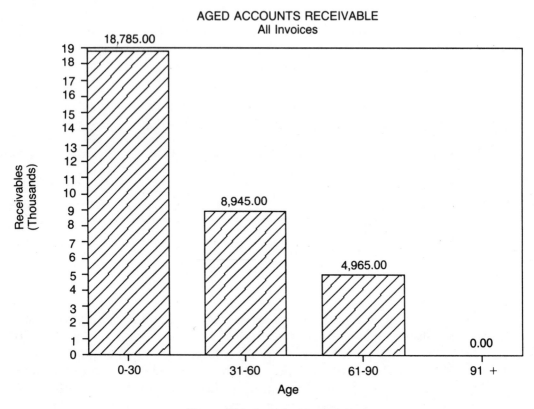

Figure 15.8 *Sample AR Graph.*

Print

When you select the **Print** option from the Main Menu, you will see a submenu that gives you the following options:

```
Data Aged
```

The **Data** option branches into a submenu with the following two choices:

```
All Selected
```

The **All** option prints out every invoice record in the worksheet, including headings and rules. The **Selected** option prints out those records that were most recently extracted.

The **Aged** option branches into:

```
All Selected
```

All will print out an aging report for every invoice in the worksheet. The **Selected** option prints the aging report for the last client you selected through the **Aging** option.

File

The **File** menu choice provides three options: save and return to the worksheet (**Save**); save and leave 1-2-3 (**Put away**); and quit without saving (**Quit**).

Title

The **Title** function locks the column headings so that they are visible even when you have scrolled down beyond 20 lines. The **Title** function defaults to on, but can be removed by selecting the Title/Unlock option.

Lock-Screen

Lock-Screen freezes the control panel and the screen during macro execution. It can only be used with 1-2-3 Releases 2 and 2.01.

Common Questions and Problems

The invoice status is incorrect. The status is determined by the value of the Balance Due. If the Balance Due is greater than zero, the line item is considered Open. Otherwise it is considered Paid.

The age is incorrect. The age calculation depends on the value of the Status field. If the item is Open (balance due greater than zero), the age is the difference between the invoice date and the current date, as determined by the system date. If the system date is not set correctly, the age will be incorrectly determined. Reset the system date via the DATE command at the DOS prompt and restart Lotus 1-2-3. If the Balance Due is equal to zero, the age is the difference between the invoice date and the payment date. You must have entered valid invoice and payment dates to produce a correct age.

You can't enter blank date of payment. The date input macro will not allow a blank or zero entry for dates since this produces an error. The template has a special feature that converts the date "1/1/1" to a blank field. So to enter a blank date for line items that have received no payments, enter the "1/1/1" date at the date prompt for Date of Payment.

16 | ACCOUNTS PAYABLE

CONTENTS

Specifications

Filename **AP.WKS**

Function

- Tracks accounts payable.

Usage

- Logs bills.
- Generates aging reports of payables.
- Tracks total payables.
- Generates list of accounts paid by vendor.

Features

- Auto-entry.
- Automatically calculates balance due on partial payments.
- Sorts bills by client, invoice number, and invoice date.
- Extracts payables by vendor, open invoices, paid invoices, or age.
- Generates aging reports for selected or all vendors.
- Prints out entire payables register or selected bills.

Introduction

The Accounts Payable Template is designed to help small businesses and consulting operations keep track of their payables. While it is not designed as a substitute for a stand-alone AP package that generates purchases orders and integrates into a general ledger, it can be very effectively used by small businesses or departments. Further, by selecting by age, you can generate a list of invoices in need of payment.

The Accounts Payable Template allows you to input basic invoice data, such as invoice number and date, the vendor, a description of the work contracted for or goods bought, the total due, the amount paid, and the balance due. The template will also show you the age of each bill and the total amount you have been billed and have paid out since you began using the template. The template also allows you to list and print all bills from a particular vendor, so you can keep a running record of your business and activity with each one in the worksheet. In addition, you can reorganize the worksheet by vendor, invoice number, or date at any time. Figure 16.1 shows completed a AP template, and Figure 16.8 shows a graph of payables.

This template is very similar to the Accounts Receivable template (Chapter 15) in structure and function. If you are using an AR template now, most of the concepts will already be familiar to you.

Template Layout

The Accounts Payable Template consists of four sections (see Figure 16.2):

1. *Invoice Data.* This is where you enter the invoice number, vendor, description, invoice date, invoice amount, date paid, and amount paid.
2. *Selection Screen.* The selection screen allows you to enter a vendor name for selection. (See Extract function, later in this chapter.)
3. *Selected Records.* Once you've indicated which payables you want to extract, they will appear in this area of the template for viewing or printing.

ACCOUNTS PAYABLE

```
==============================================================================================
Invoice                        Invoice   Invoice  Date of     Payment   Balance
Number   Vendor   Description   Date      Total    Payment     Amount    Due       Age  Status
..............................................................................................
                                                                                   1=OPEN
                                Totals:  $28,197.00            $217.00   $0.00      2=PAID
..............................................................................................
Number   Vendor          Description        Date      Total     Payment     Amount   Due    Age  Status
A4387    ABC Office      Computer Supplies  12-Feb-87    217.00 10-Mar-87    217.00   0.00   26      2
A4388    XYZ Truck Lease Van Rental         15-Jan-87    350.00               0.00
A4389    Ace Plumbing    Maintenance        15-Feb-87    150.00               0.00
A4390    Carewell Ins    Fire Insurance     15-Dec-86    750.00 28-Feb-87     0.00
A4391    Zxlex           Computers          01-Jan-87  2,570.00               0.00
A4392    Able, et. al.   Legal Services     10-Jan-87  1,350.00               0.00
A4393    ABC Office      Stationery         12-Feb-87    350.00               0.00
A4394    Revbar          Food Service       30-Nov-86    455.00 02-Mar-87     0.00
A4395    Zxlex           Disk drives        27-Jan-87  1,700.00               0.00
A4396    Excellex        Plants             31-Jan-87    150.00               0.00
A4397    CBF Furniture   Desks              01-Feb-87  3,580.00               0.00
A4398    F & G Assoc     Accounting         30-Nov-86  1,200.00 10-Mar-87     0.00
A4399    CBF Furniture   Desks              30-Jan-87  1,270.00               0.00
A4400    Compusys        Payroll            17-Jan-87  4,387.00               0.00
A4401    CBF Furniture   Chairs             05-Jan-87  1,456.00               0.00
A4402    ABC Office      Supplies           15-Jan-87    275.00               0.00
A4403    Compusys        Payroll            15-Feb-87  4,387.00               0.00
A4404    CBF Furniture   Tables             17-Jan-87    750.00               0.00
A4405    Advice, Inc.    Consulting         01-Feb-87  2,500.00               0.00
A4406    ABC Truck Lease Van Rental         31-Jan-87    350.00               0.00
```

Figure 16.1 *Sample Accounts Payable Template.*

4. *Macros.* This section contains the macros that drive the menu operations and carry out sorting, extracting, printing, and saving functions.

Invoice Data	Selection Screen	Selected Records
A11..J1000	**K1..O20**	**AA11...AJ1000**

Macros
K21..Z145

Figure 16.2 *Layout of AP Template.*

Main Menu Options

The Accounts Payable Template offers the following options in the Main Menu:

`Data Extract Print Aging Sort File Title Lock-Screen`

Refer to Figure 16.3 for a view of the template's complete menu structure.

Data

When you select the **Data** option, a submenu will display the following options:

`Continue Begin Edit Delete`

Begin is only used the first time you enter data, and **Continue** is used thereafter. **Edit** allows you to manually move the cursor, and

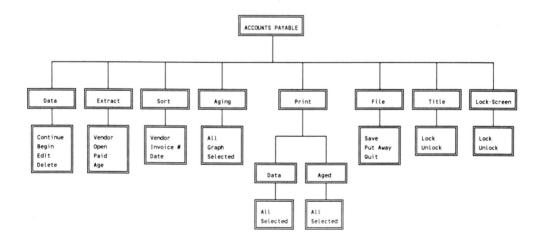

Figure 16.3 *Menu Tree, AP Template.*

Delete is a special substitute for the Lotus 1-2-3 /Worksheet Delete Row function, which can damage the template.

When you select Continue or Begin, the macro moves the template through the following sequence of cells each time you enter data and press **<RETURN>**:

```
Invoice Number (T) → Vendor (T) → Description (T) →
Invoice Date (N) → Invoice Total (N) → Date of
Payment (N) → Payment Amount (N)
T= text cell
N= numerical cell
```

To stop the auto-entry process at any time, press **CTRL-END**. If the current input request is for text characters, such as *Vendor*, pressing **ESC** will also break the macro. If the current request is for numerical data, such as *Payment Amount*, only **CTRL-BREAK** will stop the macro. (Note: With Release 2.0 or 2.01, "Error" will be displayed in the mode indicator cell after you press **CTRL-BREAK**. The error message can be cleared by pressing the **ESC** key.)

If you end the auto-entry macro in the middle of a line, you must manually enter data in the rest of the cells or erase the line entirely, since the Extract and Sort routines require complete rows of data. Caution: Do NOT use the /Worksheet Delete Row function to erase a line of data, as this may damage the macros. Instead, erase the row cell-by-cell using the /Range Erase command.

After inputting information in the *Amount Paid* cell, which is the last data entry cell in a record, the auto-entry macro returns the cell pointer to the *Date* cell of the next row, and asks whether you wish to continue data entry.

> **IMPORTANT NOTE:** The age of Open invoices and the Aging Reports are calculated by subtracting the invoice date from   today's date. It is therefore necessary that you manually enter the current date at the DOS date prompt prior to starting 1-2-3 if you don't have a built-in clock in your computer or a multifunction board with a clock. If you do have a built-in clock, make sure the date is correct.

Edit

The Data/Edit option allows you to use the cursor keys to move the pointer, so you can manually change data in cells of your choice. When you are done with your edits, press **ALT-M** to redisplay the Main Menu.

To edit a date, press **ALT-D**. You will then be prompted to enter the month, day, and year, pressing **‹RETURN›** after each. If you do not wish to use the **ALT-D** edit function for editing dates, you must use the standard Lotus 1-2-3 date format (@date(yy,mm,dd)).

Delete

The **Data/Delete** option is fully explained in Chapter 1. It is intended to be a substitute for 1-2-3's /Worksheet Delete Row command, which should never be used with Ready-to-Run templates since it can accidentally erase the macros.

Sample Data Entry

In the following example, we'll input a record for invoice number A4387 from A.B.C. Office Supplies. The bill, which totaled $217.00, was issued February 12, 1987 and paid March 10, 1987.

1. After selecting **Begin** (or **Continue** if you've already entered rows of data), the cell pointer will move to the *Invoice Number* cell (Column A), where you can input any combination of alphabetic and numeric characters. When you press **‹RETURN›**, the cell pointer will move right to the *Vendor* cell.
2. Enter the vendor's name or code in the *Vendor* cell (Col B). Be consistent in the way you abbreviate a client's name, otherwise the **Sort** and **Extract** routines will not work properly. The vendor name or "A.B.C. Office Supplies Inc" (with periods) is treated differently from "ABC Office Supplies Inc" (no periods). Note that spaces are also treated as characters, so that "ABC" is considered different from "A B C."

   If you are using Release 1A, be aware that "case-sensitivity" is an issue. Release 1A regards capital letters differently from lower case letters during the **Extract** and **Sort** routines.
3. In the *Description* cell (Col C), enter a brief comment about the nature of the invoice (e.g., "computer supplies"). If you find that the column isn't wide enough, and you have a 132 column printer, you can expand the cell using the /Worksheet Column Set command. (You will also have to increase the

right margin using the /PPOMR command. Refer to your 1-2-3 manual for assistance.)

4. The cell pointer should now be in the *Invoice Date* cell (Col D). Enter the date of the invoice as month, day, and year as instructed by the prompts in the control panel. In our example, you would enter "02" ‹**RETURN**› "12" ‹**RETURN**› "87" ‹**RETURN**›.

   When you edit the date after payment is received, you must use the **ALT-D** function or the Lotus date format @date(yy,mm,dd), then press the **F9** (calc) key. Also in Edit mode, you cannot use "1/1/1" to create a blank record date. Instead, simply add a label prefix.

5. Enter "217," the amount of the ACE Supplies' bill, in the Total Invoice (Col E) cell. Do not use dollar signs or commas. Press ‹**RETURN**› to move the cell pointer to the *Date of Payment* cell.

6. Next, in the *Date of Payment* cell (Col F), enter the date you paid the bill, March 10, 1987, as prompted by the template. If you have not paid the bill yet and want to enter a blank, you must enter "1/1/1"—the template will translate that number into a blank entry.

7. Initially, you will enter "0" for the amount paid (assuming that you will be entering bills into the template as you receive them, or in weekly batches). When the bill is paid and you update the template, you will have to manually edit the *Payment Amount* cell by pressing the **F2** key and entering the amount you paid. You must press the calc key (**F9**) after manually inputting the payment amount cell to see the correct calculation. When you print, the template will automatically recalcuate all formulas.

8. The *Balance Due* (Col H), *Age* (Col I), and *Status* (Col J) will automatically be computed when you finish data entry. The Balance Due will be the difference of the Invoice Amount and the Amount Paid. If the Balance Due is greater than zero, the status is set to Open (designated by "1"). Otherwise the status is set to paid ("2").

   The age of an invoice is determined either as the time difference between the invoice date and the current date as represented by the system date if the Status is Open (i.e., balance due is greater than zero), thus showing the age of the invoice

The age of an invoice is determined either as the time difference between the invoice date and the current date as represented by the system date if the Status is Open (i.e., balance due is greater than zero), thus showing the age of the invoice as of today. Otherwise, the invoice age is the difference between the invoice date and the date paid, showing the age of the invoice as of the date of payment. Therefore, if you create an illogical situation, such as a balance due of $0.00 with no date of payment, you may get an illogical aging display.

Once the calculations are completed, the cell pointer will move to Column "A" of the next row and prompts you to continue entering data or to abandon the data entry process.

Extract

The Extract function of the Accounts Payable Template allows you to subgroup all invoices according to the following options:

```
Vendor Paid Open Age
```

Vendor

Vendor is used to extract invoices that have the same source. When you select this option, the cell pointer will move to the Selection Screen area of the template (Figure 16.4), and you will be prompted to enter the vendor's name.

Make sure that you enter the name exactly as you have entered records (punctuation and spaces count as valid characters). Extracted records are copied into an "output range" located in the Selected Records section (refer to Template Layout, Figure 16.2). The cell pointer will automatically move to the Selected Records section, so you can view the entries. (To print the extracted entries, use the **Print/Selected** option as described later in the chapter.). When you're done viewing the extracted entries, either press **Home** to move the cell pointer back to the Invoice Date section or press **ALT-M** to invoke the Main Menu and carry out another function.

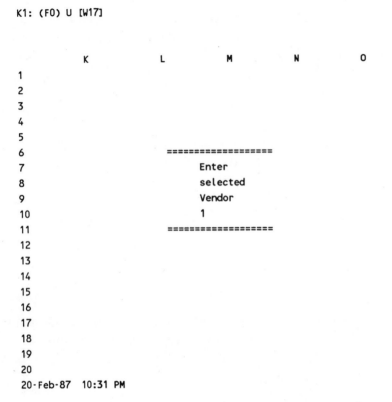

K1: (F0) U [W17]   READY

            K   L   M   N   O
1
2
3
4
5
6   ====================
7   Enter
8   selected
9   Vendor
10   1
11   ====================
12
13
14
15
16
17
18
19
20
20-Feb-87 10:31 PM

Figure 16.4 *Extract Selection Screen, AP Template.*

Paid, Open

These options do not require input into the template's Selection Screen. When you select either one, the appropriate records are copied to the Selected Records area of the template.

Age

If you decide to extract records by age, the template will display a submenu with the following age ranges:

0 – 30 31 – 60 61 – 90 91 +

Select the desired aging range and press <**RETURN**>. All invoices that fall within the specified range will be extracted (Figure 16.5).

```
ACCOUNTS PAYABLE                        31-Mar-87
          Client:
=====================================================================================================
Invoice                                 Invoice  Invoice Date of     Payment   Balance
Number    Vendor      Description        Date     Total   Payment     Amount    Due        Age  Status
.....................................................................................................
                                                                                          1=OPEN
                                        Totals:  $0.00               $0.00     $0.00       2=PAID
.....................................................................................................
Number    Vendor      Description        Date     Total   Payment     Amount    Due        Age  Status
A4387     ABC Office  Computer Supplies  12-Feb-87 217.00 10-Mar-87
A4393     ABC Office  Stationary         12-Feb-87 350.00
A4402     ABC Office  Supplies           15-Jan-87 275.00
```

Figure 16.5 *Sample Extract, AP Template.*

Sort

When you select the **S**ort option from the Main Menu, you will be given three options for reorganizing the template:

```
Vendor Invoice # Date
```

The **S**ort options reorganize all entries in the Invoice Data section of the worksheet. Alphabetic entries (**Vendor**) will be sorted alphabetically, in ascending order (A to Z). Alphanumeric entries (Invoice #) will also sort in ascending order, but numbers will appear before characters—"7023" before "ZX7023". Dates (Invoice Date) will be sorted chronologically.

You can also create a multilevel sort by running the **S**ort several times sequentially. If you wanted to create an invoice list organized chronologically by vendor, you would first select the **Date** option, and then select the **Vendor** option. As a general principle, the highest order of sorting should be the last sort you perform. (A sample sorted AP template is shown in Figure 16.6.)

```
ACCOUNTS PAYABLE                          31-Mar-87
          Client:
===============================================================================
Invoice                          Invoice   Invoice Date of    Payment   Balance
Number    Vendor   Description   Date      Total   Payment    Amount    Due        Age  Status
...............................................................................
                                                                                       1=OPEN
                                 Totals:   $0.00              $0.00     $0.00          2=PAID
...............................................................................
Number    Vendor   Description   Date      Total   Payment    Amount    Due        Age  Status
A4387     ABC Office  Computer Supplies  12-Feb-87  217.00 10-Mar-87
A4393     ABC Office  Stationary         12-Feb-87  350.00
A4402     ABC Office  Supplies           15-Jan-87  275.00
```

Figure 16.6 *Sample Sorted AP Template.*

Y25:   READY

```
             T      U       V       W       X       Y      Z
      6
      7    ================================================================
      8    *                                                         *
      9    *                                      20-Feb-87          *
     10    *                                                         *
     11    *                                                         *
     12    *      Aged Accounts Payable - All invoices               *
     13    *                                                         *
     14    *                                                         *
     15    *      0-30    31-60    61-90    91 +                      *
     16    *                                                         *
     17    *                                                         *
     18    *      0.00    567.00   275.00   0.00                      *
     19    *                                                         *
     20    *                                                         *
     21    *                                                         *
     22    *                                                         *
     23    *                                                         *
     24    ================================================================
     25
20-Feb-87  10:41 PM                                    CALC
```

Figure 16.7 *Sample AP Aging Report.*

Aging

The **Aging** option of the Main Menu offers the following submenu options:

```
All Graph Selected
```

All displays an Aged Receivables Report for all invoices in the template (Figure 16.7).

The **Graph** option generates a bar graph of all aged payables by time category (0-30, 31-60, and so forth—see Figure 16.8). The

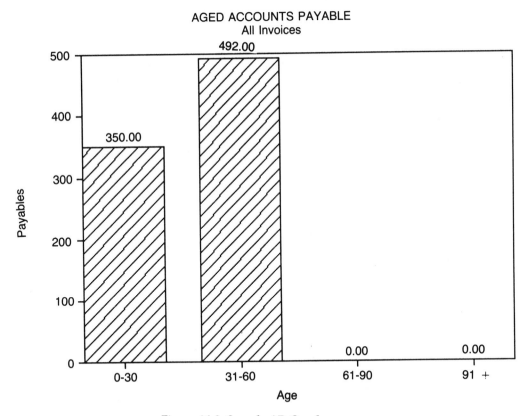

Figure 16.8 *Sample AP Graph.*

Graph option assumes that you have a graphics or color card and a graphics or color monitor.

To switch back to the worksheet after viewing the graph, press **ESC**. The template will then create a .PIC file that you can later print from the Lotus PrintGraph utility. To complete the .PIC file, the template will prompt you to enter a name. If you are planning on graphing several different sets of numbers, be sure to give each .PIC file a unique name. Otherwise, you will simply overwrite the same file.

Selected

If you choose the Selected option, the cursor will move to the Selection Screen and prompt you to enter the vendor name or code. Press **‹RETURN›** and the aging report for that client will appear on the screen. Once the report is complete, the Main Menu will appear. Choose an option or break the menu macro by pressing **ESC.** You can then press **‹Home›** to reposition the pointer to cell A1.

Print

The **Print** option from the Main Menu branches into two submenu choices:

```
Data Aged
```

The **Data** option in turn offers two submenu options:

```
All Selected
```

All option prints out every record in the worksheet, while the Selected option prints out the most recently extracted records.

Aged

Aged offers you two choices:

```
All Selected
```

All will print out an aging report for every invoice in the worksheet (see Figure 16.7). The **S**elected option prints an aging report for the last client you selected through the **A**ging option.

File

The **F**ile menu choice provides three options: save and return to the worksheet (**S**ave); save and leave 1-2-3 (**P**ut away); and quit without saving (**Q**uit).

Title

The **T**itle function locks the column headings so that they are visible even when you have scrolled down beyond 20 lines. The **T**itle function defaults to on, but can be removed by selecting the **T**itle/Unlock option.

Lock-Screen

Lock-Screen freezes the control panel and the screen during macro execution. It can only be used with 1-2-3 Release 2 and 2.01.

Common Questions and Problems

If you follow the above instructions, you are unlikely to have any difficulties with the Accounts Payable template. If you do experience any problems, refer to the last section of the Accounts Receivable template (Chapter 15)—the points discussed also pertain to the AP template.

17 | GANTT CHART

CONTENTS

Specifications

Filename **GANTT.WKS**

Function

- Gives visual representation of project schedule.

Usage

- Project planning.
- Displaying effects of changing a project schedule.

Feature

- Allows you to input project end date or alloted completion time for specific tasks.

Introduction

Gantt Charts are useful means for representing a project schedule, as they show the time relationship of all tasks and subtasks. The Gantt Chart Template allows you to input the starting date for a task, and then either input the end date or the time alloted. The time span will then be graphically depicted as a series of "plus" marks across a calendar.

While the template is not a substitute for a stand-alone project management package, it can give you a basic sense of how all the tasks in a given project are interrelated. See Figure 17.1 for a sample Gantt Chart Template.

```
Gantt Chart

=========================================================================|·········1987·······|  |·········1988········|
                    Task       Task     Task     Task
                    Start      End      Time     Time       J F M A M J J A S O N D J F M A M J J A S O N D
         Task       Date       Date     (Input)  (Calculated)  A E A P A U U U E C O E A E A P A U U U E C O E
                    (Required) (Option A)(Option B)(End·Start)   N B R R Y N L G P T V C N B R R Y N L G P T V C
                               (1/1/1=blank)(Months) (Months)  ************************************************
·····················································································  ************************************************

  1  Choose project team  02·Feb·87  28·Feb·87   0      0.9    . ++. . . . . . . . . . . . . . . . . . . . . . .
  2  Library research      15·Mar·87              3      0.0    . . +++++++++. . . . . . . . . . . . . . . . . .
  3  Interviewing          01·May·87              3      0.0    . . . . . ++++++. . . . . . . . . . . . . . . . .
  4  First draft           01·Aug·87  31·Aug·87   0      1.0    . . . . . . . . ++. . . . . . . . . . . . . . . .
  5  Review                01·Sep·87  18·Sep·87   0      0.6    . . . . . . . . . ++. . . . . . . . . . . . . . .
  6  Final draft           22·Nov·87  18·Dec·87   0      0.9    . . . . . . . . . . . . ++++. . . . . . . . . . .
  7  Graphic design        01·Nov·87  15·Nov·87   0      0.5    . . . . . . . . . . . ++. . . . . . . . . . . . .
  8  Printing              01·Dec·87              2      0.0    . . . . . . . . . . . . ++++. . . . . . . . . . .
```

Figure 17.1 *Sample Gantt Chart.*

Template Layout

The Gantt Chart Template is divided into three sections (see Figure 17.2):

1. *Task Data.* This is where you enter the description of the task, the start date, and the end date or task length.
2. *Chart Section.* This section is where the actual Gantt Chart is generated.
3. *Macros.* This section contains the various macros that drive the menu and recalculation functions of the template.

Task Data	*Chart*	*Macros*
A11..H1000	**J11..AG1000**	**AK1..AR71**

Figure 17.2 *Layout, Gantt Chart Template.*

Main Menu Options

The Gantt Chart Template offers five Main Menu choices:

`Data Print File Title Lock-Screen`

The **Data** and **Print** options are discussed in this chapter. Refer to Chapter 1 for an explanation of the **File, Title,** and **Lock-Screen** functions. Also see the Menu Tree (Figure 17.3) for a view of the template's full menu structure.

Data

The **Data** option offers three choices:

`Continue Begin Edit`

Continue and **Begin** start macros that make it easier to enter data into the template. **Edit** returns cell pointer control to the cursor and other screen navigation keys.

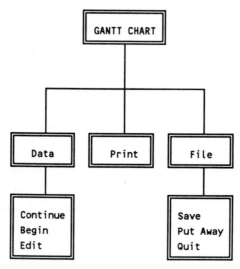

Figure 17.3 *Menu Tree, Gantt Chart.*

When you select **C**ontinue or **B**egin (only use **B**egin the first time you enter data), the template prompts you to enter appropriate information as the pointer moves through the following sequence of cells:

```
Task (T) → Task Start Date (N) → Task End Date (N) → Task
Time [Input] (N)
T = text cell
N = numeric cell
```

Whenever you are inputting data into a numeric field, the only way to stop the auto-entry macro is to press **CTRL-END**. When you are working in a text field, the macro can be broken by pressing **ESC**. If you are using Release 2.0 or 2.01, "Error" will be displayed in the mode indicator cell after you press **CTRL-BREAK**. You can clear the error message by pressing **ESC.**

After you enter information in *Task Time (Input)* and press **‹RE-TURN›,** the template will make the appropriate calculations and enter two plus signs in the Chart Section for each month that the task spans. (Note: Even if a task only includes the first day of a month, that month will be marked by plus signs—the template can only show schedules in full months.) Once the Chart Section is filled in for that row, the cell pointer will move to the *Task* cell of the next row, and ask you whether you want to continue entering data or exit from macro control.

Sample Data Entry

Suppose you're in charge of producing a report for your company. The entire project will take a year, and you wish to visually represent the span of each task in months. Table 17.1 lists the time or date requirements for each task. Some tasks have a definite start and end date. For others the date is flexible, but the time span is fixed (e.g., the printer needs eight weeks). The completed Gantt Chart for this project is shown in Figure 17.1.

Table 17.1 *An example of information included in a Gantt Chart.*

Task	Start Date	End Date	Time Span (mos)
Choose project team	Feb 2, 1987	Mar 2, 1987	
Library research	Mar 15, 1987		3
Interviewing	May 1, 1987		3
First Draft	Aug 1, 1987	Sep 1, 1987	
Review	Sep 1, 1987	Sep 18, 1987	
Final Draft	Nov 22, 1987	Dec 18, 1987	
Graphic Design	Nov 1, 1987	Nov 15, 1987	
Printing	Dec 1, 1987		8

To input this task information, select the **Data** option and the cell pointer will move to the first row. The template will automatically enter "1" as the first task number. Follow the system prompts.

1. Enter the name of the task (Col C). In the case of our example, the task would be "Choose project team."
2. Enter the *Task Start Date* (Col D) as "02" **‹RETURN›** "02" **‹RETURN›** "87" **‹RETURN›**, following the prompts at the top of the screen. If you later want to manually edit the start date, press the **F2** key and use the standard Lotus date format (@date(yy,mm,dd)). You *must* input a task start date for the template to function.
3. Enter the *Task End Date* (Col E), Feb 28, 1987, the same way as you entered the start date. Use the @date(yy,mm,dd) format to edit the task end date.
4. Enter zero for the *Task Time*. (Since you have entered an end date, the length of the task will be automatically computed in the *Task Time* cell located in Column H.)

Now enter the second task, which uses an inputted task time rather than a computed task time.

1. Select the **Data/Continue** option. The template will automatically enter #2 at the beginning of the row.
2. Enter the task, "Library research."
3. Enter the start date, "Mar 15, 1987".

4. Since the next task has a time span rather than an end date, enter a blank in the *Task End Date* cell. This is done by inputting the date as "1/1/1". The template will beep and then move the cursor to the *Task Time* cell in Column G. Input the duration of the task (e.g., 3 months). The *Calculated Task Time* cell in Column H will show a zero, since you entered a blank task end date.

If you enter both a task time and an ending date, the template will base its calculations on the longer of the two inputs.

Print

When you select the **Print** option from the Main Menu, the template will determine the print range for the Gantt Chart you have generated. The chart will be printed in condensed form.

File

The **File** menu choice provides three options: save and return to the worksheet (**Save**); save and leave 1-2-3 (**Put** away); and quit without saving (**Quit**).

Title

The **Title** function locks the column headings so that they are visible even when you have scrolled down beyond 20 lines. The Title function defaults to on, but can be removed by selecting the Title/**Unlock** option.

Lock-Screen

Lock-Screen freezes the control panel and the screen during macro execution. It can only be used with 1-2-3 Release 2 and 2.01.

Common Questions and Problems

The chart doesn't use the task time you input. The Gantt Chart allows two forms of Task Time input: the starting and stopping dates or the starting date and duration. Remember, the template selects the longer of these two time spans for plotting the chart.

The template won't accept blank dates. The date input macro will not allow a blank or zero entry for dates, since these will result in an error. The template has a special feature that converts the date "1/1/1" to a blank field. This date should be used in the *Task End Date* cell when you want to enter the task time rather than having the template compute it for you.

18 | PORTFOLIO VALUATION

CONTENTS

SPECIFICATIONS

Filename **PORTFOLI.WKS**

Function

- Tracks stock market investments.

Usage

- Keeps up-to-date portfolio valuation for planning and tax purposes.
- Tracks unrealized profits and losses from each transaction.

Features

- Auto-entry.
- Automatically calculates portfolio value, as well as long-term and short-term unrealized capital gains.
- Reports show all data needed for tax preparation.
- Update feature for changing current stock prices.

Introduction

This template is designed to make it easy for you to monitor your portfolio value, and to prepare your tax returns. Once you've entered the valuation date, you enter basic data about the transaction, such as the number of shares you own as well as the purchase price, purchase date, and commissions. Later, you can easily update the current stock price by using the template's auto-update feature.

Note that while changes in the 1986 Tax Reform Act reduced the significance of short-term versus long-term gains, many investors still prefer to monitor their investments by distinguishing short-term versus long-term movement. For this reason, the template provides the ability to separate both types of gains. If you wish to group short- and long-term gains together, you can simply set the long-term holding period to zero (see sample data entry later in this chapter).

A sample page from the Stock Portfolio Template is shown in Figure 18.1.

PORTFOLIO VALUATION

```
================================================================================================================
                                     * * Portfolio Summary * *
   Valuation Date:    20-Feb-87
                                       Cost:        $52,420.00
   Long-Term Holding                   Market:      $58,825.00
     Period in Days:   180.00          Short-Term:   $1,595.00
                                       Long-Term:    $4,810.00
================================================================================================================
```

Stock Name	Purchase Date	Number of Shares	Purchase Price/ Share	Purchase Commission	Current Price/ Share	Total Purchase Cost	Current Market Value	Short-Term Capital Gain/(Loss)	Long-Term Capital Gain/(Loss)
IBM	03-Oct-85	100	120.000	100.00	138.000	12,100.00	13,800.00	0.00	1,700.00
GlfWst	15-Sep-86	200	70.500	120.00	76.750	14,220.00	15,350.00	1,130.00	0.00
AT&T	12-Jun-86	100	18.000	90.00	23.500	1,890.00	2,350.00	0.00	460.00
Compaq	15-Jan-87	100	29.000	60.00	31.750	2,960.00	3,175.00	215.00	0.00
Zero	31-Mar-86	100	12.000	50.00	18.000	1,250.00	1,800.00	0.00	550.00
Waste	08-Aug-84	100	62.000	100.00	71.000	6,300.00	7,100.00	0.00	800.00
Litton	01-Dec-86	100	82.000	100.00	85.500	8,300.00	8,550.00	250.00	0.00
Singer	08-May-85	100	35.000	50.00	45.000	3,550.00	4,500.00	0.00	950.00
Cptvsn	06-Apr-86	100	18.000	50.00	22.000	1,850.00	2,200.00	0.00	350.00

Figure 18.1 *Sample Portfolio Valuation Worksheet.*

Template Layout

The Portfolio Valuation Template is divided into two sections (see Figure 18.2):

1. *Transaction Data.* This is where you enter the details of the purchase or sale, including price, date, and commission. You cannot view the entire section in one screen. To see the total purchase cost, the current market value, and the short-term and long-term capital gains and losses columns, you will have to move the cursor four columns to the right.
2. *Macros.* This section contains the various macros that drive the menu and recalculation functions of the template.

```
Transaction Data              Macro Section
A16..J1000                    L1..R76
```

Figure 18.2 *Layout of Portfolio Valuation Template.*

Main Menu Options

The Main Menu of the Portfolio Valuation Template offers the following options (see Menu Tree, Figure 18.3):

```
Data Print File Title Lock-Screen
```

Data

The Data option offers five choices:

```
Continue Begin Edit Update Delete
```

The **Begin** and **Continue** options invoke an auto-entry macro that moves the cell pointer through the Transaction Data section each time you make an entry and press **<RETURN>**, in the following sequence:

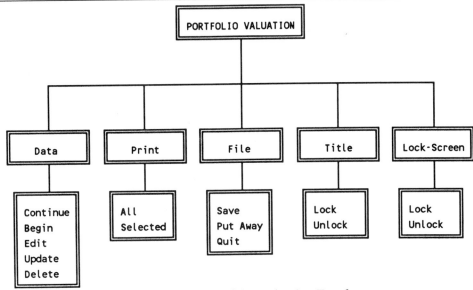

Figure 18.3 *Menu Tree, Portfolio Valuation Template.*

```
Valuation Date (N) →Long Term Holding Period (N) →
Stock Name (T) → Purchase Date (N) →Number of Shares (N) →
Purchase Price (N) → Purchase Commission (N) →
Current Price Per Share (N)
T = text cell
N = numeric cell
```

As you enter data into the template, the Portfolio Summary will be automatically updated (see Figure 18.4). The Portfolio summary shows the total cost of all stocks in the template (cell F6), the total market value (F7), the total short-term gains (F8), and the total long-term gains. (F9). After you enter information in the *Current Price Per Share* and press **<RETURN>**, the template will move the pointer to the *Stock Name* cell of the next row and display a continuation menu. Press **<RETURN>** to add another row of data, or **S**top to break the auto-entry macro and return to the Main Menu.

```
=========================
* * Portfolio Summary * *

Cost:        $52,420.00
Market:      $58,825.00
Short-Term:   $1,595.00
Long-Term:    $4,810.00

=========================
```

Figure 18.4 *Portfolio Summary Section.*

CAUTION! Begin should only be used when entering data into the template the first time you enter data. If you use it once data have already been entered, you will overwrite existing rows. Continue should be used once you have data in the template.

You can stop the auto-entry macro at any time by pressing **CTRL-BREAK**. With Release 2.0 and 2.01, this action will generate an error message. Press **ESC** to clear the message. When the pointer is in a text cell, **ESC** alone can be used to break the macro. The Main Menu can be restarted by pressing **ALT-M**.

Edit

The edit function allows you to use the cursor keys to move the cell pointer throughout the template. Press **ALT-M** when you finish your edits.

To edit a date, press **ALT-D**. You will then be prompted to enter the month, day, and year, pressing **‹RETURN›** after each. If you do not wish to use the **ALT-D** edit function for editing dates, you will have to use the standard Lotus 1-2-3 date format (@date(yy,mm,dd)).

Delete

Delete is a special function designed to replace the /Worksheet Delete Row function. If you use /WDR function with Ready-to-Run templates, you may erase lines of the macros and cause the template to function improperly.

You should use the **Data/Delete** function when you sell a stock and need to eliminate a specific transaction from your template. (Alternately, you can overwrite the transaction with a new one.)

Sample Data Entry

As an example, suppose you purchased 100 shares of IBM stock on October 3, 1985 at $120 per share. The commission on the transaction was $100. On February 19, 1987, you wanted to determine the unrealized capital gain from the purchase. Here is how you would use the Portfolio Valuation Template to make that determination.

1. After you select **Data/Begin**, the cell pointer will automatically move to the *Valuation Date* cell (B5). Enter the date as of which you would like to value your portfolio. You will be prompted to enter the month, day, and last two digits of the year. Enter "02" **‹RETURN›** "19" **‹RETURN›**"87" **‹RETURN›** for the example.

    Note: If you always want to value the portfolio as of "Today," you can insert the Lotus 1-2-3 function "@ Today" for Release 1A or "@ Now" for Release 2 or 2.01 in cell B5. If you do not have a built-in clock in your computer, make sure that you correctly enter the date at the DOS prompt when you first boot up.

2. The cell pointer will now be in the *Long-Term Holding Period* cell (B8). Enter "180," (the long-term holding period defined prior to the 1986 Tax Reform Act). If you do not want to separate long- and short-term gain, set the holding period to zero and all gains will appear as long-term.

3. The cell pointer will now have moved down to the *Stock Name* cell (Col A). Enter "IBM" and press **‹RETURN›**.

4. Now enter the date you bought the stock in the *Purchase Date* cell (Col B), again following the prompts. In the case of our example, you would enter "10" **‹RETURN›**, "03," "85" **‹RETURN›**.

5. Next, enter the number of shares you bought in the *Number of Shares* cell (Col C). Enter "100."

6. The cell pointer should now be in the *Purchase Price* cell (Col D). Enter the amount, without dollar signs or commas, and press **<RETURN>** to continue. You must enter in decimal format. You can use 3 decimal places to properly represent fractions (e.g., 52 1/8 would be 52.125). In our example, enter "120." (No dollar signs or commas are used with 1-2-3 numeric inputs).

7. Enter the commission charge, "100" in the *Purchase Commission* cell (Col E). Press **<RETURN>**.

8. Finally, input the appropriate amount in the *Current Price Per Share* (Col F). In our example, enter "138." When you press **<RETURN>** the template will automatically calculate the total purchase cost (Col G), the current market value (Col H), the short-term (Col I) and long-term (Col J) unrealized capital gains and losses (refer to Figure 18.1). To view these on the screen, you will have to use the right arrow key to move the cell pointer four columns to the right.

When you finish entering information in the *Current Price Per Share* cell, the cell pointer will then move to the *Stock Name* cell of the next row. At this point, you will be asked if you wish to continue or stop. Press **<RETURN>** to select **C**ontinue or select **S**top to end data input and return to the Main Menu.

Update (Current Stock Prices)

The **U**pdate option moves the cell pointer to the *Current Price Per Share* cell in the first transaction row. If you want to change the price, enter a new value and press **<RETURN>**. The cell pointer will move down to the *Current Price Per Share* cell in the next row. If you don't want to change the price, simply press **<RETURN>** and the cursor will move on. Discontinue the update process by pressing **CTRL-BREAK** if you are using Release 1A and **CTRL-BREAK** and then **ESC** if you are using Release 2. You can update the stock prices by using the manual entry mode.

Print

When you select the **Print** option from the Main Menu, the template will determine the print range for the table you have generated, and print the report. See Figure 18.1 for a sample report.

File

The **File** menu choice provides three options: save and return to the worksheet (**Save**); save and leave 1-2-3 (**Put** away); and quit without saving (**Quit**).

Title

The **Title** function locks the column headings so that they are visible even when you have scrolled down beyond 20 lines. The Title function defaults to on, but can be removed by selecting the Title/Unlock option.

Lock-Screen

Lock-Screen freezes the control panel and the screen during macro execution. It can only be used with 1-2-3 Release 2 and 2.01.

Common Questions and Problems

What do I do with stock splits. The template has no facility for handling stock splits or other transactions. You must edit the data to reflect any changes in position.

I can't input fractions. The template does not accept fractions since Lotus cannot calculate with them in Release 1A. All fractions must be first converted to decimals. If you want, Lotus 1-2-3 can perform the conversion for you by using its ability to accept a formula as numeric input. For example, you could enter "25 1/8" as "25 + 1/8" which will result in the decimal value 25.125.

19 | BUSINESS PLANNING AND ANALYSIS SERIES

CONTENTS

SPECIFICATIONS

Filename **MASTER.WKS**

Functions

- Provides ongoing reports on the financial condition of a business.
- Links income statement and balance sheet data.
- Produces monthly and year-to-date financial ratios from current financial statement data.
- Generates breakeven analysis from current financial statement information.

Usage

- Evaluates financial condition of a business. Offers business forecasting and planning.

Features

- Calendarized and integrated financial statements.
- Automatic calculation of breakeven range, breakeven point, and financial ratios.
- Numerous graphs and print options.
- Automated link between cash flow forecast and pro forma balance sheet.
- Easy-to-use menus, customized entries, simplified data input.

Filename **CASHFLOW.WKS**

Functions

- Forecasts cash inflows and outflows monthly over a one-year period.
- Illustrates monthly cash balances and projections.

Usage

- Provides cash forecasting for business planning.
- Analyzes "what-if" assumptions about cash flow.

Features

- Accommodates anticipated delays in accounts payable and accounts receivable.
- Easy data entry.
- Optional link to balance sheet in Master Financial Analyzer.
- Graphs and print options.

Filename **RATIOS.WKS**

Functions

- Calculates financial ratios from selected income statement and balance sheet data.
- Tracks trends in financial ratios over three-year period and compares with industry norms.

Usage

- Facilitates analysis of year-end financial statements.
- Identifies trends in business financial condition.

Features

- Calculates and graphs eight different ratios and quantities.
- Easy data entry and customization.

Filename **BRKEVEN.WKS**

Functions

- Determines breakeven revenue point from year-end costs and revenues information.

Usage

- Separates fixed and variable costs for breakeven analysis.
- Facilitates breakeven analysis.
- Provides graphic illustration of breakeven point, profit, and profit margin.

Features

- Easy data entry.
- Prints or graphs results.
- Flexible structure can be used with many projects.

Introduction

This chapter presents a series of templates for use in financial planning: MASTER, the Master Financial Analyzer, records and combines a calendarized income statement and balance sheet, and produces a breakeven analysis, financial ratios, and numerous graphs and printed reports to assist in the financial analysis of a business. CASHFLOW, the Cash Flow Planner, facilitates cash forecasting. RATIOS, the Financial Ratios Calculator, and BRKEVEN, the Breakeven Analyzer, are freestanding templates for financial ratio and breakeven analysis.

Master Financial Analyzer

The Master Financial Analyzer consists of four main subjects arranged vertically on the worksheet: an *Income Statement*, showing the revenues and expenses of a business on a monthly basis for an entire year; a *Balance Sheet*, also calendarized monthly for a year and tied to the Income Statement by a Statement of Retained Earnings; the *Financial Ratios* resulting from the above information, calculated and graphed; and a *Breakeven Analysis* derived from income statement data.

Income Statement

An income statement is a record of the revenue earned and expenses incurred by a business over a period of time. The Income Statement portion of this worksheet is organized in a standard accounting fashion, allowing you to customize revenue and expense items and track them on a monthly basis for an entire year. Totals, both monthly and yearly, are automatically calculated, and each revenue and expense item is shown as a percentage of net revenue. A graph illustrates several key revenue and expense items over the year. Finally, an automated report function prints the Income Statement, in either 8.5 × 11 inch format or on wide carriage paper.

> *Example.* Figure 19.1 illustrates an income statement with numbers entered for the ABC Corp. The following discussion explains how the worksheet was built.

First, the ABC Corp. controller went to the upper-left corner of the worksheet and entered the name of the business in cell A2. Since this cell is highlighted, she was able to overwrite it. (Remember, cells that are not highlighted are protected and therefore cannot be changed.)

Next, the controller selected **Date** from the main menu. (See "Using the Master Financial Analyzer, page 247 for a summary of the main menu selections.) This menu selection prompted her for the entry of a beginning month, day, and year for the worksheet data. In response, she entered "1", "1", and "87" and the worksheet filled in the column headings with "Jan-86" "Feb-86" and so forth (see Figure 19.2).

The Income Statement consists of two main sections: Revenues and Expenses. The Revenues section is itself divided into Gross Revenues (or Gross Sales) and Costs of Goods Sold. Gross revenues are the gross sales receipts of the business. Costs of goods sold (COGS) are often the principle *variable* expenses ofa business; they tend to increase in direct proportion to the volume of sales.

> *Example.* In the case of the ABC Corp., there were three types of costs of goods sold expense (Figure 19.3): labor (wages), supplies (raw materials for manufacturing), and freight (to ship the materials to the ABC factory). The controller entered these labels into the highlighted cells and the Revenues section of the worksheet was ready for data entry. Each month, the data operator entered gross sales and COGS data into the worksheet. By subtracting total costs of goods sold from net revenues, the worksheet generates a gross profit figure. This gross profit, when divided by net revenue, yielded the gross margin percent. Gross margin percent is that portion of each revenue dollar that becomes gross profit.

The second portion of the Income Statement is devoted to Operating Expenses. Many times these are essentially *fixed* expenses—rent, insurance, and other overhead items. The business must pay these expenses regardless of sales volume.

```
INCOME STATEMENT          Jan-86      to       Dec-86
ABC Corp.
================================================================================

                          Jan-86    Feb-86    Mar-86    Apr-86    May-86
................................................................................

REVENUES

  Gross Revenues          $40,000   $40,250   $40,500   $40,750   $41,000
    Less: Discounts & Credits  500      550       580       580       620
                          --------  --------  --------  --------  --------
  Net Revenues            39,500    39,700    39,920    40,170    40,380

  Cost of Goods Sold
    Labor                 12,000    12,250    12,250    12,400    12,450
    Supplies               8,500     8,700     8,700     8,800     8,850
    Freight                1,200     1,250     1,280     1,300     1,400
                          --------  --------  --------  --------  --------
    Total Cost of Goods Sold  21,700  22,200   22,230    22,500    22,700

  Gross Profit            17,800    17,500    17,690    17,670    17,680
  Gross Margin Percent       45%       44%       44%       44%       44%
................................................................................

OPERATING EXPENSES

  Rent                     2,400     2,400     2,400     2,400     2,400
  Depreciation             1,170     1,170     1,170     1,170     1,170
  Insurance                2,380     2,380     2,380     2,380     2,380
  Maintenance                600       600       600       600       600
  Advertising              3,000     2,000     2,000     2,000     2,000
  Utilities                  900       900       900       900       900
  General Administration   2,300     1,300     1,300     1,300     1,300
  Item                         0         0         0         0         0
  Item                         0         0         0         0         0
  Item                         0         0         0         0         0
  Item                         0         0         0         0         0
  Item                         0         0         0         0         0
                          --------  --------  --------  --------  --------
  Total Operating Expenses 12,750    10,750    10,750    10,750    10,750
                          ========  ========  ========  ========  ========

OPERATING INCOME (LOSS)    5,050     6,750     6,940     6,920     6,930
................................................................................

  Other Income
    Item                       0         0         0         0         0
    Item                       0         0         0         0         0
                          --------  --------  --------  --------  --------
    Total                      0         0         0         0         0

  Other Expenses
    Item                       0         0         0         0         0
    Item                       0         0         0         0         0
                          --------  --------  --------  --------  --------
    Total                      0         0         0         0         0
                          ========  ========  ========  ========  ========

Pre-tax Profit (Loss)      5,050     6,750     6,940     6,920     6,930
Taxes                      1,515     2,025     2,082     2,076     2,079
================================================================================
  NET INCOME (LOSS)       $3,535    $4,725    $4,858    $4,844    $4,851
```

	Jun-86	Jul-86	Aug-86	Sep-86	Oct-86	Nov-86	Dec-86	Total	% of Net Revenues
	$41,250	$41,500	$41,750	$42,000	$42,250	$42,500	$42,750	$496,500	102%
	690	740	790	850	850	900	970	8,620	2%
	40,560	40,760	40,960	41,150	41,400	41,600	41,780	487,880	100%
	12,450	12,500	12,600	12,600	12,600	12,650	12,800	149,550	31%
	8,800	8,800	8,800	8,850	8,900	8,900	8,950	105,550	22%
	1,400	1,450	1,550	1,550	1,580	1,680	1,600	17,240	4%
	22,650	22,750	22,950	23,000	23,080	23,230	23,350	272,340	56%
	17,910	18,010	18,010	18,150	18,320	18,370	18,430	215,540	44%
	44%	44%	44%	44%	44%	44%	44%	44%	
	2,400	2,400	2,400	2,400	2,400	2,400	2,400	28,800	6%
	1,170	1,170	1,170	1,170	1,170	1,170	1,170	14,040	3%
	2,380	2,380	2,380	2,380	2,380	2,380	2,380	28,560	6%
	600	600	600	600	600	600	600	7,200	1%
	2,000	2,000	2,000	2,000	2,000	2,000	2,000	25,000	5%
	900	900	900	900	900	900	900	10,800	2%
	1,300	1,300	1,300	1,300	1,300	1,300	1,300	16,600	3%
	0	0	0	0	0	0	0	0	0%
	0	0	0	0	0	0	0	0	0%
	0	0	0	0	0	0	0	0	0%
	0	0	0	0	0	0	0	0	0%
	0	0	0	0	0	0	0	0	0%
	10,750	10,750	10,750	10,750	10,750	10,750	10,750	131,000	27%
	7,160	7,260	7,260	7,400	7,570	7,620	7,680	84,540	17%
	0	0	0	0	0	0	0	0	0%
	0	0	0	0	0	0	0	0	0%
	0	0	0	0	0	0	0	0	0%
	0	0	0	0	0	0	0	0	0%
	0	0	0	0	0	0	0	0	0%
	0	0	0	0	0	0	0	0	0%
	7,160	7,260	7,260	7,400	7,570	7,620	7,680	84,540	17%
	2,148	2,178	2,178	2,220	2,271	2,286	2,304	25,362	5%
	$5,012	$5,082	$5,082	$5,180	$5,299	$5,334	$5,376	$59,178	12%

Figure 19.1 *Sample Income Statement.*

```
A1: [W3] 'INCOME STATEMENT                                              READY


        A       B           C           D       E       F
  1   INCOME STATEMENT                         Jan-86    to     Dec-86
  2   ABC Corp.
  3   ================================================================
  4
  5                                           Jan-86  Feb-86  Mar-86
  6   ..........................................................
  7   REVENUES
  8
  9     Gross Revenues                          $0      $0      $0
 10       Less: Discounts & Credits             $0      $0      $0
 11                                           ........ ........ ........
 12       Net Revenues                           0       0       0
 13
 14     Cost of Goods Sold
 15       Item                                   0       0       0
 16       Item                                   0       0       0
 17       Item                                   0       0       0
 18                                           ........ ........ ........
 19       Total Cost of Goods Sold              0       0       0
 20
```

Figure 19.2 *Income Statement—Date Headings.*

Example. In the case of ABC Corp., the controller again entered labels for the expense categories appropriate to this particular business. As data are entered, the worksheet subtracts total operating expenses from gross profit to get the firm's operating income.

When entering data, the controller found it convenient to use the Titles option from the Main Menu. This made it possible to see the column headings (the months) when entering numbers farther down in the operating expenses section of the statement, and to see the revenue and expense labels when working on months beyond March. See Figure 19.4 for an illustration.

C7: [W17]   READY

```
        A      B              C        D        E        F
 1    INCOME  STATEMENT              Jan-86    to     Dec-86
 2    ABC Corp.
 3    ================================================================
 4
 5                                   Jan-86   Feb-86   Mar-86
 6    ------------------------------------------------------------
 7    REVENUES
 8
 9      Gross Revenues            $40,000  $40,250  $40,500
10        Less: Discounts & Credits   500      550      580
11                                  --------  --------  --------
12      Net Revenues               39,500   39,700   39,920
13
14    Cost of Goods Sold
15      Labor                      12,000   12,250   12,250
16      Supplies                    8,500    8,700    8,700
17      Freight                     1,200    1,250    1,280
18                                  --------  --------  --------
19      Total Cost of Goods Sold   21,700   22,200   22,230
20
                                                      CALC
```

Figure 19.3 *Income Statement—COGS Labels and Data.*

After adding other nonoperating revenues (such as investment income) and subtracting other nonoperating expenses, the income statement shows pretax profit. After taxes are subtracted, the bottom line is Net Income.

A graph of selected Income Statement data has been built into the Master Financial Analyzer. This graph shows gross revenue, gross profit, and net income for each month of the year. It can be viewed by selecting **Graph** from the worksheet main menu and then selecting Income from the first submenu.

The ABC Corp. Income Statement Graph is shown in Figure 19.5.

```
H27: (,0) U [W10] 1170                                            READY


    A    B            H         I         J         K         L
 1  INCOME STATEMENT
 2  ABC Corp.
 3  =============================================================
 4
 5                   May-86    Jun-86    Jul-86    Aug-86    Sep-86
 6  ...........................................................
24  OPERATING EXPENSE
25
26     Rent          2,400     2,400     2,400     2,400     2,400
27     Depreciation  1,170     1,170     1,170     1,170     1,170
28     Insurance     2,380     2,380     2,380     2,380     2,380
29     Maintenance     600       600       600       600       600
30     Advertising   2,000     2,000     2,000     2,000     2,000
31     Utilities       900       900       900       900       900
32     General Admin. 1,300     1,300     1,300     1,300     1,300
33     Item              0         0         0         0         0
34     Item              0         0         0         0         0
35     Item              0         0         0         0         0
36     Item              0         0         0         0         0
37     Item              0         0         0         0         0
20-Feb-87   12:23 AM                                CALC
```

Figure 19.4 *Income Statement—Titles Lock.*

Balance Sheet

The Balance Sheet of a business shows the results of the activity illustrated in the income statement. That is, it reports the financial holdings (the assets) and the financial obligations (the liabilities) of the
business at a defined point in time, rather than the revenue and expense activities that have produced these holdings and obligations. In
a stock and flow model, the balance sheet shows the stock and the
income statement shows the flow.

In the Master Financial Analyzer, a calendarized balance sheet follows along with the Income Statement. The dates for each month are
automatically brought down from the Income Statement. The Balance Sheet is laid out vertically, with Assets above Liabilities. A separate Statement of Retained Earnings is included below the Balance
Sheet. There, net income for each month (the bottom line of the
Income Statement) is brought down and added to the existing retained earnings. Any dividends paid are subtracted, and the new
retained earnings value is added to the current month's balance
sheet. As with the Income Statement, an automated report function
prints the Balance Sheet on either wide carriage or 8.5 × 11 inch
paper.

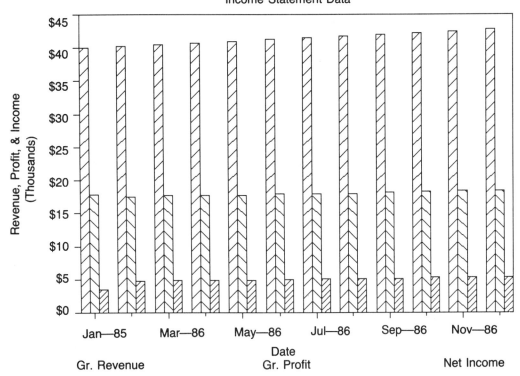

Figure 19.5 *Income Statement—Graph.*

Example. In the case of the ABC Corp., the controller used the **Express** option from the menu to move quickly to the Balance Sheet section of the Master Financial Analyzer. The column headings were carried down from the Income Statement by the worksheet, so she simply entered the company name and began to examine the labels along the left side of the worksheet. The worksheet supplies a number of commonly used asset and liability labels and organizes them into the appropriate sections of the Balance Sheet. They are all unprotected however, and can be written over to suit the needs of your particular business.

Sections of the Balance Sheet

The Balance Sheet is divided into the following sections (refer to Figure 19.6):

1. *Assets*. This section includes Current Assets (those that are relatively liquid, such as cash, receivables, and inventory), Fixed Assets (such as buildings and equipment, which cannot be turned into cash as readily as current assets), and Intangible Assets (such as trademarks and goodwill), which cannot be converted into cash but which have real value to potential investors, purchasers, and others evaluating the business.
2. *Liabilities*. The Liabilities section consists of Current Liabilities (obligations that must be met within a year or less) and Long-Term Liabilities (such as loans being paid over more than a year's time). Since the assets and the liabilities sections of the balance sheet must, by definition, be equal, any remaining financial claims on the business are some form of equity. The Stockholder's Equity section, which falls on the liabilities side of the Balance Sheet, has been designed to provide for a variety of sources of capital, including repurchased stock (Treasury Stock). Many small businesses will not need all of these line items.
3. ***Statement of Retained Earnings***. This is a schedule that generates the Retained Earnings line in the above Stockholders Equity section. A starting value for the year must be supplied; it is the retained earnings from the close of the previous year. After that, the worksheet brings down the net income each month from the Income Statement, subtracts any dividends paid, calculates the resulting retained earnings, and sends this number back up to the Balance Sheet.

The Financial Ratios

This section of the Master Financial Analyzer calculates a number of useful financial ratios, based on the data entered in the income statement and balance sheet above it. For each month, two numbers are shown. The first is the ratio resulting from the current

BALANCE SHEET   Jan-86   to   Dec-86
XYZ Business, Inc.

	Jan-86	Feb-86	Mar-86	Apr-86	May-86	Jun-86	Jul-86	Aug-86	Sep-86	Oct-86	Nov-86	Dec-86
ASSETS												
Current Assets												
Cash	$37,534	$38,213	$36,879	$40,466	$33,219	$36,418	$38,956	$43,523	$30,421	$36,793	$40,530	$45,345
Accounts Receivable	31,672	36,508	44,516	44,211	31,062	32,906	35,503	38,192	31,241	31,999	34,734	36,884
Less: Allowance for bad debt	1,627	1,566	1,671	1,711	1,703	1,645	1,605	1,543	1,562	1,600	1,637	1,550
Notes Receivable	0	0	0	0	0	0	0	0	0	0	0	0
Inventory	48,756	48,442	46,003	48,251	47,888	48,446	49,860	47,332	47,889	47,325	46,799	47,968
Prepaid Expenses:												
Security Deposit	4,800	4,800	4,800	4,800	4,800	4,800	4,800	4,800	4,800	4,800	4,800	4,800
Item	0	0	0	0	0	0	0	0	0	0	0	0
Item	0	0	0	0	0	0	0	0	0	0	0	0
Other	0	0	0	0	0	0	0	0	0	0	0	0
Other	0	0	0	0	0	0	0	0	0	0	0	0
Other	0	0	0	0	0	0	0	0	0	0	0	0
Other	0	0	0	0	0	0	0	0	0	0	0	0
Other	0	0	0	0	0	0	0	0	0	0	0	0
Total Current Assets	121,135	126,397	130,527	136,017	115,266	120,925	127,514	132,304	112,789	119,317	125,226	133,447
Fixed Assets												
Buildings and Equipment	325,000	325,000	325,000	325,000	350,000	350,000	350,000	350,000	375,000	375,000	375,000	375,000
Less: Accumulated Depreciati	22,200	22,200	22,200	22,200	22,200	22,200	22,200	22,200	22,200	22,200	22,200	24,200
Land	1,260	1,260	1,260	1,260	1,260	1,260	1,260	1,260	1,260	1,260	1,260	1,260
Other	0	0	0	0	0	0	0	0	0	0	0	0
Other	0	0	0	0	0	0	0	0	0	0	0	0
Other	0	0	0	0	0	0	0	0	0	0	0	0
Total Fixed Assets	304,060	304,060	304,060	304,060	329,060	329,060	329,060	329,060	354,060	354,060	354,060	352,060
Intangible Assets												
Trademarks	0	0	0	0	0	0	0	0	0	0	0	0
Other	0	0	0	0	0	0	0	0	0	0	0	0
Other	0	0	0	0	0	0	0	0	0	0	0	0
Total Intangible Assets	0	0	0	0	0	0	0	0	0	0	0	0
TOTAL ASSETS	$425,195	$430,457	$434,587	$440,077	$444,326	$449,985	$456,574	$461,364	$466,849	$473,377	$479,286	$485,507

Figure 19.6(A) *Sample Balance Sheet (Assets).*

Figure Note: *The balance sheet shown on pages 237–238 will be printed on one 8.5 × 11 page when you use this template.*

```
BALANCE SHEET              Jan-86    to      Dec-86
XYZ Business, Inc.
======================================================================================================================
```

	Jan-86	Feb-86	Mar-86	Apr-86	May-86	Jun-86	Jul-86	Aug-86	Sep-86	Oct-86	Nov-86	Dec-86
LIABILITIES												
Current Liabilities												
Accounts Payable	$47,995	$48,241	$47,444	$47,500	$46,433	$46,910	$47,777	$46,900	$47,229	$48,003	$47,864	$48,209
Notes Payable	6,000	6,000	6,000	6,000	6,000	6,000	6,000	6,000	6,000	6,000	6,000	6,000
Wages Payable	12,250	12,250	12,400	12,450	12,450	12,500	12,600	12,600	12,600	12,650	12,800	13,000
Income Taxes Payable	5,415	5,706	5,625	6,165	6,630	6,750	7,290	7,875	7,851	8,256	8,820	9,120
Other	0	0	0	0	0	0	0	0	0	0	0	0
Other	0	0	0	0	0	0	0	0	0	0	0	0
Other	0	0	0	0	0	0	0	0	0	0	0	0
Other	0	0	0	0	0	0	0	0	0	0	0	0
Other	0	0	0	0	0	0	0	0	0	0	0	0
Other	0	0	0	0	0	0	0	0	0	0	0	0
Other	0	0	0	0	0	0	0	0	0	0	0	0
Other	0	0	0	0	0	0	0	0	0	0	0	0
Total Current Liabilities	71,660	72,197	71,469	72,115	71,513	72,160	73,667	73,375	73,680	74,909	75,484	76,329
Long-Term Liabilities												
Bank Notes Payable	100,000	100,000	100,000	100,000	100,000	100,000	100,000	100,000	100,000	100,000	100,000	100,000
Other	0	0	0	0	0	0	0	0	0	0	0	0
Other	0	0	0	0	0	0	0	0	0	0	0	0
Other	0	0	0	0	0	0	0	0	0	0	0	0
Other	0	0	0	0	0	0	0	0	0	0	0	0
Total Long-Term Liabilitie	100,000	100,000	100,000	100,000	100,000	100,000	100,000	100,000	100,000	100,000	100,000	100,000
TOTAL LIABILITIES	171,660	172,197	171,469	172,115	171,513	172,160	173,667	173,375	173,680	174,909	175,484	176,329
STOCKHOLDERS EQUITY												
Preferred Stock	0	0	0	0	0	0	0	0	0	0	0	0
Common Stock	150,000	150,000	150,000	150,000	150,000	150,000	150,000	150,000	150,000	150,000	150,000	150,000
Additional Paid-In Capital	0	0	0	0	0	0	0	0	0	0	0	0
Retained Earnings (see Statement of Retained Earnings)	103,535	108,260	113,118	117,962	122,813	127,825	132,907	137,989	143,169	148,468	153,802	159,178
Less: Treasury Stock	0	0	0	0	0	0	0	0	0	0	0	0
TOTAL STOCKHOLDERS EQUITY	253,535	258,260	263,118	267,962	272,813	277,825	282,907	287,989	293,169	298,468	303,802	309,178
TOTAL LIABILITIES AND STOCKHOLDERS EQUITY	$425,195	$430,457	$434,587	$440,077	$444,326	$449,985	$456,574	$461,364	$466,849	$473,377	$479,286	$485,507

```
STATEMENT OF RETAINED EARNINGS
------------------------------
```

	Jan-86	Feb-86	Mar-86	Apr-86	May-86	Jun-86	Jul-86	Aug-86	Sep-86	Oct-86	Nov-86	Dec-86
Retained Earnings, start:	$100,000	$103,535	$108,260	$113,118	$117,962	$122,813	$127,825	$132,907	$137,989	$143,169	$148,468	$153,802
Add: Net Income This Period	$3,535	$4,725	$4,858	$4,844	$4,851	$5,012	$5,082	$5,082	$5,180	$5,299	$5,334	$5,376
	$103,535	$108,260	$113,118	$117,962	$122,813	$127,825	$132,907	$137,989	$143,169	$148,468	$153,802	$159,178
Less: Dividends	$0	$0	$0	$0	$0	$0	$0	$0	$0	$0	$0	$0
Retained Earnings for Period	$103,535	$108,260	$113,118	$117,962	$122,813	$127,825	$132,907	$137,989	$143,169	$148,468	$153,802	$159,178

Figure 19.6(B) *Sample Balance Sheet (Liabilities and Retained Earnings).*

month's data. (In the case of inventory turnover, return on assets, and return on equity, it is the annualized projection from the current month's data.) The second number is a moving average, based on year-to-date averages of balance sheet data. The moving average for each ratio is graphed over the entire one-year period.

The following ratios are calculated by the worksheet:

1. *Current Ratio*. This is the current assets divided by the current liabilities (both from the balance sheet). It is a measure of the ability of a business to meet its current financial obligations. A current ratio of about 2:1 is a healthy standard for most businesses.

2. *Quick Ratio*. This is a more stringent version of the current ratio in that inventory is subtracted from current assets before dividing by current liabilities. It thus tests the ability of the business to meet current financial obligations using only immediately available financial assets. A ratio of about 1:1 is safe for most businesses.

3. *Inventory Turnover*. This number is arrived at by dividing the total cost of goods sold for the year (from the income statement) by the value of the inventory on hand at year's end (from the balance sheet). To get the monthly number, the current month's COGS is multiplied by 12 and divided by the average inventory value to date; it is a forecast based on current data. The Inventory Turnover number estimates the number of times your business will completely replace, or turn over, its inventory during the year. Standard inventory turnover ratios vary enormously from industry to industry. In general, however, a high turnover rate is desirable because it suggests that resources are being used efficiently and capital is not being tied up in inventory.

4. *Debt to Equity*. This is the total liabilities of the business divided by the owner's or stockholders' equity. It is a measure of how highly leveraged a business is, since it compares the amount of debt carried by the firm to the amount of capital contributed by the owners. Acceptable debt to equity ratios vary widely, though clearly the higher the ratio the greater the risk carried by the firm's creditors.

5. *Return on Assets*. This is pretax profit divided by total assets. It measures the return on funds invested in a business and,

therefore, is of great interest to potential investors. As with Inventory Turnover, the monthly number represents an annual projection based on pretax profit for the month, divided by average total assets to date. The moving average value is the average profit to date divided by the average value for total assets to date. Generally, the return on assets should be better than the return one could expect from a passive investment such as a Treasury bill—the riskier the business, the higher the expected return.

6. *Return on Equity*. This is the firm's net income divided by the stockholders equity. It is essentially a measure of how effectively the equity has been used. Generally a return of 15 percent or better is considered healthy. Again, the worksheet presents an annualized projection of current data in the monthly column and a year-to-date average in the column next to it.

7. *Working Capital*. This is current assets minus current liabilities. It is a measure of the liquidity of a business, and should always be positive. Working capital is not the same as cash.

8. *Net Worth*. Net worth is what remains when total liabilities are subtracted from total assets. It is the dollar value of the owner's/stockholders' share of the business. In order to be solvent, a business must have a positive net worth.

> *Example*. The Controller of the ABC Corp. wanted to evaluate the financial condition of the business, given the Income Statement and Balance Sheet data that had been entered for the year. So, again using the Express option from the menu, she moved directly to the Ratios section of the Master Financial Analyzer to study the table of financial ratios. She pressed **F9**, the recalculation key on the left of the keyboard, to make sure that all of the calculations in the spreadsheet were up-to-date.
>
> A quick scan of the numbers in the table was encouraging. The current ratio was generally around 1.7 or 1.8— nearly twice as much in current assets as in current liabilities. Similarly, the quick ratio was always around 1; the business had enough cash to cover current liabilities. Inventory turnover varied from month to month, but averaged a healthy 3 to 1 for the year. The business was

carrying very little debt (a debt to equity ratio of .6), and the returns on equity and assets were strong. The financial ratios table is shown in Figure 19.7.

FINANCIAL RATIOS CALCULATION:
YTD Average, and
Current Month

	Jan-87	YTD Average	Feb-87	YTD Average	Mar-87	YTD Average	Apr-87	YTD Average	May-87	YTD Average	Jun-87
1. Current Ratio	1.7	1.7	1.8	1.7	1.8	1.8	1.9	1.8	1.6	1.8	1.7
2. Quick Ratio	1.0	1.0	1.1	1.0	1.2	1.1	1.2	1.1	0.9	1.1	1.0
3. Inventory Turnover*	5.3	5.3	5.5	3.0	5.8	3.1	5.6	3.1	5.7	3.1	5.6
4. Debt to Equity	0.7	0.7	0.7	0.7	0.7	0.7	0.6	0.7	0.6	0.7	0.6
5. Return on Assets*	14.3%	14.3%	18.8%	16.5%	19.2%	17.4%	18.9%	17.8%	18.7%	18.0%	19.1%
6. Return on Equity*	16.7%	16.7%	22.0%	19.4%	22.2%	20.3%	21.7%	20.7%	21.3%	20.8%	21.6%
7. Working Capital	$49,475	$49,475	$54,200	$51,838	$59,058	$54,244	$63,902	$56,659	$43,753	$54,078	$48,765
8. Net Worth	$253,535	$253,535	$258,260	$255,898	$263,118	$258,304	$267,962	$260,719	$272,813	$263,138	$277,825

* Monthly column shows annualized forecast from current data.

	Jul-87	YTD Average	Aug-87	YTD Average	Sep-87	YTD Average	Oct-87	YTD Average	Nov-87	YTD Average	Dec-87	YTD Average
	1.7	1.7	1.8	1.7	1.5	1.7	1.6	1.7	1.7	1.7	1.7	1.7
	1.1	1.1	1.2	1.1	0.9	1.1	1.0	1.0	1.0	1.0	1.1	1.1
	5.5	3.1	5.8	3.1	5.8	3.1	5.9	3.1	6.0	3.1	5.8	3.1
	0.6	0.6	0.6	0.6	0.6	0.6	0.6	0.6	0.6	0.6	0.6	0.6
	19.1%	18.3%	18.9%	18.4%	19.0%	18.5%	19.2%	18.5%	19.1%	18.6%	19.0%	18.6%
	21.6%	21.0%	21.2%	21.1%	21.2%	21.1%	21.3%	21.1%	21.1%	21.1%	20.9%	21.1%
	$53,847	$53,286	$58,929	$53,991	$39,109	$52,338	$44,408	$51,545	$49,742	$51,381	$57,118	$51,859
	$282,907	$268,060	$287,989	$270,551	$293,169	$273,064	$298,468	$275,605	$303,802	$278,168	$309,178	$280,752

Figure 19.7 *Financial Ratios Table.*

In order to study graphs of these ratios, the controller selected **Graph Ratios** from the menu. Each of the financial ratios is graphed, using the year-to-date figure for each month. Several of these graphs for the ABC Corp. are shown in Figures 19.8–19.10.

Breakeven Analysis

There are two kinds of breakeven analysis customarily done by businesses. The first is a calculation of the number of units that must be sold in order to break even—the breakeven volume. The

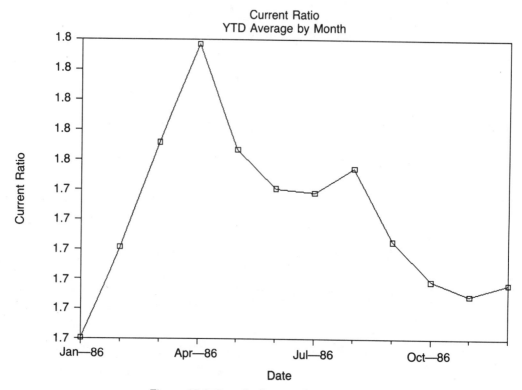

Figure 19.8 *Sample Current Ratio Graph.*

second is a calculation of the overall revenue that must be generated by the business to break even—the breakeven revenue. The
Master Financial Analyzer generates the second type of calculation,
a breakeven revenue analysis.

The breakeven revenue analysis on this worksheet makes two
important simplifying assumptions. First, it assumes that all of the
costs of goods sold are *variable costs.* Second, it assumes that all of
the operating expenses are *fixed costs.* In general, these will be reasonable assumptions for many small businesses. A precise
breakeven analysis, however, requires the examination of each expense item to determine if it is variable or fixed, or whether it is
partly variable and partly fixed. (The separate Breakeven Analysis
template can be helpful for this purpose.) Therefore, be cautious
when interpreting the breakeven figures from this worksheet. The
closer your situation matches the above assumptions about fixed

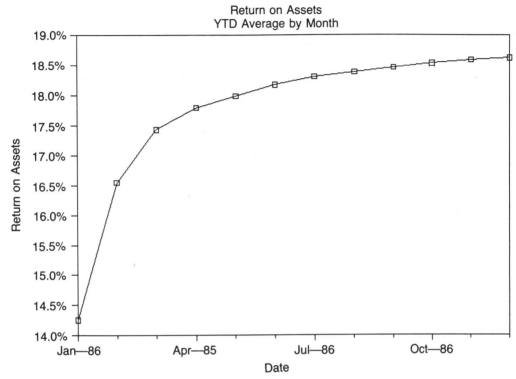

Figure 19.9 *Sample Return on Assets Graph.*

and variable costs, the more accurate your breakeven analysis numbers will be.

The Master Financial Analyzer illustrates the breakeven revenue point in two general ways. The first is a graph of monthly breakeven points for the year under study. This tracks the breakeven point as it is generated from each month's operations. The second is a set of graphs showing the average breakeven point for the year. In this option, three different graphs are created for a revenue range, which you supply. Net profit, costs and revenues, and profit margin are then illustrated.

Example—Tracking the Breakeven Point (Figure 19.11).
ABC's controller wanted to study the range over which the business's breakeven point had varied during the year. To do this, she selected **Graph Breakeven Track** (Figure 19.11)

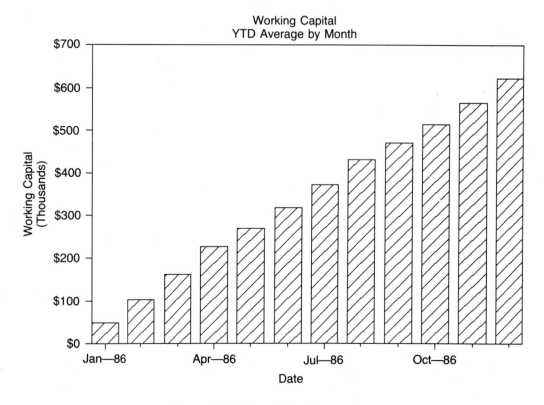

Figure 19.10 *Sample Working Capital Graph.*

from the worksheet menu. There was a pause while the worksheet recalculated all of its formulas and then Graph 1 of the Breakeven Analysis section appeared.

The numbers that create this graph are derived as follows: For each month, the worksheet brings down the fixed expenses (i.e., operating expenses) and the gross margin percentage, both from the Income Statement, and calculates the resulting breakeven point. This is done by dividing the fixed expenses by the gross margin percentage. The resulting stream of breakeven points is then graphed. These numbers can be seen in the Breakeven Analysis section of the Master Financial Analyzer. They are shown for the ABC Corp. in Figure 19.12.

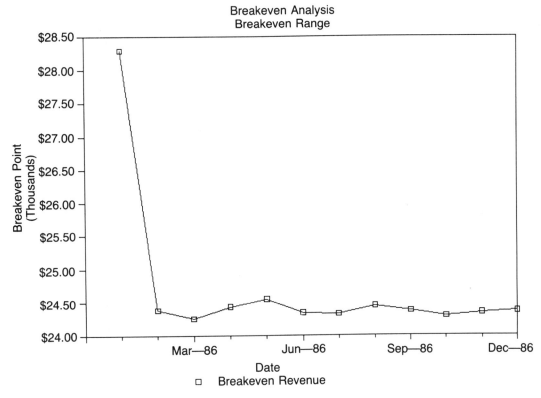

Figure 19.11 *Monthly Breakeven Point Graph.*

The second way in which the Master Financial Analyzer illustrates a breakeven revenue point is by creating a range of revenue values and showing corresponding costs, profit, and profit margin for the business, again using data from the income statement on the worksheet. For these breakeven calculations, the worksheet uses average numbers—either year-end or year-to-date—whichever is appropriate.

Example—Average Breakeven Point Graphs. ABC Corp's controller wanted to study the average breakeven point for the year. She selected Graph Breakeven Point Average from the worksheet menu, and was prompted to enter a starting value and an increment value for a revenue range. After some experimentation, she selected a starting value of $18,000 and an increment value of $1,500, since these

BREAKEVEN ANALYSIS

Graph 1: Breakeven Range over Time

	Jan-86	Feb-86	Mar-86	Apr-86	May-86	Jun-86
Fixed Expenses	$12,750	$10,750	$10,750	$10,750	$10,750	$10,750
Gross Margin Percentage	45%	44%	44%	44%	44%	44%
Breakeven Point	$28,294	$24,387	$24,259	$24,438	$24,552	$24,345

	Jul-86	Aug-86	Sep-86	Oct-86	Nov-86	Dec-86
	$10,750	$10,750	$10,750	$10,750	$10,750	$10,750
	44%	44%	44%	44%	44%	44%
	$24,329	$24,449	$24,373	$24,293	$24,344	$24,370

On your computer, this graph will be displayed spread across the screen, with July through December following June.

Figure 19.12 *Monthly Breakeven Analysis Data.*

produced a series of numbers in the Profit (Loss) column of the Graph 2 table that started negative and turned positive. In other words, by starting with a revenue value that was less than the average breakeven point and advancing to a value that was more than the average breakeven point, a meaningful set of graphs could be created. Graphs created in this way will show cost and revenue lines that intersect, and profit lines that start below zero and cross above it.

Once these values are processed by the worksheet, three graphs are available for viewing: a net profit graph, a costs/ revenues graph, and a profit margin graph.

The net profit graph, Figure 19.13, shows net profit as a straight line function, from less than zero at less than breakeven revenue levels to greater than zero above the breakeven point. It illustrates the amount of *pretax profit* that a given amount of *net revenue* will produce. In the case of the ABC Corp., about $25,000 in net revenue is necessary to breakeven.

The costs/revenues graph illustrates the same breakeven point from a different perspective. It shows fixed costs, total costs, and net revenues. You can thus study both the point at which revenue is adequate to cover fixed costs as well as the point at which total

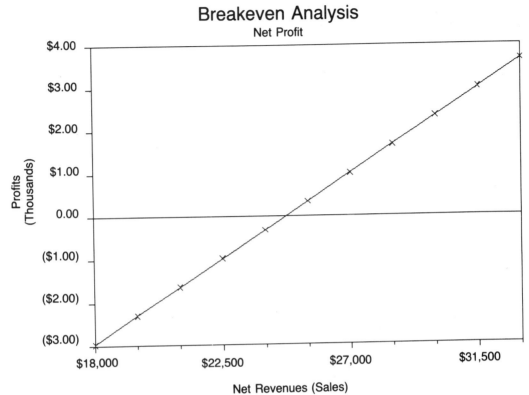

Figure 19.13 *Breakeven Graph—Net Profit.*

costs and net revenues cross. The Costs/Revenues graph for the ABC Corp. is shown in Figure 19.14.

The final graph, Profit Margin, shows the rate at which profitability increases above the breakeven point. The ABC Corp. version of this graph is shown in Figure 19.15.

Breakeven Analysis

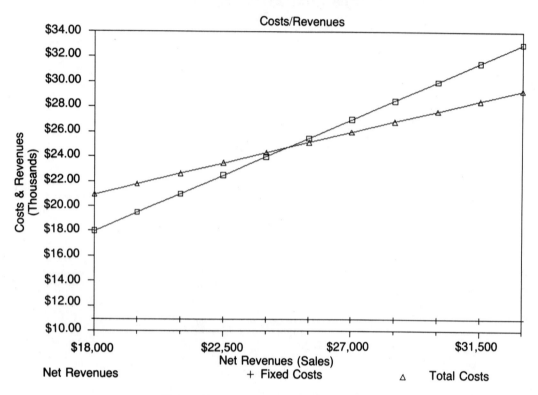

Figure 19.14 *Breakeven Graph—Costs/Revenues.*

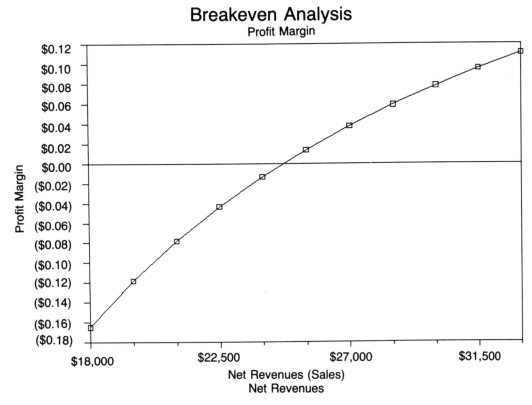

Figure 19.15 *Breakeven Graph—Profit Margin.*

Using the Master Financial Analyzer

Main Menu Options

The Main Menu of the Master Financial Analyzer Template offers the following choices:

```
Date Express Title Print Graph Link File
```

Date

This option automates the entry of monthly date headings across the top of the income statement and other sections of the worksheet. When you select **Date**, you will be prompted to enter a month using a number from 1 through 12, a day using a number from 1 through 31, and a year using two digits from 00 through 99. Entry of an invalid date will bring an error message and an opportunity to try again.

Express

This option is designed to facilitate getting around the rather large worksheet. It brings up the following submenu:

```
Income Balance Earnings Ratios Analysis
```

Each of these headings is a defined section of the worksheet to which you can move with just a keystroke.

Titles

Titles is another convenience selection. It allows you to freeze the column and row headings on either the Balance Sheet or the Income Statement. This makes it easier to read the worksheet when you are out in months beyond March or in rows that would ordinarily leave the monthly headings off the screen. The Titles submenu offers the following choices:

```
Income Balance Unlock
```

Income locks the title in the income portion of the spreadsheet, and Balance locks the title in the balance sheet portion. Unlock frees the title in any portion of the template.

Print

This selection produces printed reports of either the Income Statement, the Balance Sheet, or the Financial Ratios. Each section can be printed on either wide carriage paper or 8.5 × 11 inch paper; the 8.5 × 11 inch option simply breaks the printed report into more pages. All reports are printed in compressed type (15 pitch). The macro assumes that you are connected to an Epson compatible printer (one that uses the setup string /015 to generate compressed print) and that you have continuous feed paper. The **Print** submenu offers choices for printing the following sections of the template:

```
Income Balance Ratios
```

Each of these items offers the following submenu.

```
Wide Regular
```

Graph

This menu option leads to the creation and viewing of a variety of graphs. Its submenu is:

```
Breakeven Income Ratios Save Exit
```

Breakeven

The **Breakeven** selection allows you either to view the Breakeven Range graph, or to create and view the several Breakeven Point graphs. Its submenu is:

```
Track Average
```

Selecting **Track** brings up Graph 1 on the worksheet. This graph shows the breakeven point for each month over the course of the year. Selecting **Average** brings up two choices:

`Create View`

The **Create** option helps you design three average Breakeven Point graphs. The **View** option allows you to see these graphs if they have already been created.

Three graphs are created under the **Breakeven Average Create** option: Net Profit, Costs/Revenues, and Profit Margin. These are as described earlier.

Income

One Income Statement graph is available. It plots net revenues, gross profits, and net income over time (refer to Figure 19.5).

Ratios

Eight graphs are available under the **Ratios** item, one for each of the eight financial ratios created on the worksheet. In each case, the numbers that are graphed are the year-to-date average values shown on the worksheet.

One important note regarding the graphs: Most of the macros that generate these graphs call for the worksheet to be recalculated before the data are graphed. Thus you will experience a 5 or 6 second delay, while the sign "Wait" flashes in the upper-right hand corner of the screen, before the graph appears.

Save is included in the graph menu for those users who wish to print out a graph. Printing a graph in Lotus 1-2-3 is a two step operation. First, you have to save the graph to a special kind of file—a .PIC file—for later printing. That is the purpose of this menu item. To print the graph once it has been saved, you will have to leave the worksheet and call up the PrintGraph function of Lotus. This process is explained in the Lotus manual.

When you select **Save** from the Graph menu, you will be saving *the graph you have most recently viewed*. Be sure, therefore, to look at the graph you want to save first. One convenient way of checking to see the current graph is to press **F10**. This will always show the graph that Lotus regards as current—the most recent graph you have viewed. Then, select **Save**. You will be asked to supply a name for your graph. This name can be no more than eight characters long.

Link

Link is an option that brings monthly cash flow data into the balance sheet. It is designed to assist in the preparation of pro forma financial statements.

A pro forma income statement or balance sheet is a statement of plans rather than a record of results. The Cash Flow Planner (next section) is a separate template that is used to plan and forecast the cash transactions of a business. When preparing a complete set of pro forma financial statements, the monthly cash balances of the cash flow planner become the monthly cash entries in the balance sheet.

The Link option automatically transfers the monthly cash balances from a specified Cash Flow Planner into the balance sheet of the Master Financial Analyzer. When you select Link, you will be asked to specify the *name of the file* containing the cash flow data you want to add. Simply point to the name of the file in the list displayed (or type the file name directly) and press **‹RETURN›**.

File

The main menu **File** option brings up a submenu for saving and/or exiting from the worksheet file. The options are:

```
Save Put Away Quit
```

Save

When you select **Save**, you will be asked to confirm the name of the file under which your worked is to be saved. If such a file already exists you will have to confirm that you wish to replace the contents of the existing file with the worksheet data as it appears on the screen.

Put Away

This selection combines saving and quitting. After executing the save routine, the macro will pause. Press the **‹RETURN›** key and the macro will continue exiting from 1-2-3.

Quit

As with **Save**, **Quit** is the worksheet menu counterpart to the **Quit** selection in the Lotus 1-2-3 main menu. As a precaution against loss of data, you will have to confirm that you wish to leave the worksheet.

Refer to Figure 19.16 for a diagram of the menu tree for this template and to Figure 19.17 for a diagram of the template layout.

Common Questions and Problems

I seem to be "stuck" in a macro; I can't get out of the command mode. Ordinarily, you can break a macro or menu by pressing **ESC**. If that does not work, press and hold **CTRL** and press **BREAK** at the same time. This will always terminate the Command mode. If you are using Release 2 or 2.01, pressing **CTRL-BREAK** will generate an error message—press **ESC** to clear it.

How do I know what "starting value" and "increment value" to pick for my breakeven graphs? Explore values that will "bracket" your breakeven point. These will be revenue numbers that result in a loss at first and then increase until they show a profit. There is no one correct set of numbers. The breakeven point has already been determined; it is just a matter of illustrating it effectively.

Can I add and delete rows in the Income Statement and Balance Sheet? Yes, but we don't encourage it. If you add too many rows the reports will not fit on the vertical length of a single page. Lotus 1-2-3 will break up the printed output for you so it will all be there in a logical fashion, but it can be cumbersome to assemble. If you want to delete (or insert) a row, use the Lotus /Worksheet **Row** Insert or /Worksheet **Row** Delete option. The integrity of the formulas and macros will be preserved.

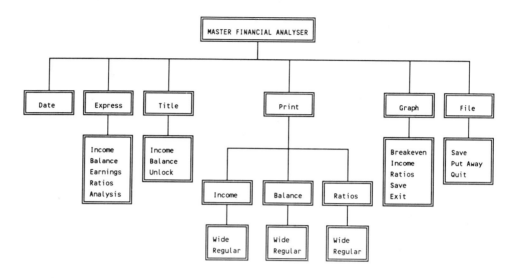

Figure 19.16 *Menu Tree, Master Business Analyzer.*

Income Statement
A1..Q61

Balance Sheet
A66...O180

Financial Ratios
A184..AA200

Breakeven Analysis and Graphs
A203..O250

Macros
A253..O400

Figure 19.17 *Template Layout, Master Business Analyzer.*

Cash Flow Planner

This is a free-standing planning template, showing an entire year of itemized monthly cash inflows and outflows (refer to Figure 19.18). Essentially, it is a forecasting device that guides you in the planning of cash receipts and disbursements for your business. You supply the assumptions guiding the flow of receipts and disbursements.

The template conveniently handles anticipated delays in both the collection of credit sales and the payment of credit purchases. A special summary section at the bottom of the worksheet shows the net cash flow for each month and the closing cash balance for that month. Both monthly net cash flow and monthly closing cash balances can be viewed on graphs supplied by the worksheet.

Like the Income Statement and Balance Sheet, the Cash Flow Planner is structured with inflow and outflow items along the left side of the worksheet and months across the top. The same **Date** function in the main worksheet menu automates the entry of monthly column headings.

The Inflows section of the worksheet is divided into Sales Receipts and Other Cash Receipts. The Sales Receipts section is designed to accommodate credit sales or other situations where the date of the sale is different from the date of cash collection. The four percentage figures on the left allow you to designate what percentage of each month's sales will become cash receipts during the current month, one month later, two months later, and three months later. If you have no credit sales, enter "100" in the Current cell, since 100 percent of your sales are cash receipts.

Other Cash Receipts items are highlighted so that you may enter any particular items that apply to your business. Simply overwrite the highlighted entry, "Other Cash Receipt," and enter the appropriate numbers for each month. *When entering numbers you must not input commas or dollar signs.*

The Outflows section is divided in a similar manner. The first portion is used for Credit Purchases—situations where the actual cash payment takes place after the expense has been incurred. As with the Sales portion of Cash Inflows, you designate a percentage of purchases to be paid currently, one month later, two months later, or three months later. The remainder of the *Outflows* section is used for other cash disbursements that you customize.

> *Example.* Filling in the Cash Flow Planner is very similar to filling in the Income Statement or Balance Sheet. The ABC Corp. controller first entered the company name in the highlighted cell, then selected **Date** from the main menu to fill in the column headings. From experience, she knew that only about 20 percent of the ABC Corp.'s sales were cash sales; about 30 percent were collected within one month and another 30 percent within two months. The remaining 20 percent were collected within three months. Accordingly, she entered these percentages in the Cash Collection Rate section under Sales.
>
> Next, the controller did the same for payment delay rate under Credit Purchases in the Cash Outflows section, entering percentage numbers as appropriate. Labels were entered for the appropriate ABC Corp. expense categories down the left side of the worksheet. The worksheet was then ready to receive data.

Figure 19.18 presents the annual cash flow projections for the ABC Corp. Notice that the business is anticipating steady sales, yet the cash flow worksheet shows several months with negative cash results. This would be a fairly typical picture for a new business, caused by the delay in receivables collection at the start of operations. It could also be experienced by any seasonal business.

Notice also that the ABC Corp. has taken out a short-term loan so as to avoid going cash negative during the early months of the year. This demonstrates the potential value of cash flow planning: By forecasting cash flow using current business assumptions, trouble spots can be identified and appropriate action planned. In this case, a short-term loan was the solution.

To view the graphs of ABC's cash flow, the controller selected **Graph** from the main menu. Two viewing options were presented: Flow and Balance. These graphs are shown in Figures 19.19 and 19.20.

```
CASH FLOW PLANNER                    Jan-87    to      Dec-87
ABC Corp.
===============================================================================
                              Jan-87   Feb-87   Mar-87   Apr-87   May-87
===============================================================================
CASH INFLOWS
--------------------
Sales                        $23,250  $23,250  $23,250  $23,250  $23,250
  Cash collection rate
    Current:          20%      4,650    4,650    4,650    4,650    4,650
    1 month lag:      30%               6,975    6,975    6,975    6,975
    2 month lag:      30%                        6,975    6,975    6,975
    3 month lag:      20%                                 4,650    4,650
       Check:        100%    -------  -------  -------  -------  -------
Sales Receipts                 4,650   11,625   18,600   23,250   23,250
---------------------------------------------------------------------------

Loan                           5,000        0        0        0        0
Other Cash Receipt                 0        0        0        0        0
                             -------  -------  -------  -------  -------
TOTAL CASH INFLOWS             9,650   11,625   18,600   23,250   23,250
===============================================================================

CASH OUTFLOWS
--------------------
Credit Purchases              15,000   15,000   15,000   15,000   15,000
  Payment delay rate
    Current:          25%      3,750    3,750    3,750    3,750    3,750
    1 month lag:      50%               7,500    7,500    7,500    7,500
    2 month lag:      25%                        3,750    3,750    3,750
    3 month lag:       0%                                     0        0
       Check:        100%    -------  -------  -------  -------  -------
Purchase Payments              3,750   11,250   15,000   15,000   15,000
---------------------------------------------------------------------------

G & A                          5,000    5,000    5,000    5,000    5,000
Taxes                            750      750      750      750      750
Interest                          50       50       50       50       50
Loan Repayment - Principal         0        0        0        0        0
Other Cash Disbursement            0        0        0        0        0
Other Cash Disbursement            0        0        0        0        0
Other Cash Disbursement            0        0        0        0        0
Other Cash Disbursement            0        0        0        0        0
Other Cash Disbursement            0        0        0        0        0
Other Cash Disbursement            0        0        0        0        0
Other Cash Disbursement            0        0        0        0        0
                             -------  -------  -------  -------  -------
TOTAL CASH OUTFLOWS           $9,550  $17,050  $20,800  $20,800  $20,800
===============================================================================

     SUMMARY

Net Monthly Cash Flow           $100  ($5,425) ($2,200)  $2,450   $2,450
Plus: Opening Cash Balance    $8,000   $8,100   $2,675     $475   $2,925
                             -------  -------  -------  -------  -------
Closing Cash Balance          $8,100   $2,675     $475   $2,925   $5,375
```

Jun-87	Jul-87	Aug-87	Sep-87	Oct-87	Nov-87	Dec-87	Total
$23,250	$23,250	$23,250	$23,250	$23,250	$23,250	$23,250	$279,000
4,650	4,650	4,650	4,650	4,650	4,650	4,650	55,800
6,975	6,975	6,975	6,975	6,975	6,975	6,975	76,725
6,975	6,975	6,975	6,975	6,975	6,975	6,975	69,750
4,650	4,650	4,650	4,650	4,650	4,650	4,650	41,850
23,250	23,250	23,250	23,250	23,250	23,250	23,250	244,125
0	0	0	0	0	0	0	5,000
0	0	0	0	0	0	0	0
23,250	23,250	23,250	23,250	23,250	23,250	23,250	249,125
15,000	15,000	15,000	15,000	15,000	15,000	15,000	180,000
3,750	3,750	3,750	3,750	3,750	3,750	3,750	45,000
7,500	7,500	7,500	7,500	7,500	7,500	7,500	82,500
3,750	3,750	3,750	3,750	3,750	3,750	3,750	37,500
0	0	0	0	0	0	0	0
15,000	15,000	15,000	15,000	15,000	15,000	15,000	165,000
5,000	5,000	5,000	5,000	5,000	5,000	5,000	60,000
750	750	750	750	750	750	750	9,000
50	50	50	50	50	50	50	600
0	0	0	0	0	0	5,000	5,000
0	0	0	0	0	0	0	0
0	0	0	0	0	0	0	0
0	0	0	0	0	0	0	0
0	0	0	0	0	0	0	0
0	0	0	0	0	0	0	0
0	0	0	0	0	0	0	0
0	0	0	0	0	0	0	0
$20,800	$20,800	$20,800	$20,800	$20,800	$20,800	$25,800	$239,600

							Total
$2,450	$2,450	$2,450	$2,450	$2,450	$2,450	($2,550)	$9,525
$5,375	$7,825	$10,275	$12,725	$15,175	$17,625	$20,075	
$7,825	$10,275	$12,725	$15,175	$17,625	$20,075	$17,525	

Figure 19.18 *ABC Corp. Cash Flow Planner.*

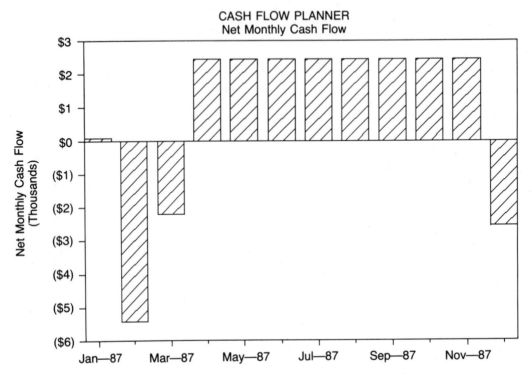

Figure 19.19 *Cash Flow Graph 1.*

Using the Cash Flow Planner

Main Menu Options

The Main Menu of the Cash Flow Planner is identical to that of the Master Financial Analyzer:

`Date Express Title Print Graph File`

Date facilitates the entry of column headings. Express facilitates movement from section to section in the worksheet. Title freezes row labels and column headings for reading convenience on the screen. Print allows for both wide carriage reports and standard 8.5 × 11 inch paper, both in compressed (15 pitch) type.

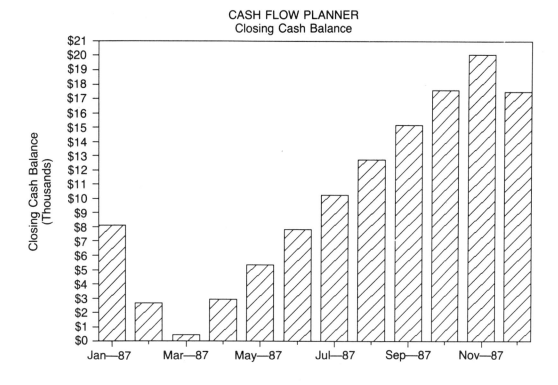

Figure 19.20 *Cash Flow Graph 2.*

Two graphs are generated by the worksheet: the Net Monthly Cash Flow, and the monthly Closing Cash Balance. As with the Master Financial Analyzer, a Save function within the graph menu allows you to save a current graph to a .PIC file for printing with the Lotus PrintGraph utility.

Data Entry

When you are entering percentages, either in the collection of sales receipts or the payout of credit purchases, just enter the number—the worksheet will supply the percent sign and convert the number to the proper percent value. Thus, "75 percent" should be entered as "75" and "50 percent" as "50". The "%" sign is already in the worksheet and the number you enter will be processed as a percent.

Also, when entering numbers into the worksheet, just type the number; do not add commas or dollar signs. The worksheet will supply these for you.

Refer to Figure 19.21 for a diagram of the menu tree for this template and to Figure 19.22 for a diagram of the template layout.

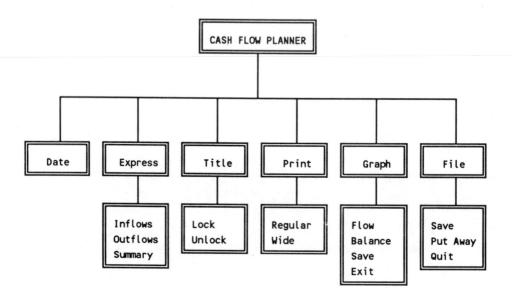

Figure 19.21 *Menu Tree, Cash Flow Planner.*

```
Cash Flow Planner
A1..O58

Macros
D72..R105
```

Figure 19.22 *Template layout, Cash Flow Planner.*

Common Questions and Problems

Don't forget to recalculate your spreadsheet. To speed up data entry on these spreadsheets, the recalculation mode has been set to manual. That means that numbers you type in are not calculated until you press **F9**, the recalculation key. The CALC sign in the bottom of the screen is a reminder that the worksheet needs to be recalculated.

How can I quickly see the last graph I was studying? Press **F10**. The most recently viewed graph will be displayed.

Financial Ratios Calculator

This template enables you to examine the same financial ratios that were generated by the Master Financial Analyzer, tracking them over a period of several years. When you enter year-end data from the Income Statements and Balance Sheets of a company over several years, the template calculates and graphs a table of eight financial ratios. In addition, a column is provided in which you may enter industry norms for comparison.

The worksheet is divided into three sections:

1. *Data From Income Statement.* In this section you enter four numbers, taken directly from the year-end income statement of a business: the total Costs of Goods Sold, the Operating Income, the Pretax Profit, and the Net Income.

2. *Data From Balance Sheet.* In this section you enter six numbers from the year-end balance sheet of a business: the value of the Inventory at cost, the total Current Assets, the total Current Liabilities, the Total Assets, the Total Liabilities, and the Owner (or Stockholders) Equity.

3. *Financial Ratios.* This is the table of financial ratios that is generated by the preceeding figures. It includes the following nine items: Current Ratio, Quick Ratio, Inventory Turnover, Debt to Equity Ratio, Return on Assets, Return on Equity, Working Capital, and Net Worth.

Example. Figure 19.23 shows a sample financial ratios analysis. It covers a three-year period for the ABC Corp. Note that just four numbers from each year's income statement and six from each year's balance sheet were needed in order to prepare the ratios calculation table.

In addition to the table of numbers, a·graph is available for each of the calculated ratios, just as with the Master Financial Analyzer. These graphs are accessed by the **Graph** selection in the Main Menu. As with the **Graph** selection in the other templates, a special **Graph Save** option creates a .PIC file of the most recently viewed graph. You may then switch to the Lotus PrintGraph utility to print a hard copy of your graphs.

Using the Financial Ratios Calculator

Main Menu Options

The menu of this template consists of the following items:

```
Express Print Graph File
```

The function of each selection is the same as in the other business planning templates. **Express** moves you quickly from one section of the worksheet to another. **Print** generates a one-page report on 8.5 × 11 inch paper. **Graph** allows you to see a graph of each ratio calculated by the worksheet. **File** offers a submenu from which you may save your work and/or quit 1-2-3.

Data entry is straightforward. The highlighted cells may be written over, cells in regular intensity may not. No commas or dollar signs are necessary when typing in amounts. The year headings are typed exactly as they appear—i.e., "1986" "1987" and so forth.

Refer to Figure 19.24 for a diagram of the menu tree for this template and to Figure 19.25 for a diagram of the template layout.

```
FINANCIAL RATIOS WORKSHEET
       COMPANY: Your Company
===================================================================


Data From Income Statement (Annual Totals)
-------------------------------------------
                            Year 1:    Year 2:    Year 3:

                            ------     ------     ------
   1. Cost of Goods Sold    $149,550   $175,600   $195,500
   2. Operating Income       $84,450   $105,200   $119,000
   3. Pre-Tax Profit         $84,540   $105,200   $119,000
   4. Net Income             $59,178    $76,650    $89,250


Data From Balance Sheet (Year End)
----------------------------
                            Year 1:    Year 2:    Year 3:

                            ------     ------     ------
   1. Inventory (at cost)    $47,968    $57,300    $65,450
   2. Current Assets        $133,447   $150,245   $185,650
   3. Current Liabilities    $76,329    $95,545   $106,355
   4. Total Assets          $485,507   $525,300   $553,650
   5. Total Liabilities     $176,329   $185,450   $197,600
   6. Owner Equity          $309,178   $347,650   $375,420




                       FINANCIAL RATIOS
===================================================================

                            Year 1:    Year 2:    Year 3:

                            ------     ------     ------
   1. Current Ratio            1.75       1.57       1.75
   2. Quick Ratio              1.12       0.97       1.13
   3. Inventory Turnover       3.12       3.06       2.99
   4. Debt to Equity           0.57       0.53       0.53
   5. Return on Assets       17.41%     20.03%     21.49%
   6. Return on Equity       19.14%     22.05%     23.77%
   7. Working Capital        $57,118    $54,700    $79,295
   8. Net Worth             $309,178   $339,850   $356,050


===================================================================
```

Figure 19.23 *Financial Ratios.*

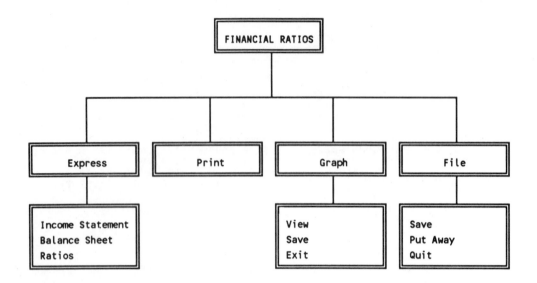

Figure 19.24 *Menu Tree, Financial Ratios Calculator.*

Data from Income Statement
A6..F15

Data from Balance Sheet
A18..F28

Finacial Rations
A34..G50

Macros
A60..F93

Figure 19.25 *Template Layout, Financial Ratios Calculator.*

Breakeven Analyzer

It was noted earlier that the breakeven analysis generated by the Master Financial Analyzer was constrained by the assumptions that all costs of goods sold are variable and all operating costs are fixed. The Breakeven Analyzer accommodates a more precise effort at identifying the fixed and variable costs of an operation or business unit. It allows you to itemize these costs independently of their location on the income statement.

The breakeven worksheet computes your gross margin percentage (gross profit as a percentage of sales revenue) using the sales revenue data that you supply. This number is then used to calculate the breakeven revenue level. As with the Master Financial Analyzer, a special table generates three graphs that give different views of the breakeven analysis.

Of course, the Breakeven Analyzer still assumes that your gross margin percentage is relatively steady over time, and that fixed expenses divided by GMP is a reasonable way to generate the breakeven point.

The Breakeven Analyzer is divided into four major sections:

1. *Fixed and Variable Costs Calculation Tables.* In these two tables you itemize your fixed and variable costs.
2. *Gross Margin Percentage Calculation.* In this section you enter sales revenue data. Your gross margin percentage is determined from this information and the preceding costs calculations.
3. *Breakeven Calculation.* This is where your breakeven revenue level is calculated and displayed.
4. *Breakeven Graph Table.* This table generates graphs that allow you to study the implications of different revenue levels for the profitability of your business.

Using the Breakeven Analyzer

Main Menu Options

The Main Menu of the Breakeven Analysis template offers the following choices:

```
Date Express Print Graph  File
```

Each option is similar to those in the other templates in the Business Planning and Analysis Series.

Date

This option automates the entry of a date at the top of the worksheet. Selecting **Date** prompts you to enter a month, a day, and a year, all entered as digits ("mm,dd,yy" format). An invalid entry brings an error message and an opportunity to start again.

Express

The Express option brings up a submenu with the following options:

```
Fixed Variable Margin Breakeven Table
```

Each of these options is a defined section of the worksheet. Express moves the cell pointer directly to the specified section.

1. **Fixed**. This section of the worksheet itemizes your fixed costs, whatever the project or business. To enter data, simply type over the highlighted cells, replacing the labels with those of your own choosing. If you already have data in the cells, simply overwrite it with the new numbers you wish to test. When entering numbers do not use dollar signs or commas; the template will supply these.
2. **Variable**. This section of the worksheet itemizes your variable costs. Again, simply type over the highlighted areas with your labels and numbers. The worksheet will supply the totals for you.

3. **Margin**. This is the table where gross margin percentage is calculated. Enter the total net revenue for the period of time during which the fixed and variable costs were incurred. The table first determines your gross profit, by subtracting variable costs from sales revenue. Then it calculates your gross margin percentage by dividing gross profit by total sales revenue. The result is a figure that represents the percentage of each sales revenue dollar that is available to cover fixed costs. Once fixed costs have been covered, this same percentage of each sales dollar is available as profit.

4. **Breakeven**. In this section, all of the cost and margin information is pulled together to calculate your breakeven level. By dividing fixed expenses by gross margin percentage, the table calculates the amount of revenue needed to cover fixed costs.

5. **Table**. This section generates the three graphs of the breakeven analysis. To use the table, you need to supply a range of net revenue levels to be tested. You do this by entering a starting value and an incremental value.

Print

A **Print** option in the Main Menu enables you to generate a report that includes fixed and variable costs, gross margin percentage calculation, and the breakeven point itself. This report prints out in compressed type and fits on standard 8.5 × 11 inch paper.

Graph

The **Graph** option calls up the following submenu:

```
Create View
```

Create

The **Create** option facilitates creation of the graphs by automating the entry of a revenue starting point and a revenue increment value. You do not need to use this option to enter these numbers; if you wish, you may proceed directly to the Breakeven Graph Table and enter your numbers in the highlighted cells. Remember, you do not need to type in commas or dollar signs.

View

The View option calls a submenu of three graphs. See the Master Financial Analyzer section for a complete discussion.

```
Net Profit Costs/Revenues ProfitMargin Save Quit
```

Net Profit

The Net Profit graph shows net profit as a straight line function, from less than zero at less than breakeven revenue levels to greater than zero above the breakeven point.

Costs/Revenues

The Costs/Revenues option illustrates the same breakeven point shown in Net Profit, but from a different perspective. It displays fixed costs, total costs, and net revenues. You can thus study both the point at which revenue is adequate to cover fixed costs as well as the point at which total costs and net revenues cross.

Profit Margin

This graph shows the rate at which profitability increases above the breakeven point.

Save

The Save option is included in the graph menu for those users who wish to print out a graph. As previously described, printing a graph in Lotus 1-2-3 is a two-step operation. First, you have to save the graph to a .PIC file for later printing with the Lotus PrintGraph utility. Refer to your Lotus manual for details.

Note: When you select Save from the Graph menu, you will be saving *the graph you have most recently viewed*. Be sure, therefore, to look at the graph you want to save first. Then, select Save. You will be asked to supply a name for your graph. This name can be no more than eight characters long.

Exit

This option allows you to leave the graph menu directly.

File

As in the other templates, the Main Menu File option allows you to save and exit in various ways.

Refer to Figure 19.26 for a diagram of the menu tree for this template and to Figure 19.27 for a diagram of the template layout.

Summary

These four templates can assist you in the analysis of your current business operations and the planning of your future activities. The Breakeven Analyzer and Financial Ratios Calculator templates are handy utilities that speed analysis of information at hand. The Cashflow Template is an important aid to cash forecasting. It is easy to use yet provides a valuable structure for cash planning. The Master Financial Analyzer is the largest and most complex template of the group. It is intended to integrate financial statement information, tracking ongoing operations to study their implications for the future. It may also be used along with the cash flow planner to produce pro forma financial statements for business planning. Together, these templates constitute a useful tool for the analysis and management of a business.

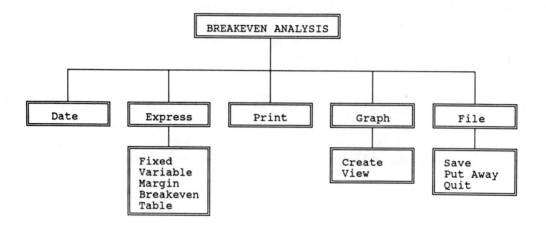

Figure 19.26 *Menu Tree, Breakeven Analyzer.*

Fixed and Variable Costs Calculations
A1..I23

Gross Margin Percentage Calculation
A27..J37

Breakeven Graphs Table
A46..G65

Macros
A70..F160

Figure 19.27 *Template Layout, Breakeven Analyzer.*

APPENDIX A: READY TO RUN MACROS, IN ALPHABETICAL ORDER

Chart A.1, on page 279, lists the macros used in each template.

/M

This macro is used to restart the Main Menu. The name /M is translated by Lotus to mean **ALT-M** and is the only way to start any of the macros from the keyboard.

/0

This is the autoexec macro that is automatically initiated every time the worksheet is loaded. It is used to display the copyright title page and start the Main Menu.

Autoburst

In order to save space on the distribution diskette, the Budget Template is compressed by removing repetitive formulas. The autoburst macro detects that this worksheet is being loaded for the first time, and automatically copies the necessary formulas to the appropriate cells. Once the worksheet is saved and recalled, the program will skip the autoburst and go directly to the Main Menu

Date1

"DATE1" is used to prompt the user to input the date in "mm dd yy" format. It then converts the input to standard Lotus "@date(mm yy dd)" format, checks the validity of the date entered, and places the result in the current cell. DATE1 can also be invoked with the ALT-D initiator in many of the templates.

Edit

The "Edit" macro is used to edit header data. It uses the (?) input format in order to permit the user to retain the current value in a cell by pressing **‹RETURN›**.

Express

The "EXPRESS" macro allows the user to move quickly to various sections of the worksheet by means of the {goto} range name.

Extract

The "EXTRACT" macro (named "Find") uses several techniques to extract data from the main data file. In order to allow different fields of the worksheet to be used as the selection criteria, the macro copies the name of the selected field into the criteria range and then requests the user to input the value for that field. This completes the criteria range. These functions of the macro are completed when you choose an option from the Extract menu. The macro then copies the name of the fields from the main data file using the data range named SOURCE to the target area named TAR. This coincides with the output range defined as OU. The macro next executes a Data Query Extract to select the matching records. Finally, it copies the header information on top of the output labels and copies the selection criteria to the header, thus completing the picture.

File

"FILE" is a menu with three options for saving and exiting the worksheet. The first option, Save, allows the user to save the current worksheet and return to the Main Menu. The second option, Put Away, is a combination of the Save and Quit options, allowing the user to save the current worksheet and exit to DOS. The third option, Quit, allows the user to exit the current worksheet without saving.

Flags

The Loan Amortization template provides the option to calculate the monthly payment only. (This is the Payment option from the Recalc submenu.) Even though a monthly payment or series of payments can be calculated and displayed without generating a new table, data from the previously generated loan table will remain on the screen and printouts. To minimize the possibility of someone printing out the incorrect loan table, the system displays a warning "flag" on the screen and indicates that the tables may not be correct. This flag is displayed whenever the data entry option is used and is cleared when the table is recalculated.

Forecast

The "FORECAST" macro is used in the Sales Forecast Template to generate new data points into the future period. It does this by adding the largest period value to each of the data points entered. These new values are appended to the original set of data points to create a new set twice as large. The sales figures are projected from these data points using the formula calculated for the line fit.

Graph

The "GRAPH" macro is used to generate on-screen bar and line graphs. The key feature of the Graph macro is its ability to automatically size itself to the range of data to be graphed. In addition, the graph option automatically creates a .PIC file for later printing with the PrintGraph function.

Input

This macro uses two levels of logic. The first uses a menu to select between the various methods of data entry. The second recursively moves the cell pointer between the data entry cells. The **Begin** option moves the cell pointer to the first cell and passes control to the recursive continue loop below it for actual data entry, using the "XN" or "XL" input prompt to ensure proper input.

The Continue choice moves the cell pointer to the first blank line after the data and then recursively moves the pointer from cell to cell, automatically formatting the cells as it progresses and inserting a single quote (') label prefix to ensure no cells are left blank. Continue also uses the "XN" and "XL" input to prompt for correct input. When it finishes a line, the macro moves the cell pointer back to the start of the next line and then calls the "CONT" menu, which offers the user the choice of continuing or stopping. The Stop option returns to the Main Menu.

Insert (New Employees)

This macro accomplishes the difficult task of inserting a column for a new employee. It is complicated since it is necessary to ensure that all ranges are properly incremented to include the new employee. By inserting a column, moving the data of an existing employee to the new column and then copying it back to its original position, all formulas, ranges, and formats are properly initialized. This macro finishes by zeroing the numeric fields and erasing the employee name.

Lock-Screen

The "LOCK-SCREEN" macro uses a sleight of hand to accomplish the goal of locking the screen during recalculations in Release 2 while not causing an error in Release 1A. The problem arises in that Release 2 provides two useful macro commands that are not recognized by Release 1A—(window on/off) and (panelon/off). In order to use them, two substitute macros, "SCREENON" and "SCREENOFF" were created. These are initially just named ranges, but become functional when the windowson and panelon commands are copied into the named range. The SCREENON macro is called with an "/xc" command after "windowon" and "panelon" returns control to the calling macro with the "/xr" command. To clear the Lock-Screen for Release 1A, the reverse logic is used and a simple "/xr" is inserted into the SCREENON range, causing the macros to loop back to the calling macros without any effect and without causing an error.

Multiple Month Printouts

Since the Budget template represents many months of data, it is likely that the user will want to print out more than one month's data at a time. The MULTIPLE MONTH PRINTOUT macro uses the following technique to accomplish this. First, it assumes that the user will want the year-to-date and appropriate quarter's printouts as well as the number of months selected. It determines the number of pages to print by multiplying the requested number of months by 1.33333 and truncating the result to an integer. This will produce an additional page for each three months or quarter. By adding 1 to the result, the YTD page is included as well. The number of pages to print is translated into specific print commands by copying the commands one row at a time from column CA to column CB. By properly ordering column CA, the correct choices are obtained. The terminating line from the data range END is copied to the bottom of column CB to conclude the multiple month print command. Finally, we pass control to the newly created macro by /xg to the first line of CB called PRNRNG.

Print

The "PRINT" macros use the ENDUP command to locate the bottom right corner of the data and then the HOME command to describe the entire data area for print. In the case of the selected records, the HOME is followed by an ENDRIGHT to skip to the beginning of the selected records.

Recalc (Loan Amortization Template)

Since the objective of RECALC is to both copy the correct number of rows of formulas and calculate their values for the current principal and interest, it must first determine the correct number of rows. It does this by adding the starting point (row 14) to the total term to arrive at row 62, for a 48-month term, for example. It then knows that it must copy the formulas found in row 14 down to row 62 to produce a complete table. By placing the value 62 within the macro itself via a Data Fill command, the macro is able to (goto) A62. It places a marker in this cell called a "flag" and then moves back to cell A14. It copies row 14 all the way down to the flag using the ENDDOWN command. In this way, it quickly creates an amortization table of the correct size. Finally, it invokes the CALC to recalculate the value of each cell.

Recalc (Sales Forecast Template)

This "RECALC" macro goes beyond the standard Lotus F9 recalc function. It checks the number of data points (period/-sales) entered and automatically adjusts the number of formulas used in the calculation of the slope and intercept. This is required since the "sum of squares" line-fit technique needs the sum of X^2 and Y^2 as well as $X *$

Y. The macro creates columns $X * X$, $X * Y$, and $Y * Y$. The length of the columns must correspond to the length of the input column. The formulas then simply use the @ sum of each column.

Selected Month Printouts

The SELECTED MONTH PRINTOUT macro uses the fact that each of the months is a named data range. It asks the user for the desired month and then prints the range with that name. By using the borders command in the print routine, the labels are automatically included.

Sort

The "SORT" macro is invoked by selecting Sort from the Main Menu. The macro is a function of the standard Data Sort feature of 1-2-3. It is unique, however, in that it autosizes the data and primary key fields to the number of records in the data base. This is accomplished through the use of the (END)(DOWN) macro command. Because of this, no blank entries can occur in the data range, and "empty" cells must have a label prefix to ensure that the range is properly calculated.

Title

Since the user will be moving all over the worksheet to enter and edit data, the system provides a simple way to lock the row titles. The system create a temporary range at the calling location called TEMP, skips to the left margin, locks the titles, returns to the range named TEMP, and finally deletes the range name TEMP. If the user is using Release 2 with the Lock-Screen function invoked, this movement is masked.

What If

This macro allows for quick reinputting of the header data via (?) input, which allows the user to retain the current value by pressing **<RETURN>**.

Zap

This macro erases all payment data by the /RE command.

Chart A.1 *Macros used in Ready-to-Run Templates*

Macro / Chapter	2	3	4	5	6	7	8	9	10	11	12	13	14	15	16	17	18	19
/M	X	X	X	X	X	X	X	X	X	X	X	X	X	X	X	X	X	X
/O	X	X	X	X	X	X	X	X	X	X	X	X	X	X	X	X	X	X
Autoburst													X					
Datel	X	X	X	X	X	X	X	X	X	X				X	X	X	X	X
Delete			X			X	X	X	X					X	X		X	
Edit			X		X	X	X	X	X			X		X	X		X	
Exit	X	X	X	X	X	X	X	X	X	X	X	X	X	X	X	X	X	X
Express								X			X							X
Extract			X			X	X		X					X	X			
Flags	X																	
Forecast													X					
Graph												X	X	X	X	X		X
Input	X	X		X						X	X					X		
Insert										X								
LockScreen	X	X	X		X	X	X		X			X	X	X	X		X	X
Menu	X	X	X	X	X	X	X	X	X	X	X	X	X	X	X	X	X	X
Multiple Month Printouts													X					
Print	X	X	X		X	X	X	X	X	X	X	X	X		X	X	X	X
Recalc (Amort)		X			X													
Recalc (Forecast)													X					
Selected Month Printout													X					
Sort						X	X		X					X	X			
Title			X		X	X	X	X	X	X			X	X	X		X	X
What If					X													
Zap					X													

APPENDIX B: RANGE NAMES USED IN READY-TO-RUN TEMPLATES

Table B.1 *Range Names Used in Loan Amortization Template (Chapter 2)*

Range Name	Cell Address	Type	Function
DATE1	K28..K30	Macro	Date input macro
DY	M27	Data Range	Day used for date input
EDIT	K16	Macro	Data input without prompts
ENTER	K13	Menu	Data entry submenu
EXIT	N52..P54	Menu	Save or Quit worksheet submenu
FLAG1	K24	Data Range	Recalculation flag
FLAG2	K25	Data Range	Recalculation flag
INPUT	K9..L11	Macro	Data input macro with prompts
INTRO	K83..K101	Screen	Introductory screen
LOCK	K44	Macro	Copies screen locking data into screenon & screenoff
LOCK1	M48..M50	Data Range	Screen locking data
LOCKSCREEN	K40..L42	Macro	Screen locking submenu
LOOPSUM	K35	Macro	Looping point for RECALC
MENU	K4..P7	Menu	Master menu
MO	K27	Data Range	Month used for date input
PRINT	K18	Macro	Prints amortization table
PROC	K62..K80	Macro	Processing data screen
RECALC	K32	Macro	Recalculation macro
REMENU	K20..L22	Menu	Recalculation submenu
SCREENOFF	K50	Macro	Turns lockscreen off
SCREENON	K48	Macro	Turns lockscreen on
TERM	C5	Data Range	Term of loan
TLOCK	K58	Macro	Locks worksheet titles
TUNLOCK	K60	Macro	Unlocks worksheet titles
UNLOCK	K46	Macro	Screen unlocking data
UNLOCK1	L48..L50	Data Range	Screen unlocking submenu
WIND	K52..L54	Menu	Title lock menu
YR	L27	Data Range	Year used for date input
\0	K1	Macro	Autoexec macro showing INTRO and starting MENU
\M	K2	Macro	Calling macro for MENU

Table B.2 *Range Names Used in Depreciation Schedule Template (Chapter 3)*

Range Name	Cell Address	Type	Function
DATE1	P55..P57	Macro	Date input macro
DY	R60	Data Range	Day used for date input
EDIT	P15	Macro	Input without prompts
ENTER	P13	Menu	Enter submenu
EXIT	Q19..S21	Menu	Save or Quit worksheet submenu
FACTOR10	T63..W73	Data Range	Table of depreciation factors
FACTOR15	Y42..AB57	Data Range	Table of depreciation factors
FACTOR20	Y60..AB80	Data Range	Table of depreciation factors
FACTOR3	T42..W44	Data Range	Table of depreciation factors
FACTOR5	T47..W51	Data Range	Table of depreciation factors
FACTOR7	T54..W61	Data Range	Table of depreciation factors
FACTORS	K7..N20	Data Range	Table of depreciation factors
FORMULA	P19..P20	Data Range	Formula for calculating sum of the year's digits
INPUT	P9..Q11	Macro	Input with prompts
INTRO	V1..W19	Screen	Introductory screen
LIFE	D5	Data Range	Depreciable life of product in years
LOCK	P46	Macro	Copies screen locking data into screenon & screenoff
LOCK1	R51..R53	Data Range	Screen locking data
LOCKSCREEN	P42..Q44	Menu	Screen locking submenu
MENU	P4..S6	Menu	Master menu
MO	Q60	Data Range	Month used for date input
PRINT	P17	Macro	Print macro
PROC	V20..W38	Screen	Processing data screen
PURCHASE	D4	Data Range	Purchase price
RECALC	P23..P36	Macro	Recalc macro
SCREENOFF	P53	Macro	Turns lockscreen off
SCREENON	P51	Macro	Turns lockscreen on
SUMDIG	P21	Data Range	Counter for sum of the years digits
UNLOCK	P48	Macro	Copies screen unlocking data into screenon & screenoff
UNLOCK1	Q51..253	Data Range	Screen unlocking data
XGOTO	P26	Data Range	Target cell for self altering macro
YR	P60	Data Range	Year used for date input
\0	P1	Macro	Autoexec macro showing INTRO and starting MENU
\M	P2	Macro	Calling macro for MENU

Table B.3 *Range Names Used in Capital Asset Inventory Template (Chapter 4)*

Range Name	Cell Address	Type	Function
BEGIN	L34	Macro	Moves to starting entry for data entry
CONT	O38	Data Range	Input range for "continue data input?" response
CONTINUE	L35	Macro	Recursively cycles through input cells for data entry
CRIT	L9..L10	Data Range	Criteria range for data selection
DATE1	L83	Macro	Date input macro
DEL1	L77	Macro	Deletes data
DELETE	L73..L75	Menu	Deletion submenu
DY	R80	Data Range	Day used for date input
ENTER	L30..N32	Menu	Data entry submenu
EXIT	L79..N81	Menu	Save or Quit worksheet submenu
FIND	L40..L41	Macro	Executes data query extract
INP	A5..I1000	Data Range	Input range for find
INTRO	L87..M105	Screen	Introductory screen
LOCK	L59	Macro	Copies screen locking data into screenon and screenoff
LOCK1	N64..N66	Data Range	Screen locking data
LOCKSCREEN	L55..M57	Macro	Screen locking submenu
MENU	L25..O27	Menu	Master menu
MO	Q80	Data Range	Month used for date input
OU	S10..AC10	Data Range	Output range for find
PRINT	L43..M45	Menu	Print submenu
PRINTALL	L47..L49	Macro	Prints all data
PRINTSEL	L51..L53	Macro	Prints selected data
PROC	L108..L126	Screen	Processing data screen
SCREENOFF	L66	Macro	Turns lockscreen off
SCREENON	L64	Macro	Turns lockscreen on
SOURCE	A5..I5	Data Range	Source of data name for output range OU
TAR	S10	Daat Range	Location to which data names are copied from SOURCE
TLOCK	O68	Macro	Locks titles
TUNLOCK	O70	Macro	Unlocks titles
UNLOCK	L61	Macro	Copies screen unlocking data into screenon and screenoff
UNLOCK1	M64..M66	Data Range	Screen locking data
WIND	L68..M70	Macro	Title locking submenu
YR	P80	Data Range	Year used for data input
\0	L22	Macro	Autoexec macro showing INTRO and starting MENU
\M	L23	Macro	Calling macro for MENU

Table B.4 *Range Names Used in Net Present Value—Continuous Flow Template (Chapter5)*

Range Name	Cell Address	Type	Function
DATE1	G18..G20	Macro	Date input macro
DY	I23	Data Range	Day used for date input
EDIT	G16	Data Range	Data input without prompts
ENTER	G13..G14	Menu	Data input menu
EXIT	G25..I27	Menu	Save or Quit worksheet submenu
INPUT	G9..H11	Macro	Data input with prompts
INTRO	G30..H48	Screen	Introductory Screen
MENU	G4..I6	Menu	Master menu
MO	H23	Data Range	Month used for date input
YR	G23	Data Range	Year for date input
\0	G1	Macro	Autoexec macro showing INTRO and starting MENU
\M	G2	Macro	Calling macro for MENU

Table B.5 *Range Names Used in Net Present Value—Variable Flow Template (Chapter 6)*

Range Name	Cell Address	Type	Function
BEGIN	G17..G21	Macro	Moves to starting record for data entry
CONT	I21	Data Range	Input range for "continue data input?" response
CONTINUE	G19	Macro	Recursively cycles through input cells for data entry
DATE1	G23..G25	Macro	Data input macro
DY	I28	Data Range	Day used for date input
ENTER	G12..I14	Menu	Data entry submenu
EXIT	G30..I32	Menu	Save or Quit worksheet submenu
INTRO	G45..K64	Screen	Introductory screen
MENU	G5..L7	Menu	Master menu
MO	H28	Data Range	Month used for date input
PRINT	G10	Macro	Worksheet print macro
TLOCK	J40	Macro	Locks worksheet titles
TUNLOCK	J42	Macro	Unlocks worksheet titles
WHATIF	G38	Macro	Data entry macro for what-if analysis
WIND	G40..H43	Menu	Title lock submenu
YR	G28	Data Range	Year used for date input
ZAP	G34..H36	Macro	Clears payment section of worksheet
\0	G2	Macro	Autoexec macro showing INTRO and starting MENU
\M	G3	Macro	Calling macro for MENU

Table B.6 *Range Names Used in the Time Billing Template (Chapter 7)*

Range Name	Cell Address	Type	Function
BEGIN	U97	Macro	Moves to starting entry for data entry
CLIENT	U56	Macro	Sort by client
CONT	W102	Data Range	Input range for "continue data input?" response
CONTINUE	U98	Macro	Recursively cycles through input cells for data entry
CRIT	W9..W10	Data Range	Criteria range for find
DATA	A1..R12	Data Range	Header data
DATE	U54	Macro	Sort by date
DATE1	U104..U106	Macro	Date input macro
DEL1	U95	Macro	Deletes specified range
DELETE	U91..U93	Menu	Deletion submenu
DY	X108	Data Range	Day used for date input
EMPLOYEE	U60	Macro	Sort by employee
ENTER	U29..V31	Menu	Data entry submenu
EXIT	X36..Z38	Menu	Save or Quit worksheet submenu
FIND	U70..U71	Macro	Executes data query extract
INP	A5..R1000	Macro	Input range for find
INTRO	T112..U130	Screen	Introductory screen
LOCK	U77	Macro	Copies screen locking data into screenon & screenoff
LOCK1	W82..W84	Data Range	Screen locking data
LOCKSCREEN	U73..V75	Macro	Screen locking submenu
MENU	T24..X26	Menu	Master menu
MO	W108	Data Range	Month used for date input
NUMBER	U52	Macro	Sorts by number
OU	AB10..AS10	Data Range	Output range for find
PRINT	U36..V38	Menu	Print submenu
PRINTALL	U40..U42	Macro	Prints all data
PRINTSEL	U44..U46	Macro	Prints selected data
PROC	T131..T150	Screen	Processing data screen
PROJECT	U58	Macro	Sort by project
SCREENOFF	U84	Macro	Turns lockscreen off
SCREENON	U82	Macro	Turns lockscreen on
SELECT	U65..X68	Menu	Find submenu
SORT	U48..Z50	Menu	Sort submenu
SOURCE	A5..R5	Data Range	Source of data names for output range OU
TAR	AB10	Data Range	Location to which data names are copied from SOURCE
TASK	U62	Macro	Sort by task
TLOCK	X86	Macro	Lock title
TUNLOCK	X88	Macro	Unlock title
UNLOCK	U79	Macro	Copies screen unlocking data into screenon & screenoff

Table B.6 *(continued)*.

Range Name	Cell Address	Type	Function
UNLOCK1	V82..V84	Data Range	Screen unlocking data
WIND	U86..V88	Menu	Title lock submenu
YR	V108	Data Range	Year used for date input
\0	U21	Macro	Autoexec macro showing INTRO and starting MENU
\M	U22	Macro	Calling macro for MENU

Table B.7 *Range Names Used in the Mileage Template (Chapter 8)*

Range Name	Cell Address	Type	Function
BEGIN	N33	Macro	Moves to starting entry for data entry
CLIENT	N56	Macro	Sorts data in client order
CODE	N58	Macro	Sorts data in code order
CONT	Q38	Data Range	Input range for "continue data input?" response
CONTINUE	N34	Macro	Recursively cycles through input cells for data entry
CRIT	P9..P10	Data Range	Criteria range for data selection
DATE	N54	Macro	Sorts data in date order
DATE1	N40..N42	Macro	Date input macro
DEL1	N74	Macro	Deletes data by row
DELETE	N70..N72	Menu	Deletion submenu
DESTIN	N52	Macro	Sorts data in destination order
DY	Q45	Data Range	Day used for date input
ENTER	N29..P31	Menu	Data entry submenu
EXIT	Q96..S98	Menu	Save or Quit worksheet submenu
FIND	N60..N61	Macro	Executes data query find
INP	A5..I1009	Macro	Input range for find
INTRO	M105	Screen	Introductory screen
LOCK	N86	Macro	Copies screen locking data into screenon and screenoff
LOCK1	P91..P93	Macro	Screen locking data
LOCKSCREEN	N82..O84	Menu	Screen locking submenu
MENU	M24..Q26	Menu	Master menu
MO	P45	Data Range	Month used for date input
OU	U10..AN10	Data Range	Output range for find
PRINT	N96..O98	Menu	Print submenu
PRINTALL	N100..N101	Macro	Prints all data
PRINTSEL	N103..N104	Macro	Prints selected data
PROC	M124..M143	Screen	Processing data screen
SCREENOFF	N93	Macro	Turns lockscreen off
SCREENON	N91	Macro	Turns lockscreen on

Table B.7 *(continued).*

Range Name	Cell Address	Type	Function
SELECT	N64..P67	Macro	Find submenu
SORT	N48..S50	Macro	Sort submenu
SOURCE	A5..I5	Macro	Source of data names for output range OU
TAR	U10	Macro	Location to which data names are copied from SOURCE
TLOCK	Q76	Macro	Locks titles
TUNLOCK	Q78	Macro	Unlocks titles
UNLOCK	N88	Macro	Copies screen unlocking data into screenon and screenoff
UNLOCK1	O91..O93	Macro	Screen unlocking data
WIND	N76..O78	Menu	Title locking submenu
YR	O45	Data Range	Year used for date input
\0	N21	Macro	Autoexec macro showing INTRO and starting MENU
\M	N22	Macro	Calling macro for MENU

Table B.8 *Range Names Used in the Travel Expense Template (Chapter 9)*

Range Name	Cell Address	Type	Function
ADVANCE	AD38	Macro	Data entry for cash advance data
BEGIN	AD13	Macro	Moves to starting record for data
CONT	AF20	Data Range	Input range for "continue data input?" response
CONTINUE	AD14	Macro	Recursively cycles through input cells for data input
DATE1	AD21..AD23	Macro	Date input macro
DEL1	AD36	Macro	Deletes data
DELETE	AD32..AD34	Menu	Delete submenu
DY	AG25	Data Range	Day used for date input
ENTER	AD9..AI11	Menu	Data entry submenu
EXIT	AD66..AF68	Menu	Save or Quit worksheet submenu
INTRO	AD46..AE64	Screen	Introductory screen
JUMP	AD41..AF43	Macro	Go to submenu
MENU	AD4..AG6	Menu	Master menu
MO	AF25	Data Range	Month used for date input
TLOCK	AG26	Macro	Locks titles
TUNLOCK	AG28	Macro	Unlocks titles
WIND	AD26..AE28	Macro	Title lock submenu
YR	AE25	Data Range	Year used for date input
\0	AD1	Macro	Autoexec macro showing INTRO and starting MENU
\M	AD2	Macro	Calling macro for MENU

Table B.9 *Range Names Used in the 1099 Template (Chapter 10)*

Range Name	Cell Address	Type	Function
BEGIN	H34	Macro	Moves to starting record for data entry
CODE	H55	Macro	Sorts data by code
CONT	R40	Data Range	Input range for "continue data input?" response
CONTINUE	H35	Data Range	Recursively cycles through input
CRIT	J9..J10	Data Range	Criteria range for FIND
CT	K43	Data Range	Input range for "continue data input?" response
DATE	H57	Macro	Sorts data by date
DEL1	H96	Macro	Deletes data
DELETE	H92..H94	Menu	Deletion submenu
DY	J43	Data Range	Day used for date input
ENTER	H29..J31	Menu	Data entry submenu
EXIT	K72	Menu	Save or Quit worksheet submenu
FIND	H61..H62	Macro	Execute data query extract
INP	A5..E999	Data Range	Input range for FIND
INTRO	G101..H119	Screen	Introductory screen
LOCK	H77	Macro	Copies screen locking data into screen on and screen off
LOCK1	J82..J84	Macro	Screen locking data into screen on and screen off
LOCKSCREEN	H72..I74	Menu	Screen locking submenu
MENU	G24..K26	Menu	Master menu
MO	I43	Data Range	Month used for data input
OU	O10..AF10	Data Range	Output range for FIND
PRINT	L65..M67	Menu	Print submenu
PRINTALL	H44..H45	Macro	Prints all data
PRINTSEL	H47..H48	Macro	Prints selected data
PROC	G120..G138	Screen	Processing data screen
SCREENOFF	H84	Macro	Turns Lockscreen off
SCREENON	H82	Macro	Turns Lockscreen on
SELECT	H65..I68	Menu	Find submenu
SORT	H50..M53	Menu	Sort submenu
SOURCE	A5..E5	Data Range	Source of data names for output
TAR	O10	Data Range	Location to which data names are copied from SOURCE
TLOCK	K86	Macro	Locks titles
TUNLOCK	K88	Macro	Unlocks titles
UNLOCK	H79	Macro	Copies screen unlocking data into screen on and screen off
UNLOCK1	I82..I84	Data Range	Screen unlocking data
VENDOR	H59	Macro	Sorts data by Vendor
WIND	H86..I88	Menu	Title locking submenu
YR	H43	Data Range	Year used for date input
\0	H21	Macro	Autoexec macro showing INTRO and starting MENU
\M	H22	Macro	Calling macro for MENU

Table B.10 *Range Names Used in Commission Calculator Template (Chapter 11)*

Range Name	Cell Address	Type	Function
DATE1	O38..O40	Macro	Date input macro
DY	T41	Data Range	Day used for date input
EDIT	O51..O53	Macro	Data input without prompts
ENTER	O6	Menu	Data entry submenu
EXIT	O10..Q12	Menu	Save or Quit worksheet submenu
INIT	O29..O35	Macro	Data input with prompts
INPUT1	O55..P57	Macro	Initialization submenu
INSERT	O19	Macro	Column insertion macro
INTRO	O59..Q78	Screen	Introductory screen
MENU	O1..Q3	Menu	Master menu
MO	S41	Data Range	Month used for date input
NEW	O17	Macro	Column insertion macro
POSITION	O25..O27	Menu	Column position menu
PRINT	O8	Macro	Print worksheet
SAVE	O11	Macro	Save worksheet
TLOCK	O46	Macro	Locks titles
TUNLOCK	O48	Macro	Unlocks titles
WIND	O42..P44	Menu	Title locking submenu
YR	R41	Data Range	Year used for date input
\0	O14	Macro	Autoexec macro showing INTRO and starting MENU
\M	O15	Macro	Calling macro for MENU

Table B.11 *Range Names Used in the Direct Mail Template (Chapter 12)*

Range Name	Cell Address	Type	Function
AUTOBURST	H100..H103	Macro	Copies repetitive formulas into cells first time
EXIT	C134..E136	Menu	Save or Quit worksheet submenu
EXPENSES	A4..F27	Data range	Used for printing
FIRST	H105	Data Range	Flag for first time , used for AUTOBURST
GRAPH	H96	Macro	Graphs profit data
GROSS REVENU	A31..G59	Data Range	Used for printing
INTRO	H110..M127	Screen	Introductory screen
LOCMENU	B114..D123	Menu	Jump to specified location
MENU	C109	Menu	Master Menu
NET REVENUE	A62..G89	Data Range	Used for printing
PRINTMENU	C125..D132	Menu	Print Submenu
REVENUES	A31..G89	Data Range	Used for printing
\0	B105..B106	Macro	Autoexe macro showing INTRO and starting MENU
\M	B107	Macro	Calling macro for MENU

Table B.12 *Range Names Used in Sales Forecast Template (Chapter 13)*

Range Name	Cell Address	Type	Function
BEGIN	Q13	Macro	Moves to starting entry for data entry
CONT	T18	Data Range	Input range for "continue data input?" response
CONTINUE	Q14	Macro	Recursively cycles through input cells for data entry
ENTER	Q9..S11	Menu	Data entry submenu
EXIT	T32..V34	Menu	Save or Quit worksheet submenu
FLAG1	S21	Data range	Recalc required flag
FLAG2	S22	Data range	Clear recalc flag
FORECAST	Q47..Q52	Macro	Forecasts fitted line to twice the input X range
FORMULA	Q23	Data range	Formula used to forecast data
GRAPHDATA	Q32..Q39	Macro	Graph actual data and fitted line
GRAPHFORE	Q56..Q62	Macro	Graphs forecast
GRAPHMENU	Q17..R19	Menu	Graph menu
INTRO	Q78..R96	Screen	Introductory screen
LOCK	Q68	Macro	Copies screen locking data into screenon & screenoff
LOCK1	S73..S75	Data range	Screen locking data
LOCKSCREEN	Q64..R66	Menu	Screen locking submenu
MAXIMUM	Q21	Macro	Last number input in X range
MENU	Q4..X6	Menu	Master menu
PRINT	Q42..Q43	Macro	Print actual and forecast data
PROC	Q98..R116	Screen	Processing data screen
RECALC	Q25..Q30	Macro	Recalculate line fit using auto-scaling feature
SCREENOFF	Q75	Macro	Turns lockscreen off
SCREENON	Q73	Macro	Turns lockscreen on
SORT	Q45	Macro	Sort data input into ascending X order
UNLOCK	Q70	Macro	Copies screen unlocking data into screenon & screenoff
UNLOCK1	R73..R75	Data range	Screen unlocking data
\0	Q1	Macro	Autoexec macro showing INTRO and starting MENU
\M	Q2	Macro	Calling macro for MENU

Table B.13 *Range Names Used in the Budget Template (Chapter 14)*

Range Name	Cell Address	Type	Function
APR	R3..T59	Data Range	Print range for month
AUG	AH3..AJ59	Data Range	Print range for month
CNT1	CF48	Data Range	Counter used to copy data into blank months
DEC	AX3..AZ59	Data Range	Print range for month
END	BY3	Macro	Terminal macro used to end multiple print
ENTER	BW32	Menu	Enter submenu
EXIT	BZ27..CB29	Menu	Save or Quit worksheet submenu
FEB	J3..L59	Data Range	Print range for month
FIRST	BY2	Data range	Flag used to determine if first time use
FLAG	CF49	Data range	Flag showing expansion in process
GRAPH	CA46..CC48	Macro	Graphs monthly summary
INIT	CF51	Macro	Initiating macro used to expand spreadsheet and fill in formulas
INTRO	BX58..CC75	Screen	Introductory screen
INTRO1	BX78..CC95	Screen	First time use introductory screen
JAN	F3..H59	Data Range	Print range for month
JUL	AD3..AF59	Data Range	Print range for month
JUN	Z3..AB59	Data Range	Print range for month
LOCK	BW49	Macro	Copies screen locking data into screenon & screenoff
LOCK1	BY54..BY56	Data Range	Screen locking data
LOCKSCREEN	BW45..BX47	Menu	Screen locking submenu
LOOP	BW16	Macro	Looping point for multiple month printout macro
LP1	CF54	Macro	Looping point for INIT initializing macro
MAR	N3..P59	Data Range	Print range for month
MAY	V3..X59	Data Range	Print range for month
MENU	BW40..CB43	Menu	Master menu
MONTH	BY1	Data Range	Counter for multiple month printout macro
MONTHINP	CF13	Data Range	Input range for number of month to print
MULTIPLE	BW12	Macro	Multiple month printout macro
NOV	AT3..AV59	Data Range	Print range for month
OCT	AP3..AR59	Data Range	Print range for month
PRINTMENU	BW23..BY25	Menu	Print submenu
PRNRNG	CB1..CB18	Macro	Dynamic range used to determine which months are printed my MULTIPLE
QRT1	BF3..BH59	Data Quarter	Print range for month
QRT2	BJ3..BL59	Data Quarter	Print range for quarter
QRT3	BN3..BP59	Data Quarter	Print range for quarter
QRT4	BR3..BT59	Data Quarter	Print range for quarter

Table B.13 *(continued).*

Range Name	Cell Address	Type	Function
SCREENOFF	BW56	Macro	Turns Lockscreen off
SCREENON	BW54	Macro	Turns lockscreen on
SEP	AL3..AN59	Data Range	Print range for month
SINGLE	BW21	Macro	Single month print macro
SUMM	CJ1..CS33	Data Range	Monthly summary data used for print and graph
SUMMARY	BW27		
TLOCK	BZ34	Macro	Locks titles macro
TUNLOCK	BZ36	Macro	Unlocks titles macro
UNLOCK	BW51	Macro	Copies screen unlocking data to screenon & screenoff
UNLOCK1	BX54..BX56	Data Range	Screen unlocking data
VER	CA88	Data Range	Input range for Lotus release used to lockscreen for release 2 on start up
WIND	BW34..BX36	Macro	Screen locking submenu
YTD	BB3..BD59	Data Quarter	Print range for quarter
\0	BW5	Macro	Autoexec macro showing INTRO(1) and branching to INIT or MENU
\M	BW8	Macro	Calling macro for MENU

Table B.14 *Range Names Used in the Accounts Receivable Template (Chapter 15)*

Range Name	Cell Address	Type	Function
AGE	T81..V83	Menu	Aged report selection menu
AGEDALL	T6..Y24	Screen	Display screen for all aged
AGEDNAME	T28..Y46	Screen	Display screen for selected aged
BEGIN	M34	Macro	Moves to starting entry for data entry
CLIENT	T107	Macro	Sorts data in client order
CLNT	M10	Data Range	Criteria range for selection
CONT	P40	Data Range	Input range for "continue data input?" response
CONTINUE	M35	Macro	Recursively cycles cursor through input cells for data entry
CRIT	M9..M10	Data Range	Criteria range for selection
CRIT120	U56..V57	Data Range	Criteria range for @DSUM used in aging report
CRIT30	S51..T52	Data Range	Criteria range for @DSUM used in aging report
CRIT60	U51..V52	Data Range	Criteria range for @DSUM used in aging report
CRIT90	S56..T57	Data Range	Criteria range for @DSUM used in aging report

Table B.14 *(continued)*.

Range Name	Cell Address	Type	Function
DATE	T111	Macro	Sorts data in date order
DATE1	M41..M43	Macro	Date input macro
DEL1	M82	Macro	Deletes data
DELETE	M78..M80	Menu	Deletion submenu
DY	046	Data Range	Day used for date input
ENTER	M30..O32	Macro	Data entry submenu
EXIT	P44..R46	Menu	Save or Quit worksheet submenu
FIND	M48..M49	Macro	Executes data query extract
INP	A10..J1000	Data Range	Input range for find
INTRO	L84..M102	Screen	Introductory screen
LOCK	T92	Macro	Copies screen locking data into screenon & screenoff
LOCK1	V97..V99	Data Range	Screen locking data
LOCKSCREEN	T88..U90	Macro	Screen locking submenu
MENU	K25..R27	Macro	Master menu
MO	N46	Data Range	Month used for date input
NCRIT120	T76..V77	Data Range	Criteria range for @DSUM used in aging report
NCRIT30	T61..V62	Data Range	Criteria range for @DSUM used in aging report
NCRIT60	T66..V67	Data Range	Criteria range for @DSUM used in aging report
NCRIT90	T71..V72	Data Range	Criteria range for @DSUM used in aging report
NUMBER	T109	Macro	Sorts data in numerical order
OPEN	M68..M69	Macro	Selects entries based on OPEN status
OPEN1	M75..M76	Data Range	Criteria range for OPEN selection
OU	AA10..AJ10	Data Range	Output range
PAID	M71..M72	Macro	Selects entries based on PAID status
PAID1	N75..N76	Data Range	Criteria range for PAID selection
PRINT	M52..N54	Menu	Print Submenu
PRINT1	Q64..R66	Menu	Print Submenu
PRINT2	O56..P58	Macro	Print Submenu
PRINTALL	M56..M58	Macro	Prints all data
PRINTSEL	M60..M62	Macro	Prints selected entries
PROC	L105..M123	Screen	Processing data screen
SCREENOFF	T99	Macro	Turns Lockscreen off
SCREENON	T97	Macro	Turns Lockscreen on
SELECT	M64..O66	Menu	Find submenu
SORT	T103..V105	Menu	Sort submenu
SOURCE	A5..J5	Data Range	Source of data names for output range OU
TAR	AA10	Data Range	Location to which data names are copied from SOURCE
TLOCK	W113	Macro	Locks titles
TUNLOCK	W115	Macro	Unlocks titles

Table B.14 *(continued)*.

Range Name	Cell Address	Type	Function
UNLOCK	T94	Macro	Copies screen unlocking data into screenon & screenoff
UNLOCK1	U97..U99	Data Range	Screen unlocking data
WIND	T113..U115	Menu	Title locking submenu
YR	M46	Data Range	Year used for date input
\0	M22	Macro	Autoexec macro showing INTRO and starting MENU
\M	M23	Macro	Calling macro for MENU

Table B.15 *Range Names Used in the Accounts Payable Template (Chapter 16)*

Range Name	Cell Address	Type	Function
AGE	T81..V83	Menu	Aged report selection menu
AGEDALL	T6..Y24	Screen	Display screen for all aged
AGEDNAME	T28..Y46	Screen	Display screen for selected aged
BEGIN	M34	Macro	Moves to starting entry for data entry
CLIENT	T107	Macro	Sorts data in client order
CLNT	M10	Data Range	Criteria range for selection
CONTINUE	M35	Macro	Recursively cycles cursor through input cells for data entry
CRIT	M9..M10	Data Range	Criteria range for selection
CRIT120	V56..W57	Data Range	Criteria range for @DSUM used in aging report
CRIT30	S51..T52	Data Range	Criteria range for @DSUM used in aging report
CRIT60	V51..W52	Data Range	Criteria range for @DSUM used in aging report
CRIT90	S56..T57	Data Range	Criteria range for @DSUM used in aging report
DATE	T111	Macro	Sorts data in date order
DATE1	M41	Macro	Date input macro
DEL1	M82	Macro	Deletes data
DELETE	M79..M80	Menu	Deletion submenu
DY	O46	Data Range	Day used for date input
ENTER	M30..O32	Macro	Data entry submenu
EXIT	O74..Q76	Menu	Save or Quit worksheet submenu
FIND	M48..M49	Macro	Executes data query extract
FIND 120	M97..M98	Macro	Executes data query extract
FIND 30	M88..M89	Macro	Executes data query extract
FIND 60	M91..M92	Macro	Executes data query extract
FIND 90	M94..M95	Macro	Executes data query extract

Table B.15 *(continued).*

Range Name	Cell Address	Type	Function
FINDAGE	M84..P86	Macro	Executes data query extract
INP	A10..J1000	Data Range	Input range for find
INTRO	L101..Q127	Screen	Introductory screen
LOCK	T92	Macro	Copies screen locking data into screenon & screenoff
LOCK1	V97..V99	Data Range	Screen locking data
LOCKSCREEN	T88..U90	Macro	Screen locking submenu
MENU	K25..R27	Macro	Master menu
MO	N46	Data Range	Month used for date input
NCRIT120	T76..V77	Data Range	Criteria range for @DSUM used in aging report
NCRIT30	T61..V62	Data Range	Criteria range for @DSUM used in aging report
NCRIT60	T66..V67	Data Range	Criteria range for @DSUM used in aging report
NCRIT90	T71..V72	Data Range	Criteria range for @DSUM used in aging report
OPEN	M68..M69	Macro	Selects entries based on OPEN status
OPEN1	M75..M76	Data Range	Criteria range for OPEN selection
OU	AA10..AJ10	Data Range	Output range
PAID	M71..M72	Macro	Selects entries based on PAID status
PAID1	N75..N76	Data Range	Criteria range for PAID selection
PRINT	M52..N54	Menu	Print Submenu
PRINT1	P44..Q46	Menu	Print Submenu
PRINT2	O56..P58	Macro	Print Submenu
PRINTALL	M56..M58	Macro	Prints all data
PRINTSEL	M60..M62	Macro	Prints selected entries
PROC	L122..M140	Screen	Processing data screen
SCREENOFF	T99	Macro	Turns Lockscreen off
SCREENON	T97	Macro	Turns Lockscreen on
SELECT	M64..O66	Menu	Find submenu
SORT	T103..V105	Menu	Sort submenu
SOURCE	A5..J5	Data Range	Source of data names for output range OU
TAR	AA10	Data Range	Location to which data names are copied from SOURCE
TLOCK	W113	Macro	Locks titles
TUNLOCK	W115	Macro	Unlocks titles
UNLOCK	T94	Macro	Copies screen unlocking data into screenon & screenoff
UNLOCK1	U97..U99	Data Range	Screen unlocking data
WIND	T113..U115	Menu	Title locking submenu
YR	M46	Data Range	Year used for date input
\0	M22	Macro	Autoexec macro showing INTRO and starting MENU
\M	M23	Macro	Calling macro for MENU

Table B.16 *Range Names Used in the Gantt Chart (Chapter 17)*

Range Name	Cell Address	Type	Function
BEGIN	AL16	Macro	Data entry macro from beginning
CONTINUE	AL18	Macro	Continuing data entry macro
DATE1	AL21..AM24	Macro	Date input macro
DY	AP20	Data Range	Day used for data input
ENTER	AL12..AN14	Menu	Enter submenu
EXIT	AL28..AN30	Menu	Save or Quit worksheet menu
INTRO	AL32..AQ50	Screen	Introductory screen
MENU	AL6..AN8	Menu	Master menu
MO	AO20	Data Range	Month used for date input
PRINT	AL26	Macro	Print macro
TEMP	AQ24	Data Range	Input range for "continue data input?" response
YR	AN20	Data Range	Year used for date input
\0	AL3	Macro	Autoexec macro showing INTRO and starting MENU
\M	AL4	Macro	Calling macro for MENU

Table B.17 *Range Names Used in Portfolio Valuation Template (Chapter 18)*

Range Name	Cell Address	Type	Function
BEGIN	M17	Macro	Moves to starting entry for data entry
CONT	P22	Data Range	Input range for "continue data input?" response
CONTINUE	M19	Macro	Recursively cycles through the input cells for data entry
DATE1	M50..M52	Macro	Date input macro
DEL1	M48	Macro	Deletes data
DELETE	M44..M46	Menu	Deletion menu
DY	Q53	Data Range	Day used for date input
ENTER	M11..QN14	Menu	Data entry submenu
EXIT	M54..O56	Menu	Save or Quit worksheet submenu
INTRO	M58..Q76	Screen	Introductory screen
LOCK	M35	Macro	Copies screen locking data to screenon and screenoff
LOCK1	O40..042	Data Range	Screen locking data
LOCKSCREEN	M31..N33	Macro	Screen locking submenu
MENU	M7..O8	Menu	Master menu
MO	P53	Data Range	Month used for date input
SCREENOFF	M42	Macro	Turns lockscreen off
SCREENON	M40	Macro	Turns lockscreen on
TLOCK	P26	Macro	Locks titles
TUNLOCK	P28	Macro	Unlocks titles

Table B.17 *(continued).*

Range Name	Cell Address	Type	Function
ULP	M24	Macro	Looping point for update macro
UNLOCK	M37	Macro	Copies screen unlocking data to screenon and screenoff
UNLOCK1	N40..N42	Data Range	Screen unlocking data
UPDATE	M23	Macro	Recursively cycles throughout current market price data cells for price updates
WIND	M26..N28	Menu	Title locking submenu
YR	O53	Data Range	Year used for date input
\0	M3	Macro	Autoexec macro showing INTRO and starting MENU
\M	M4	Macro	Calling macro for MENU

Index

ABOUT THE AUTHORS

Steven J. Bennett is a professional writer and computer consultant. Educated at the University of Rochester and Harvard University, he has written numerous technical publications and is the author of *Playing Hardball with Soft Skills* (Bantam). He is also the coauthor of *dBase III Plus™ to Go* (Brady), *The HAL Handbook* (Brady), *Executive Chess* (New American Library), and *Inner Lightning* (New American Library).

Peter G. Randall is president of Ariel Enterprises, Inc., a software development and consulting firm. Prior to the start-up of Ariel, he served as president of ESIS International, an international marketing subsidiary of Cigna Corporation. Mr. Randall, who holds a BSE degree in systems engineering from Princeton Univerisity and an MBA degree from Wharton School of Business (specializing in operations management), has written more than 30 major applications programs for use in business. He is the coauthor of *dBASE III Plus™ to Go* and *The HAL Handbook (Brady)*.

Alan P. Wichlei is a business consultant with nationwide experience teaching and designing spreadsheet application programs. He holds degrees from both Harvard and Yale and was for 10 years the executive director of a multistate health services agency in New England. During that time he supervised the introduction of microcomputer managed operations into the organization, both designing major Lotus applications programs and training staff in their use.

Important! Read Before Opening Sealed Diskette
END USER LICENSE AGREEMENT

The software in this package is provided to You on the condition that You agree with SIMON & SCHUSTER, INC. ("S&S") to the terms and conditions set forth below. **Read this End User License Agreement carefully. You will be bound by the terms of this agreement if you open the sealed diskette.** If You do not agree to the terms contained in this End User License Agreement, return the entire product, along with your receipt, to *Brady, Simon & Schuster, Inc., One Gulf + Western Plaza, New York, NY 10023, Attn: Refunds*, and your purchase price will be refunded.

S&S grants, and You hereby accept, a personal, nonexclusive license to use the software program and associated documentation in this package, or any part of it ("Licensed Product"), subject to the following terms and conditions:

1. License

The license granted to You hereunder ..., pursuant to a separate End User License Agreement ...

2. Term

This End User License Agreement is ... terminated. You may terminate this End User License ... made by You or received by You. Your right to use of ... of this End User License Agreement. Upon such ter...

3. Restriction Against Tra...

This End User License Agreement ... o another party unless the other party agrees to acc... duct, You must at the same time either transfer all ... ot transferred.

4. Restrictions Against Co...

The Licensed Product is copyrighted ... ake one copy for backup purposes provided You rep... is in violation of this Agreement and may also const... minal suit. **You may not use, transfer, mod... xcept as expressly permitted in this E...**

5. Protection and Securit...

You shall take all reasonable steps ... to it and that no unauthorized copy of any part of i...

6. Limited Warranty

If You are the original consumer pu... nclude problems relating to the nature or operation o... refund your purchase price) within 30 days followi... replace any such defective diskette upon payment o... anty Registration Card has been filed within 30 days... ompanied by the original defective diskette and pro... refund your purchase price) based on claims of d...

The software program ... implied, including but not limited to ... se. The entire risk as to the quality ... ective, You (and not S&S) assume t...

Some states do not all... pply to You. This warrant gives You s... ate to state.

S&S does not warrant ... or that the operation of the program ... en involved in the creation or produc... al or consequential damages, wheth... arranty, and S&S shall have no resp... r, at its option, provide a refund o...

No sales personnel or other re... make any warranties with respect to the diske... **ot constitute warranties,** shall not be relie... mbodied in this Agreement.

7. General

If any provision of this End User ... deemed omitted and the remaining provisions sh... trued in accordance with the laws of the State ...

1-2-3® Ready-to-Run!

REPLACEMENT ORDER FORM

Please use this form when ordering a replacement for a defective diskette.

A. If Ordering within Thirty Days of Purchase
If a diskette is reported defective within thirty days of purchase, a replacement diskette will be provided free of charge. *This card must be totally filled out and accompanied by the defective diskette and a copy of the dated sales receipt.* In addition, please complete and return the Limited Warranty Registration Card.

B. If Ordering after Thirty Days of Purchase but within One Year
If a diskette is reported defective after thirty days but within one year of purchase and the Warranty Registration Card has been properly filed, a replacement diskette will be provided to you for a nominal fee of $5.00 (send check or money order only). *This card must totally filled out and accompanied by the defective diskette, a copy of the dated sales receipt, and a $5.00 check or money order made payable to Simon & Schuster, Inc.*

NAME _____ PHONE NUMBER (_____) _____

ADDRESS _____

CITY _____ STATE _____ ZIP _____

PURCHASE DATE _____

PURCHASE PRICE _____

COMPUTER BRAND & MODEL _____

Please send all requests to: Technical Support Center, Simon & Schuster, Inc., Route 9W, Englewood Cliffs, NJ 07632; ATTN: Replacements

NOTE: Simon & Schuster reserves the right, at its option, to refund your purchase price in lieu of providing a replacement diskette.

0–13–93988–6

1-2-3® Ready-to-Run!

LIMITED WARRANTY REGISTRATION CARD

In order to preserve your rights as provided for in the limited warranty, this card must be on file with Simon & Schuster within thirty days of purchase.

Please fill in the information requested:

NAME _____ PHONE NUMBER (_____) _____

ADDRESS _____

CITY _____ STATE _____ ZIP _____

COMPUTER BRAND & MODEL _____ DOS VERSION _____ MEMORY _____ K

Where did you purchase this product?

DEALER NAME _____

ADDRESS _____

CITY _____ STATE _____ ZIP _____

PURCHASE DATE _____ PURCHASE PRICE _____

How did you learn about this product? (Check as many as applicable.)

STORE DISPLAY _____ SALESPERSON _____ MAGAZINE ARTICLE _____ ADVERTISEMENT _____

OTHER (Please explain) _____

How long have you owned or used this computer?

LESS THAN 30 DAYS _____ LESS THAN 6 MONTHS _____ 6 MONTHS TO A YEAR _____ OVER 1 YEAR _____

What is your primary use for the computer?

BUSINESS _____ PERSONAL _____ EDUCATION _____ OTHER (Please explain) _____

Where is your computer located?

HOME _____ OFFICE _____ SCHOOL _____ OTHER (Please explain) _____

0–13–93988–6

Simon & Schuster, Inc.
Brady Books
One Gulf + Western Plaza
New York, NY 10023

ATTN: **PRODUCT REGISTRATION**